CLERGY RETIREMENT:
Every Ending a New Beginning for Clergy, Their Family, and the Congregation

Rabbi Daniel Roberts
and Dr. Michael Freidman

Death, Value, and Meaning Series
Series Editor: Darcy L. Harris

Baywood Publishing Company, Inc.
AMITYVILLE, NEW YORK

Baywood Publishing Company, Inc.
26 Austin Avenue
P.O. Box 337
Amityville, NY 11701
(800) 638-7819
E-mail: baywood@baywood.com
Web site: baywood.com

Library of Congress Catalog Number:
ISBN: 978-0-89503-910-1 (cloth : alk. paper)
ISBN: 978-0-89503-911-8 (paper)
ISBN: 978-0-89503-912-5 (e-pub)
ISBN: 978-0-89503-913-2 (e-pdf)
http://dx.doi.org/10.2190/CLE

Library of Congress Cataloging-in-Publication Data

Names: Roberts, Daniel A. (Daniel Alan), 1942- author.
Title: Clergy retirement : every ending a new beginning for clergy, their family, and the congregation / authors, Rabbi Daniel Roberts and Dr. Michael Freidman.
Description: Amityville : Baywood Publishing Company, Inc., 2016. | Series: Death, value, and meaning series | Includes bibliographical references and index.
Identifiers: LCCN 2015043333| ISBN 9780895039101 (clothbound : alk. paper)| ISBN 9780895039118 (paperbound : alk. paper) | ISBN 9780895039132 (epdf : alk. paper) | ISBN 9780895039125 (epub : alk. paper)
Subjects: LCSH: Clergy--Retirement.
Classification: LCC BL635 .R63 2016 | DDC 253/.20846--dc23
LC record available at http://lccn.loc.gov/2015043333

Permissions

Addison, H. A. (2006). *Berur: How do you know if it's God?" In Jewish spiritual direction: An innovative guide from traditional and contemporary sources.* H. A. Addison and B. E. Breitman (Eds.). Woodstock, VT: Jewish Lights. Permission granted by Jewish Lights Publishing, Woodstock, VT.

Bridges, W. (2009). *Managing transitions: Making the most of change.* Philiadelphia, PA: Da Capo Press. Reprinted by permission of Perseus Books Group.

Darling, C. (2004). Understanding stress and quality of life for clergy and clergy spouses. *Stress and Health 20,* published on line www.interscience.wiley.com. Used by permission of John Wiley and Sons.

Doka, K. (2002). *Disenfranchised grief: Recognizing hidden sorrow.* Lexington, MA: Lexington Press.

Frankl, V. (1984). *Man's Search for Meaning.* New York: Washington Square Press. Used with permission.

Grollman, E. (1967). *Explaining death to children.* Boston: Beacon Press. Used with permission.

Heschel, A. J. (1972). *Insecurity of freedom.* New York, Schocken Books. Copyright by Silvia Heschel. reprinted by permission of Farrar, Strauss and Giroux, LLC.

Hileman, L. (2008). The unique needs of protestant clergy families: Implications for marriage and family counseling. *Journal of Spirituality in Mental Health.* Reprinted by permission of the publisher, Taylor & Francis, Ltd.

Kemper, R. (1988). *Planning for ministerial retirement.* New York: The Pilgrim Press. Used with permission.

Koenig, H. G. (2002). *Purpose and power in retirement: New opportunities for meaning and significance.* Templeton Press, Philadelphia, PA. Used with permission.

Krause, N. (1992). Providing support to others and well-being in later life. *Journal of Gerontology*, 47(5), 300-311.

Levy, N. (2002). "A retirement blessing" and "A prayer at retirement" from *Talking to God: Personal prayers for times of joy, sadness, struggle, and celebration,* New York, NY. Used by permission of Alfred A. Knopf, and imprint of the Knoph Doubleday Publishing Group, a division of Random House LLC. All rights reserve.

Lynch, Merrill. *Americans' perspectives on new retirement realities and the longevity bonus: A 2013 Merrill Lynch retirement study, conducted in partnership with Age Wave.* New York: Merrill Lynch/Bank of America Corporation. Permission from PARSINTL.com

Matt, D. (1996). *The essential Kabbalah.* San Francisco: HarperCollins Publishers. Reprinted by permission HarperCollins Publishers.

Merton, T. (1999). *Thoughts in solitude.* NY: Farrar, Straus, and Giroux. Reprinted by permission of Farrar, Strauss and Giroux, LLC.

Neimeyer, R. (2006). *Lessons of loss: A guide to coping, Memphis:* Center of the Study of Loss and Transition. reproduced by permission of Taylor & Frances Group, LLC, a division of Informa pic.

Shapiro, R. (1988). *Tangents: Selected poems,* Miami, FL: ENR Wordsmith. Used with permission.

Table of Contents

PART 3
For the People in Your Life
(Chapters You Will Want to Share) 103

PART 4
Conclusion 175

Foreword

I am a Professor with a focus on gerontology (the study of aging) and thanatology (the study of death) at the Graduate School of The College of New Rochelle. The College of New Rochelle defines itself as "historically Catholic"—proud of its heritage as a college originally for women, founded by the Ursuline Sisters. With such a tradition, I often have members of the clergy as students. Father Thomas Rainforth was one of my early students. Teaching is often mutual learning, with faculty and students, particularly graduate students, trading insights, knowledge, and wisdom. I learned much from Father Tom. He had come to the College at the request of his Bishop to assist in a diocesan project on clergy retirement.

In many ways, the term *clergy retirement* is almost an oxymoron. For many clergy, being a priest, minister, pastor, rabbi, or imam is more than a job—it is a calling, a part of our identity. It is not as much what we *do* as what we *are*. How then can we retire from ourselves? Father Tom noted the great difficulty, even resentment, that many Catholic priests experienced as they were compelled to retire.

Rabbi Roberts' first chapter indicates that the grief and adjustments to retirement are not unique to priests. Having been involved in the lives, crises, illnesses, and deaths of so many of our congregants, it is difficult to find a sense of meaningfulness in golf or fishing.

Losing such a meaningful role is in itself a cause of the grief that Dan Roberts explores so well in his book. This quest to find a meaningful place within the congregation as mentor is unappreciated. Yet, while retirement may engender a sense of loss and grief, it is a grief that is often disenfranchised or unrecognized and supported by others. *Clergy Retirement* enfranchises and validates that loss.

Roberts and Freidman, though, offer more than validation. *Clergy Retirement* offers suggestions and advice that can assist clergy in planning a retirement that is meaningful.

Years ago I was a consultant to IBM, assisting in their preretirement programs. These programs were designed for employees at all levels who were a decade away from eligibility for retirement. At that point, IBM had a generous retirement program. While the program reviewed their financial options, IBM realized the psychological and social issues that arise as part of retirement planning.

For example, most of us spent nearly 60–70 hours involved with work, including the time spent commuting, preparing, even dressing. *How will we fill those hours as we retire?* Often participants would offer some leisure activity such as fishing, golf, or tennis. Yet could we really do that for 60–70 hours a week? We asked participants to consider whether their retirement plans were realistic, balanced, meaningful, and consistent with past activities and interests.

There was also more. Work meets deep psychological and social needs. For some, the needs may simply be social—work provides an opportunity to be with others. In such a case, membership in a club or senior center may satisfy that need. For others, though, there may be great satisfaction in the power of one's work role. Here one may need to run the Center or club.

In short, there is more than financial planning to retirement—a fact well addressed in Roberts' and Freidman's book. They note the spiritual needs that have to be met in clergy retirement. Ministry is something we do—it is not something we can retire from doing. The quest becomes how we can redefine our ministry even as we retire from one role.

Clergy, I think, will find this book an extraordinary guide even as they contemplate retirement as the next stage of life. In fact, it is a road map—not just for clergy but also spouses, families, and even congregational leaders. All will find specific chapters in this extraordinary guide to assist them in dealing with this significant transition. *Clergy Retirement* should be required reading for clergy, their families, and congregational leaders. It should become a well-worn book in every clergy and congregational library. Roberts and Freidman offer not only sensitivity to their loss but the great truth that thanatologists are constantly rediscovering that even in loss there are great opportunities for growth.

Kenneth J. Doka, PhD, MDiv.
Professor, The Graduate School of The College of New Rochelle
Senior Consultant, The Hospice Foundation of America
Lutheran Clergyman (Ret.)

Acknowledgments

Dan Roberts

I sometimes wonder if I could have ever written this book were it not for my mother. She once related to me how she used a dictionary and a thesaurus when, as its business manager, wrote articles for the Youngstown Symphony. As a single parent, she was a role model for me and encouraged me to be the best human being I could be, living up to my potential. I think back also to some of my English teachers in high school and college who were very liberal with their red markers, decorating my papers with corrections and I am deeply appreciative to them for making me a better writer. I think about all those who have been patient and kind to me, like my loving wife, Elaine, who found ways to make corrections and suggestions for improvements without hurting my delicate ego. I am also indebted to my former administrative assistant and continued devotee, Audrey Katzman, who has labored over each and every word and comma and did a lot of judicial editing to make my writings better. I thank Ruth Lester as well for making additional corrections to the final document, as well as to all of my friends and colleagues who made comments about topics that should be included in this book.

Of course, I would not be writing this book at all if it were not for my friend, colleague and mentor, Rabbi Earl Grollman, who not only encouraged me to become credentialed in the area of Thanatology, but suggested that a short article I had written on my retirement experience, should be shared with others by writing a book. He continued to make suggestions and encouraged me to complete this project. It is with gratitude that I dedicate this book to him. I also thank my co-author, Michael Freidman, who graciously offered suggestions to clarify my wording and was willing to argue his point when he thought I was wrong in my thinking. I am thankful to the many clergy who responded to our questionnaire and gave us material that would exemplify certain chapters. I also wish to thank Bishop Patrick White for his encouragement and his admonishment to never forget our own sense of spirituality that got us to this point. And we thank Linda Thal for her insights about spiritual practice so as not to dismiss this aspect of our lives. We also thank the entire Baywood Publishing Company staff for their help in bringing this book to fruition. And, of course, we are grateful to others who have written about this subject of retirement that gave us fodder for the various chapters.

Michael Freidman

This book is the result of Rabbi Dan Roberts' inspiration and determination. Without his dedicated conceptualization of retirement as a significant loss in the lives of clergy, this book would never have evolved into a comprehensive resource on the topic. I am indebted to him for graciously inviting my partnership in his venture and for his ability to accept my sometimes differing perspectives as complimentary to his own. I never would have embarked on such a project myself and am grateful for the experience and opportunity to learn from him as we worked together. Although my reasons are different from Danny's, I too largely credit the roots of my engagement in this venture to my mother, Henrietta Peyser Freidman, z"l. She introduced me to the riches that a religious home life can offer while modeling the value of engagement in our family's congregation and the responsibility of volunteering for causes in which one believes. Perhaps equally important was her ability and desire to work with others and thereby develop mutually enriching relationships. Upon this foundation, I grew to know and respect numerous rabbis and cantors through every stage of my life while respecting the differences of other religions and their clergy. My life has been truly enriched by these personal and professional relationships which have fueled my interest and commitment to the issues addressed in this book.

I must express my appreciation to all those clergypersons who have shared their lives with me as colleagues, clients and friends. I too add my thanks to Linda Thal for her addition of a spiritual dimension to my own thinking and this book and to Audrey Katzman and the Baywood Publishing Company staff for their editorial guidance.

INTRODUCTION
Clergy Retirement: Endings and New Beginnings

> Yes, my child, life is a beginning; but everything in life is a new beginning.
> Elie Wiesel (2010, p. 177)

RETIREMENT THROUGH THE EYES OF A THANATOLOGIST

A thanatologist studies the medical, psychological, and sociological aspects of death and the ways that people deal with it. I became a thanatologist at age 10 when my father died and I was face to face with a "major" death for the first time. I became a thanatologist before I knew what it meant or even how to spell the word.

I truly became a thanatologist during seminary when my philosophy professor defined religion as *man's response to his finitude, his infinite striving, and his finite factuality.* In essence, as human beings, we want to live forever, yet we know we are mortal and we deal with our mortality every day of our lives, and religion helps us to reconcile this knowledge. On each birthday we inch a bit closer to the inevitable understanding that we are aging. We confront it when some life-threatening scenario occurs, such as a car accident or a medical emergency. We face it when deciding whether or not to buy life insurance or when making estate plans.

Finally, I became a thanatologist when I attended my first International Conference of Death and Dying in London, Ontario, with Dr. Jack Morgan. Learning from some of the pioneers in the field, I was sold on this being a critical area of study for anyone who wants to make the most of their days left. I was reminded that one has to fully confront one's finitude so as to live life with meaning and purpose and as fully as possible each and every day.

Along the way I discovered that many of us only associate grief and mourning with the death of a person, but psychosocial losses can equally drive us into depression and lead to stress and melancholy. Darcy Harris reminds us in *Counting Our Losses* that we need to consider the losses when something dies within us (Harris, 2011). We need to consider that when we are forced to view

1

our-selves differently and are challenged to rethink our self-esteem, then we often enter the grieving process. We may or may not recognize this, and our sense of loss may consume us, but ultimately we will come out of this period a changed person.

Nonfinite loss is usually precipitated by a major life change that dashes our dreams and changes our sense of self. We feel sorrow as aging or health crises cause a loss of physical or intellectual function. We mourn the death of a loved one and grieve a divorce and/or loss of a relationship. Grief can occur when we move from our home, leaving behind a lifetime of memories. At retirement we often find it agonizing to adjust to the new rhythms of life, even though we looked forward to this time. Some find it distressing to leave behind colleagues and those to whom we ministered in times of crisis and celebration.

Just because we plan for retirement and think we are ready does not lessen a whole host of emotions during the transition. A person should not be surprised that it feels like something inside has died. He/she should not be surprised that like other losses, we find ourselves lamenting what was, and fearful of what will be. One is a precipitous decline in self-esteem around the time of retirement. In their longitudinal study, Ulrich Orth and associates at University of Basel in Switzerland suggest that the relative stability of career and family life in middle age contributes to high self-esteem, but that retirement, declining health, and an "empty nest" can all detract from it (Orth, Trzesniewski, & Robins, 2010a). In retirement, we leave a piece of ourselves behind and enter a new phase without the *me* we once knew. Anticipation, planning, and reading this book may soften the blow, yet they cannot completely preclude despair when our career has ended. If you are aware, however, of what is normal during the days ahead, and if you are willing to allow yourself to grieve the loss of your former self rather than ignoring it, then indeed your journey to an enriched life in the final chapters of your book of life will be made easier and more comprehendible.

After a lifetime of counseling and advising others through life changes, it is ironic that we clergy lack a professional support system that understands the trials we endure upon retirement. Many of us confront the dilemma of with whom to share our anguish and sorrow. Some counselors comprehend ambiguous grief and some even specialize in the clergy world. However, many either do not understand or think that nonfinite grief is trivial. It would greatly help if denominational groups were to establish opportunities for retired clergy and those nearing retirement to share their experiences. The atmosphere would give permission to vent and to grieve. In such a setting, fellow colleagues would listen, not to judge or give advice, but to let others share their feelings. Writes Rabbi David Wolpe, "What loss cries for is not to be fixed or to be explained, but to be shared, and eventually, to find its way to meaning" (Wolpe, 1999, p. 15).

To help us understand how some clergy adjust to retirement, we reached out to some retired clergy from multiple denominations in an unscientific survey (see Appendix II) and throughout the book we have included some of the comments of the 130 who responded. Perhaps reflecting on others' responses will stimulate contemplation and add some clarity to your particular circumstance. We hope that the voices of fellow travelers can serve as sources of comfort to you.

Daniel Roberts

THE ESSENCE OF THIS BOOK

This book is about the usual and normal emotions experienced as one faces the adventure of retirement and the beginning of a new phase in life. It is about both ambiguous loss.

The greatest difficulty we as authors face is how to include every scenario: clergy who lead a congregation, serve as educators, or work for an organization; those who choose to retire or were "forced" out of their position; those who remain in a congregation as an emeritus; and those whose denomination requires them to absent themselves for a period of time without contacting members. We struggled with how to include female clergy and male spouses and tried to avoid he/she and him/her in the text, so we ask that you mentally make appropriate gender substitutions as you read. We hope that within these pages you will find your particular situation, can relate to the heartrending upheaval that you might possibly endure during your transition, and hopefully will be stimulated in preplanning for your future.

PART I: PERSPECTIVES ON RETIREMENT

In Chapter 1, we share a personal experience of retirement and some of its nonfinite losses.

In Chapter 2, we deal with transitions of retirement through the eyes of a psychologist, acknowledging the various opportunities it may offer.

PART II: FOR THE CLERGY

In Chapter 3, we remind you that *retirement* is not a dirty word and that you earned the right to collect Social Security and a pension and to enjoy the next stage of life.

In Chapter 4, we offer suggestions for the best ways to say goodbye to congregants.

In Chapter 5, we address the dangers of depression and residual anger that can occur during transition. We suggest means to manage the process of closing the door on one period of your life while waiting for the window to open onto the next one.

In Chapter 6, we share the importance of finding new meaning that will give your encore years intention and significance.

In Chapter 7,[1] we address the issue that leaving a position your spiritual leadership does not mean leaving the service of God. In retirement we need to find new ways to relate to the Divine as we turn our attention from nurturing our congregants' spiritual lives to further developing our own.

PART III: FOR THE PEOPLE IN YOUR LIFE
(CHAPTERS YOU WILL WANT TO SHARE)

In Chapter 8, we give insight into the emotional lives of your spouses/partners throughout your ministry. They too will experience a retirement of another sort, which should be recognized.

In Chapter 9, we suggest ways to involve your children so they can understand what you are going through. They will learn to identify and express their reactions to this significant family change and discover ways they can open conversations with you.

In Chapter 10, we share with your laity what we have learned about the upheaval in both your life as a clergy and in the lives of congregants during the transition and what they need to do to ensure a healthy changeover.

Chapter 11 is designed for Judicatories and concerns their responsibilities to retirees and how they might continue to include them so as to remove a sense of isolation.

Chapter 12 is designed to be shared with your successor. It reminds them to proceed slowly during this transition and find an appropriate way of keeping your memory alive in the congregation.

Chapter 13 explains the pros and cons of being an emeritus. Even in the midst of the complicated emotions surrounding retirement, an emeritus must continue to represent God's vision of a loving and caring steward of the congregation. We remind you that this is not your congregation, but God's.

PART IV: CONCLUSION

In Chapter 14, we give a sense of hope that a wonderful world awaits you in retirement.

In Appendix I, we provide some useful books, websites, and other resources on retirement.

In Appendix II, we provide a copy of the questionnaire we submitted to clergy of many faiths. Over 130 participated, and many of the chapters contain their anonymous responses that we hope you will find insightful.

---

[1] "Retirement as Spiritual Challenge and Opportunity" by Linda Thal, EdD; "Retirement-Exile or Promised Land" by Bishop Patrick G. White.

SUMMARY

We write this book through two primary viewpoints. Rabbi Daniel A. Roberts is a retired congregational leader who is a certified thanatologist. Michael Freidman is a psychologist who has worked with retiring clergy and who has also served as president of his congregation. Michael has also been involved with congregational leaders as they hire successors and manage the transition. Linda Thal is an educator and spiritual director who focuses on adult spiritual development; many of her students and directees are rabbis at various stages of their careers, including retirement. Bishop Patrick G. H. White, BA, MDiv, DMin, DD, and Retired Bishop of Bermuda served as a parish priest for many years and was elected Bishop in 2009 and served until 2012 when he retired.

We write this book for those who are transitioning from a lifetime of service and those with whom they have shared this journey. We hope that you will benefit by knowing that this change is often accompanied by emotional tumult, including anxiety and grief with the reward of "green pastures" of a new and different rhythm ahead. Even those who can utter, "Whew, I am glad it's over," will find this book beneficial, as it acknowledges the change of roles that one goes through. Please understand that the period of adjustment has no set timetable nor is it predictable. Taking time to reflect, grieve, plan, and talk with a close friend or a professional could provide invaluable emotional support during this time. Just putting words to emotions can be very cathartic.

We hope that you are familiar with *Man's Search for Meaning*, by Viktor Frankl 1946. In it he reveals that those who survived longer during the Holocaust felt some reason to live even if it were just to prove Hitler wrong. We've all known those who willed themselves to die because they no longer had a purpose to live. A wise person once said, "Life isn't about finding yourself, it is about creating yourself," and that is exactly what we all need to do in our retirement. We need to leave our former life behind yet build upon it as we search for new meaning and new roles.

Change is hard for many people. It requires one to grieve for a world gone by while we build a new life. It takes compassion and understanding and, most importantly, time. Just as one does not get over a death of a loved one in a few days, a few weeks, or even a year, so one does not reconcile nonfinite loss in a brief period of time either. Here at the end of a career it takes time to deal with the reality that one more chapter of our lives is complete. However, we say again that in every ending there is a new beginning, and with retirement, a new chapter opens with blank pages to be written upon by your personal hand. A new, fantastic world is awaiting you in which you have the power to include all the dreams you have had for years and even more.

REFERENCES

Frankl, V. (1946). *Man's search for meaning.* Austria: Verlag fur Jugend und Volk.

Harris, D. (Ed.). (2011). *Counting our losses: Reflecting on change, loss, and transition in everyday life.* New York, NY: Routledge, Taylor & Francis.

Orth, U., Trzesniewski, K. H., & Robins, R. W. (2010). Self-esteem development from young adulthood to old age: A cohort-sequential longitudinal study. *Journal of Personality and Social Psychology, 98*(4).

Wiesel, E. (2010). *The Sonderberg case: A novel.* New York, NY: Alfred A. Knopf.

Wolpe, D. (1999). *Making loss matter: Creating meaning in difficult times.* New York, NY: Riverhead Books.

PART I

Perspectives on Retirement

http://dx.doi.org/10.2190/CLEC1

CHAPTER 1

Grieving a Retirement: Reflections of a Thanatologist*

Two are better than one . . .
For if they fall, the one will lift up his fellow;
But woe to him that is alone when he falleth,
and hath not another to lift him up

(Ecclesiastes 4:9–10 JPS)

In his heart a man plans his course, but the Lord determines his steps.

(Proverbs 16:9 NIV)

RETIRED AT TOP OF GAME

I know that I'm just in my early 60s, but I want to leave while I'm still at the top of my game and have my health and enough energy to enjoy another version of my life. Overall, my congregants seem to appreciate me and all I have done to enrich their lives. I was surprised but pleased when the president announced to me that the Board had authorized her to negotiate an extension of my contract for another 5 years even though our current agreement doesn't expire for another year and a half. In fact, when I responded that I couldn't accept that, she interrupted and asked how much longer I'd prefer. She was shocked when I shared that I planned to retire at the end of my current term and that I thought it was time for us to begin to plan for that transition. Even though I am confident in my decision, I must admit to some mixed feelings as I think about my future.

INTRODUCTION—MY STORY

I sat alone in my office with the center drawer of my desk three quarters of the way open. Tucked in the far left corner was a collection of 25 pocket calendars that I used to carry every day in my breast pocket. I recorded every activity of my life

---

*A thanatologist studies the medical, psychological, and sociological aspects of death and the ways that people deal with it.

until I bought a PalmPilot. I couldn't go anywhere without that little book. It was my life. I sat there in loneliness staring at them. Then I slowly began leafing through each book, wondering where all the years had gone. How quickly they had flown by! The calendars contained countless appointments and, of course, family and friends' birthdates. Then there were the anniversary of family deaths that I had meticulously transferred each year. As I leafed through those little calendars, I relived so many memories.

I looked down at the many open boxes crammed full of books near my desk and I felt overwhelmed. Which books was I going to keep? Which ones might I need in the future and which ones should I give away? Who would want them, especially in this digital age? I glanced at all the certificates still hanging on the walls along with the various art pieces, many given by friends and congregants, and I contemplated what I was going to do with them. We had no room at home to hang them, and besides, my wife didn't care for many of them. But I loved them. Where could I put them? Could I give some pieces away or try to sell them? So many tiny, crushing, overwhelming decisions put me in a state of chaos. Philosopher Suzanne Langer (1996) posits that the one thing that the mind cannot deal with is chaos, and here I was right in its midst.

So many recollections; so many events happened in this office. Now, 30 years of my professional life was about to be put into crates and moved to an undetermined location. I sat in my chair by the light of the desk lamp and wanted to cry. Instead, with emotions overwhelming me, I just turned off the light, walked out of my office, and left the growing mess and decisions behind.

WHERE DO I GO FROM HERE?

Walking to my car, my thoughts raced. What was to be my new role? What was to be my future relationship with all those who will come to my retirement service? What future roles would be as meaningful to me as those I had played for the last 30 years?

I was conflicted. Unlike some of my friends who never really enjoyed the world of the rabbinate and think of retirement as a welcome relief, I loved it. But now, after so many years, I was getting tired of constantly being *on*; of constantly digging for material for new and different sermons and programs; of constantly seeing to the needs of congregants at the expense of my own family. And yet this had been the only life I had known for 30 years. What was I going to do now? How would I spend my time now that I did not have to be at the office, lead services, or officiate at sacred occasions? I had thought about this many times as I pondered retirement. I had developed a cadre of hobbies I enjoyed. However, I was greatly influenced to do more than *play* my life away when I read Abraham Joshua Heschel's article, "To Grow in Wisdom," from his book *The Insecurity of Freedom* (1972). In it he encourages the elderly to "attain the high values we failed to sense, the insights we have missed, [and] the wisdom we ignored." From this and other readings, as well as my work in the field of death, dying, and grief, I knew that to continue to live life and enjoy every minute, I had to find a sense of significance and meaning beyond the active rabbinate. But what was it to be?

As retirement arrived, the reality of changing my lifestyle frightened me, even though I had been anticipating this moment. It is similar to the person who spent hours at the bedside of a dying loved one, but when the call came announcing the death, he exclaimed, *I can't believe it!* Even though one knows the moment is coming, with the moment of death, the last hope for some kind of miracle is gone and reality sets in. In that case, it is a world without one's loved one in it; in my case, it is a world without all the things that had given me a sense of who I am, a sense of *me*, missing.

Over the years I had felt the love and respect of so very many congregants. This fact was made even more obvious at my retirement service when the sanctuary was filled to overflowing. When I received letters telling me how I had touched their lives, I was tremendously moved and did not know how to react or respond. My wife tells me that I have never believed my press. Of course, I had heard there were those who were delighted that I was retiring. You can imagine how that hurt, even though I have always known that a certain percentage of congregants will always find fault. You cannot please everyone, but like most people who want to be loved, I had tried.

Like the mourner who is angry with the deceased for leaving the survivors in such a chaotic state, I felt that mix of anger, disappointment, sadness, and relief. I became critical of those who planned my retirement weekend, thinking it could have been better designed; the speeches more laudatory and the display of gratitude for all the years I had tended to this flock more effusive. But I knew what really was gnawing at me, as with all people who are bereaved: *How and where was I to find that sense of meaning that I had enjoyed all these years?* I was in the midst of what one might call a cognitive dissonant moment—a happy/sad time.

Because I am a thanatologist, I was well aware that I was experiencing existential grief,[1] as grief counselor Kenneth Doka identifies it in his article, "Death in Life" (Doka, 2002). I had anticipated this reaction, and I knew I needed time to grieve because retirement is an existential event. I knew that I must deal with my own mortality and what to do with the rest of my life. It's strange, but anticipation and preparation do not lessen grief's intensity, they just allow for some premourning, and the shock is not as severe as suddenly being told to pack your office and get out. Think of the physician who understands the need for and risks of major surgery, yet it does not lessen his anxiety when the surgery is being performed on him.

---

[1] Existential grief is a sense of alienation, despair, pain, or deep sorrow for a loss of meaning.

So here I was, feeling the full force of the psychological, social, and physical reactions to my loss. Unlike the death of a family member that incurs sympathy and support, no one, other than my wife, seemed to understand the sadness and turmoil in my life. Everyone was congratulating me and wishing me a happy retirement, telling me how lucky I was to now have so much free time. If I had told anyone how I really felt, would they understand that I was grieving a great loss? Would they comprehend that I did not know how I was going to fill my hours or how to continue a consequential life? Would they identify with the fact that I was going from a world where my phone was constantly ringing to one where it hardly rang at all? Would they understand that I was going from a role where people valued me as a rabbi and made me the center of attention to a world where many did not feel comfortable socializing with me? I learned, too quickly, they had regarded me as someone "holier" or they felt ashamed that they didn't attend synagogue regularly and now felt uncomfortable in a social relationship with me. As Robert Neimeyer, a noted authority on bereavement and transition, points out in *Lessons of Loss: A Guide to Coping,*

> Unlike losses through death, there is no "ritual" that recognizes this loss or that provides a socially sanctioned period of grieving and recovery. If anything, social expectations run to the opposite extreme. We are expected to be relentlessly "self-motivated" and efficient in our pursuit of a new job [finding meaning is our new occupation—author's words], at the very time that we feel most depressed, full of self-doubt, and unsure of how to proceed. (2006, p. 34)

Would people think me silly because I was grieving when they were envious that I had such freedom? I was experiencing disenfranchised grief: "that is, the survivors are not accorded a 'right' to grieve . . . that grief is experienced when a loss cannot be openly acknowledged, socially sanctioned, or publicly observed" (Doka, 1989, p. 5). So I bottled my emotions and put on an appreciative face, but I knew I was in the world of melancholy. I had to undo the psychological ties binding me to a world that had provided me with security and stability, both emotionally and financially. I had to learn to live without the daily routine I once knew, even though it often changed with the single ring of a telephone. The adrenaline rush of the fast-paced life I had led for 30 years was gone. My new world would call for a redefining of my ego needs.

Like many who magically believe that their loved one will return home and is not really dead, somewhere in the recesses of my mind, I thought that the synagogue's board would beg me to stay, but they didn't. As far as I was concerned, they embraced the new rabbi far too quickly and didn't appear to miss me at all. I had worked so hard to create the vibrant congregation that it had become. Some of my dreams had come true; others were still unfulfilled. I wondered if they would ever come to fruition or would they fade away with me? Would I have to grieve for them as well?

LIFE THROUGH A NEW LENS

Suddenly I found myself on the other side of the pulpit. I had no past experiences to call upon for a life without my work. I felt a little like someone who lost their mate and thinks about reentering the dating world. It is a time fraught with anxious worry. Will I be accepted or rejected? I have never had this unending freedom. I never had to search for ways to fill my days with meaning. Just as anyone who is dying, I only wanted to be reassured that I would not be forgotten. I still wanted to be asked to contribute in small ways. My heart was heavy as I worshipped with the congregation. I sat there and thought that I would have done some things differently; I would have given a different sermon. As days went on, I did not like how some congregants were being treated. To add to my discomfort, my successor was quickly making changes. He seemed to have no need for my advice.

Each time I attended services, be it at my former congregation or another congregation, I was reminded that I was no longer needed and revisited my grieving. I have had a hard time feeling comfortable in other congregations; they simply were different from the one I had conducted over the years. Because it was not *me* on the pulpit leading others in prayer, I only felt lonelier, particularly because I was without a true worship community now.

I foolishly thought that this new rabbi would seek me out to learn about the history of the synagogue and its traditions. He would ask what programs, classes, and activities worked (or didn't). He would want background on congregants. I had over 30 years of history to share and help with the transition. Certainly there was enough work in the congregation for both of us, I thought. I would volunteer, not to undermine him but to help him succeed. I was envisioning a mentor relationship as my predecessor and I had shared. I was fortunate to have had such a good mentor in the founding rabbi of our congregation that I wanted to pay it forward. But it was not to be. Another dream was dashed.

As a thanatologist I knew that I was not the only one who was grieving. Some members of the congregation who were especially close to me were going through an adjustment period as well. They lost "their rabbi," the one they had grown up with, literally and figuratively, and now they too needed a period of time to recover.

I am well aware that some retiring colleagues never understand their own "death" within the congregation and try to control from the "grave" with behind-the-scenes maneuvering. They are experiencing complicated grief.[2] They are stuck in musing, never seeming to get past the "death." What they really need to do is to deal with their grief and begin to explore ways of reinventing themselves.

---

[2] In complicated grief, painful emotions are so long-lasting and severe that one has trouble accepting the loss and resuming life.

Like all mourners, I found myself caught between two worlds: the world that was and the world to be. To progress, I had to do the dance of grief, three steps forward and one back. I had to engage in the oscillation process that Margaret Stroebe and Henk Schut describe in their dual process of mourning where one goes back and forth between remembering the world that was and planning and moving ahead to restore balance to their world (Stroebe & Schute, 2010). From my thanatology experience, I understood that the best way to handle grief was to talk one's way through it, but to whom? My wife had heard enough. She had her own feelings about how I was treated over the years. She was contending with a new lifestyle as well. She was worried as I was whether or not the money we had set aside would be sufficient to keep us in the lifestyle we had enjoyed and last through our old age; this caused us real stress. Her role in the congregation had changed as well, and she needed to retreat into the background and allow the new rabbi's wife to shine. Although I was comfortable sharing my feelings with her, I found myself being careful about what I shared about the congregation, sifting out the things that would only anger or upset her.

As a rabbi, I have always been the counselor, the consoler, the one to whom others have come to share their most intimate feelings. Where do I go to share mine? Many of my friends are congregants, and I have no intention of telling them how I feel and how I am being treated. I do not want to turn them against the congregation. Even some of my friends outside the congregation don't seem to understand my sense of loss. Many have not yet retired, and those who are retired have left positions in industry, which is very different. As a rabbi, I have been accepted as a family member to many, have been part of every life-cycle event, and have sometimes shared the most intimate details of their lives. It creates an intense sense of being needed. I guess that is what I am grieving—that I am no longer needed. This is my loss. I have been in the field of death and dying long enough to know that if one cannot express one's emotions at a time such as this, it turns into "complicated grief."

THE GRIEF CONTINUES

It has been several years since my retirement, and I have built a new, meaningful life, but the scar of grief is still there, as it is with any mourner. At times, when I walk into the synagogue, there is an ache in the pit of my stomach. In some ways, I feel lost in this familiar place. New congregants do not know me. I realize that people I thought were my friends have never phoned, never inquired how I was doing, and never invited me to their family celebrations. I find myself hurt and angry. Then another congregant greets me with such warmth and delight that I am saved from my depression. Their loving welcome reminds me that I am not forgotten after all. Yet, too often, for the moment, I can't even remember their names. Suddenly a new fear surfaces within me. I sense that my memory is slipping, that I am not as sharp as I used to be. I fear that my mind is crumbling along with my body, for even my racquetball game is deteriorating. I am confronted with a different kind of grief, the reality that I have no control over the physical changes that are happening as I age.

Many of us only associate grief and mourning with the death of a person, but psychosocial losses can equally drive us into depression. Changing life status also leads to stress and melancholy. Just because you planned for your retirement and thought that you were ready does not take away the sorrow. As mentioned before, anticipatory grief does not prevent despair after the death of a loved one. When reality sets in, one must spend time at that moment lamenting, otherwise one will mourn later when it appears inappropriate and the support system has vanished.

Most of us do not realize that, like death, retirement brings wide emotional swings: bouts of sorrow, anger, frustration, loss of meaning, and feelings of incompetency. These are all usual, standard, and normal in bereavement. But it is wonderful to realize as well that so many who have walked the path before us have a world filled with "green pastures" full of meaning and excitement by being able to pursue all the interests, including family involvement, denied them during the hectic world of work.

SUMMARY

Unlike those who suggested that there are set stages to the mourning process, we do not believe this to be true when considering retirement. We believe each handles the crisis of this transition as they have handled other times of stress—in one's own way, in one's own style, on one's own time schedule. But we do know that just as in the grief process, one must find new things that will bring importance to his life. It will not be one single item, but there will be many meaningful new roles a person can play that will keep them alive, happy, and content.

REFERENCES

Doka, K. J. (1989). *Disenfranchised grief: Recognizing hidden sorrow.* Lexington, MA: Lexington.

Doka, K. (2002). Death in life. In K. Doka (Ed.), *Living with grief: Loss in later life.* Washington, DC: Hospice Foundation of America.

Heschel, A. J. (1972). *The insecurity of freedom.* New York, NY: Schocken.

Langer, S. (1996). *Philosophy in a new key: A study in the symbolism of reason, rite, and art* (3rd ed.). Cambridge: Harvard University Press.

Neimeyer, R. A. (2006). *Lessons of loss: A guide to coping.* Memphis, TN: Center of the Study of Loss and Transition.

Stroebe, M., & Schut, H. (2010). The dual process model of coping with bereavement: A decade on. *Omega: Journal of Death and Dying, 61*(4), 273–289.

http://dx.doi.org/10.2190/CLEC2

CHAPTER 2

Opportunities of Transition: A Psychologist's Perspective of Retirement

To everything there is a season, and a time to every purpose under heaven.

(Ecclesiastes, 3:1)

To exist is to change, to change is to mature, to mature is to go on creating oneself endlessly.

(Henri Bergson, 1912)

I am not only here to be, I am also here to become.

(Goethe)

RE-INVENTION

After a long but sometimes uncomfortable career as a congregational rabbi, Sam gratefully accepted the congregation's offer that he take early retirement. After 30 years in several urban congregations, he and his wife were anxious to return to their rural roots. They bought property in a community not far from where they had each grown up and settled down to a quieter lifestyle than they had known since leaving for college years ago. They planted their own garden to be as self-sustaining as possible, engaged in various outdoor activities, and found community programs for which they could volunteer. Life was good, but Rabbi Sam was not fulfilled; he was bored. He had always been a bit of a "tech geek" and realized that retirement had provided him with the time to reengage in this interest. He created a web-based service to provide Hebrew teaching and Torah reading tutoring for those interested Jews living in remote locations without easy access to congregations. Sam created what was for him a perfectly balanced life; he hadn't been this happy for years!

WHAT IS *RETIREMENT*?

The common dictionary definitions focus on "withdrawing from active employment, service or society," which is limiting and outdated. They reflect a period in our history when (mostly) men were granted the opportunity to be relieved of their duties as laborers. Typically, they worked hard for many years and had a much shorter life expectancy than people do today. When first introduced in the late 19th and early 20th centuries, retirement was a break, a privilege, and a reward for hard work. According to the National Center for Health Statistics (2006), when the Social Security Act was passed in 1935, with retirement benefits to start at age 65, the average life expectancy was only 61.7. Retirement was time out when working people could rest and theoretically enjoy life during their few remaining years.

Much has changed today. Life expectancy in developed parts of the world has significantly increased, while physical labor has been supplanted by work that is less strenuous or dangerous. Additionally, life itself has become easier, given the prevalence of machinery and the application of technology to virtually all of its aspects. As a result, retirement is often thought of in much different terms. Rather than a retreat into a solitary holding pattern until one dies, for many, retirement is now viewed as a new beginning—the next stage of life, which provides an opportunity to reinvent oneself, to invest in new interests, activities, and relationships. Depending on one's financial circumstances, physical condition, and mental outlook, this can be a time of expansion rather than contraction. A current advertisement says, "Retirement is paying ourselves for doing what we love!"

Nonetheless, there are still many negative associations to the term and construct of retirement. As the Baby Boom generation ages beyond the mid-60s, much now appears in the media about what retirement means today and various strategies for achieving the best it has to offer. Alternatives to the terms *senior citizens* and *retirement* are gaining popularity, such as the *next stage, bonus years, third chapter of life, encore years, and second career*. One of my favorites is *retreading* rather than *retiring*. However, more important than terminology is society's attitude about this stage of life.

Retirement really is about attitude. Has the glass of one's life been depleted, and is it now half empty? Or is it only half full with ample room for continued growth, development, and new experiences? Both as a psychologist and someone beginning to experience this stage of life, I am clear about the choice. Retirement is a time to be optimistically anticipated and embraced with enthusiasm! It is a time for growth and new beginnings! In an interview on the CBS TV show, *Sunday Morning*, Jane Pauley (2014) said of retirement, "It used to be a door marked 'exit,' but now it is more like a door that swings on a hinge, moving a person from one thing to something else."

Is Retirement to be Mourned or Celebrated?

The answer is both! As you have read, retirement brings with it significant change in one's life and for those with whom the retiree interacts. For many of us, change comes with anxiety, discomfort, or even fear of the uncertainties that the future may bring. Regarding retirement, unsettling questions about the future may include how long will I live and will I be healthy, fit, financially secure, and happy during these years? What will I do? With whom will I do it?

Newly retired (particularly men) are among the most vulnerable to depression, and unemployed men over the age of 60 are at greater risk of suicide than any other demographic group (Koenig, 2002). This situation is not necessarily caused by retirement but is often associated with increased age, deteriorating health, and decreased social involvement, which are more common at this stage of life. The healthy elderly and the retired are often just as happy and report having at least as good a quality of life as younger employed adults. This suggests that retirement itself does not necessarily lead to depression. For some, this change in employment situation is actually perceived as a relief. So what makes the difference? Why do some focus more on the problems and others on the opportunities?

PSYCHOLOGICAL PERSPECTIVES

Positive Perspective

A basic premise of positive psychology is that human beings are more prone to being drawn to the future then to the past. This seems particularly relevant to our exploration of retirement as a challenging, life-changing event (Wang, Henkens, & van Solinge, 2011). In addition, there are significant individual differences or factors that influence whether or not the retiree is drawn toward or away from a positive attitude about this significant life change. These include existing underlying personality characteristics such as optimism and resilience as well as one's personal history. Experience with previous transitions (career and otherwise), work, and leisure habits as well as experiences, social and work contexts (i.e., roles and status), and family and social networks all impact an individual's perspective about retirement (Wang & Shultz, 2010). Interestingly, one of the strongest influencing factors for making a positive adjustment to retirement transition is being in a happy marriage.

Developmental Perspective

Many have found it helpful to understand retirement as one more life stage, which brings challenges, requires adjustment, and provides opportunities for continued development. A significant difference between retirement and earlier developmental stages is that this one comes during adulthood once we have achieved significant growth and are generally independent and capable of making intentional plans and decisions to facilitate our adjustment. Like transitions between earlier stages in life, retirement involves change—change that is funda-mental to our continued evolution, for without change we would stop growing, stop living. Retirement is not the end of life; death is the inevitable final stage of that journey and both are best met with acceptance and planning (Brown, 2013).

This is not to ignore the pain and sense of loss that many feel as part of this transition. Loss of purpose, prestige, financial security, and social connection are not uncommon reactions to retirement and are therefore thoughtfully addressed throughout this book. However, retirement is about more than loss. Like other losses mourned, once one acknowledges the losses and the changes associated with retirement, the retiree is then positioned to engage in development for the future.

Retirement is not about either loss or opportunity, but both; similarly, the transition into retirement is not linear. Instead, like most stages of human development, it ebbs and flows—advancing and receding. Those of us who are parents or have worked closely with children may think of the sometimes unpredictable and extreme behavioral changes of toddlers and adolescents. What we may not recall as clearly are the times of calm between these bursts of change. Although we appreciated these periods of peace and may have thought of them as the "calm before the (next) storm," we may not have thought of their developmental importance. But it is during these periods of calm or homeostasis that the child actually grows and advances in preparation for its next stage. This phenomenon is no less true of those progressing through this stage of retirement. Between times of excitement, uncertainty, and dread, we will experience periods of seeming calm when nothing appears to be happening. Instead of considering these times of peace merely as breaks, these are times for inner reflection that fuel the process of disintegration and reintegration (Bridges, 2004) and ultimately lead to personal growth. Recognizing retirement as such a "neutral zone" in life, Linda Thal writes in Chapter 7, *Retirement as Spiritual Challenge and Opportunity*, that retirement provides a "time to learn how to move from doing to being . . . to be fully present to whatever arises in your life."

Retirement is best thought of as a *commencement* that both recognizes an end and marks a new beginning, which provides an opportunity for continued growth and new adventures. As such, this is a time for celebration! During this period with fewer responsibilities for others, we have time to reengage in activities that once brought us joy and fulfillment but had to be put aside because of other demands. Rabbi Rachel Cowan (2010), a noted scholar on aging, reminds us that at this stage of life, we have unbelievable resources of experience, energy, passion, time, and wisdom. We are no longer "building résumés" nor concerned about how others evaluate our performance. We can take risks, experiment with new activities and relationships, and not be concerned about how we look. We are free to experience life to the fullest!

"SUCCESSFUL" RETIREMENT

While the typical retiree would likely describe a successful retirement in terms of happiness, fulfillment, peace of mind, health, and economic security, some psychological researchers (Wang et al., 2011) have characterized retirement adjustment as "not [being] preoccupied with the retirement transition and being comfortable with the changed circumstances of life in retirement." Other researchers have highlighted the positive aspects of role transitions in retirement. Strengthening roles in one's family and community, involvement in non-job-related positive roles, viewing retirement as an opportunity rather than a disruption, and aligning one's goals and plans with one's various resources all facilitate a more positive adjustment to retirement.

Perhaps the most significant factor in achieving a positive adjustment to retirement is planning. If we think of human development as a personal journey, we may be reminded of the value of maps in helping us reach our destination during our more literal travel. If we don't decide on a particular destination, then how will we know when we get there? When using this metaphor for our life journeys, having a clear sense of our goals not only provides focus but also informs us about a preferred process to achieve them. Just as successful organizations start their strategic planning process with a Vision Statement, individuals will be aided in development of their life plans by articulating a Personal Vision Statement as a target for their efforts and a destination for their journey.

If anxiety is largely caused by fear of the unknown and uncertainty of the future, planning for significant life transitions can provide a reassuring sense of control. Part of this reassurance comes from being aware of and working through the various choices we face. Nonetheless, in our drive for a sense of control, we must be cautious not to *overplan* and unintentionally redesign a life that does not provide a balance between relaxation and productivity.

RETIREMENT PLANNING

Planning Process

All successful planning relies on meaningful assessment to evaluate the current status of elements critical to one's articulated vision and goals. Therefore, for retirement planning, one must begin with some form of self-assessment. Some may choose a standardized tool such as Quality of Life Inventory (QOLI) or exercises like The 27 Things I Want To Do Before I Die. Others may use a more informal form of self-reflection such as a review of one's personal journal. However, a particularly useful approach can be customized using the underlying concepts of Appreciative Inquiry (see resource below), a technique for understanding people and situations. This strength-based approach to change builds on reflection and appreciation of past events through a positive lens.

Using an Appreciative Inquiry approach, you might recall times when you were particularly happy, proud, or felt fulfilled. Analysis of these events or accomplishments and how you achieved them will generate lists of your combined strengths, abilities, and values. You may use these as you paint a mental image of the rest of your life and articulate a set of goals to achieve that vision. A deeper reflection of the high points of your life to identify particular interests, desires, and meaningful relationships will add to the richness of your goal planning. Of course, meaningful planning for retirement must also address more practical aspects of life such as finances, physical and spiritual health, and family situation and responsibilities. Thoughtfully integrating these with your goals will result in a comprehensive and realistic plan.

Preparing Yourself for Retirement

Although essential, having a vision, a set of goals, and a realistic self-assessment are only the start of preparation for retirement. Understanding and appreciating the complexity of this process are equally important. As described above, retirement is not an event but an ongoing process. It takes time and has to run its natural course—moving forward, stepping back, and experiencing periods of relative calm in between, all while coping with and even celebrating the unfamiliar.

While one's retirement is primarily about the retiree, it would be a mistake to discount the impact that this change will have on others—family, colleagues, congregants, students, or beneficiaries of the organization in which you have been professionally employed. Engaging one's family, particularly a spouse, in detailed planning about retirement may seem obvious but is so critical that it shouldn't be taken for granted. Issues extend well beyond timing and the financial implications. The impact on a clergy spouse may be almost as significant as on the clergyperson, particularly when the spouse has played an important role in the congregational community and has received much recognition for doing so. Conversely, when the spouse has a career or an active volunteer life outside of the congregation, the decision to retire, change family routines, and possibly even relocate can be even more complex and challenging (see Chapter 8 for further elaboration). This is a time when communication is invaluable not only for the impact that it may have on the decisions to be made but even more importantly on the future of the relationship itself. Similarly, retirement decisions will impact others with whom you share your personal life (i.e., children and friends) and professional life (i.e., co-workers, congregational leaders and members, other clergy, and community leaders). Clearly, not everyone should have a vote in the decisions being made; however, each in their own way deserves to be informed by you, given an opportunity to reflect on how your retirement will impact them, and share their feelings with you. Maintaining these relationships during the next stage of life will play a significant role in the overall experience and your sense of well-being.

Don't discount the importance of other seemingly more mundane decisions and arrangements to be made, for these too will impact the quality of life going forward. Culling through books, papers, and possessions in your study or office can be both daunting and therapeutic. Because they each have associated memories, the process typically takes much more time than one might imagine. Just as preparing for closing down is important, so is making arrangements for new beginnings. Arranging suitable space for a study at home or a private professional office out of the home will provide a sense of grounding as well as a place to work without disrupting ongoing family routines.

Finally, take time to think about your personal needs. Identify those supports in your life that may continue and replace those that won't. A professional coach or therapist knowledgeable about clergy life can provide invaluable assistance and guidance through this period of transition in ways that friends, family, and colleagues may not. On a more practical level, arranging for guidance in financial, legal, and insurance matters can be reassuring as you step out on your own.

Preparing the Congregation or Organization for Your Retirement

After devoting much of your life to caring for others in your clergy work, planning for retirement is not the time to lose that focus. While taking care of your own needs, it is also important to think about how your retirement will impact these others. This is a time to end strong and on a positive note and will be beneficial to co-workers, lay leaders, congregants, as well as yourself. Clear advanced communication of your basic plans will help them prepare for the resulting changes in their own lives and give them time to reflect on their feelings and the messages they would like to share with you.

Planning for your "finals" (i.e., service, sermon, study group, staff meeting, etc.) will be therapeutic for you and those with whom you have shared your life as clergy. This would be an excellent time to create rituals associated with your departure. At such times, rituals can be helpful for all those involved (including the retiree), as they provide opportunities to reflect on past joys and successes, forgive past disappointments and hurts, highlight the congregation or organization's core values, and bring the community together as endings make space for new beginnings (see Chapter 4).

Finally, the importance of the retiring clergy "letting go" cannot be over-emphasized. Hopefully you have had a successful career and are leaving a proud legacy behind. It is now time to move on and do all you can to help the congregation or organization prepare for changes just as you are doing so in your own life. Much as the gardener tills the soil as winter ends in anticipation of spring planting, the retiring clergy's generous departure can be one of his most meaningful gifts to this community.

LIFE IN RETIREMENT

If we view retirement as a stage of life rather than an event, the importance of caring for yourself during the years ahead becomes even clearer. As discussed above, planning is essential. One of the first questions prospective retirees grapple with and are asked by others is "How will you spend your time?" While the specific responses will vary, staying reasonably active is preferable to disengaging from life and being dormant.

Many retirees who are healthy and anticipating a long life ahead often seek some form of work during their retirement years. Some clergy continue in similar congregational or organizational work in a new setting or on a part-time basis that is less demanding (and possibly more gratifying) than the position from which they retired. Others prefer to find a "bridge career" that is different from their work as clergy but draws on their experience, interests, and knowledge and is more compatible with achievement of their overall goals during this next stage of life. The advantage of part-time or bridge employment is that they provide opportunities for meaningful engagement and some continued income without the demands of full-time roles. Similarly, others find volunteering provides gratifying opportunities to continue to contribute to the community while engaging with other like-minded individuals.

One of the inherent joys of retirement is the flexibility it provides to fulfill other needs as we plan for the next stage of a meaningful life. Too many in our society, including clergy, have become overly dependent on work as the primary source of fulfillment. Instead, retirement can be an opportunity to intentionally build time and space into our lives for meaningful social, spiritual, intellectual, and physical activities. The goal here is balance and alignment with one's goals for the remainder on one's life.

Finally, as mentioned elsewhere in this book and the various resources included in Appendix I, here are some strategies that will contribute to successful life during retirement:

- Join or create clergy support systems.
- Build on your existing personal network.
- Engage in journaling or other self-reflective activities.
- Maintain a healthy lifestyle through exercise, diet, and medical care.
- Continue appropriate engagement with your congregation and successor.
- Engage with a coach, spiritual director, or therapist.
- Make time for self that is reflective and not merely goal driven.
- Strive for optimism.

THE JOY OF OPPORTUNITY

For those of us who are blessed with reasonably good health and at least a modicum of financial security, it is easy to imagine retirement being a time of joy. But even for those not so blessed, the new opportunities and discoveries afforded by retirement can be a blessing in themselves. This stage of life allows us to build on our past experiences, accumulated knowledge, and self-awareness as we continue to identify and achieve our life goals. What those particular goals may be is less important than whether they fulfill our desires for meaning and comfort. We can each decide how to allocate time, strength, and resources. What a privilege to have the option of continuing work as clergy temporarily on a full- or part-time basis, finding new employment, volunteering for causes one values, exploring old or new hobbies and interests, aiding family members, studying, and self-reflecting. Retirement is truly a smorgasbord time of life!

REFERENCES

Bergson, H. (1912). *An introduction to metaphysics* (1903) (T. E. Hulme, trans.) New York: G. P. Putnam's Sons.

Bridges, W. (2004). *Transitions: Making sense of life's changes* (2nd ed.). Cambridge, MA: Da Capo.

Brown, E. (2013). *Happier endings: A meditation on life and death.* New York, NY: Simon & Schuster.

Cowan, R. (2010, Fall). Wise aging. *Contact—The Journal of the Steinhardt Foundation for Jewish Life, 13*(1).

Koenig, H. G. (2002). *Purpose and power in retirement: New opportunities for meaning and significance.* Philadelphia, PA: Templeton Press.

National Center for Health Statistics. (2006). *Health, United States, 2006.* Hyattsville, MD. Retrieved from http://www.cdc.gov/nchs/data/hus/hus06.pdf

Wang, M., Henkens, K., & van Solinge, H. (2011). Retirement adjustment—A review of theoretical and empirical advancements. *American Psychologist, 66*(3), 204–213.

Wang, M., & Shultz, K. S. (2010). Employee retirement: A review and recommendations for future investigations. *Journal of Management, 36,* 172–206.

PART II

For the Clergy

http://dx.doi.org/10.2190/CLEC3

CHAPTER 3

Retirement is Not a Dirty Word

> When one door of happiness closes, another opens; but often we look so long at the closed door that we do not see the one which has opened for us.
>
> Helen Keller (1929)

> You've got to know when to hold 'em, know when to fold 'em, know when to walk away.
>
> *The Gambler* (Schlitz, 1977) sung by Kenny Rogers

RETIRING TO A NEW IDENTITY/LIFE

Now that my retirement date is approaching, I can't wait! After all these years of living up to the expectations of others, it is time for me. Congregants keep trying to express concern for my fatigue at keeping up with the demands of a growing and busy congregation. I appreciate their concern but can't tell them the truth. My wife and I have been living a sham of a marriage for more years than I care to remember. I don't think she loves me and know that she deeply resents my intense engagement with the congregation. The only clear outcome of a year of marriage counseling was an agreement that we'd stay married until our children were out of the house and I was retired from the congregation. As much as we both want to be able to breathe and start new lives, neither of us could bear the embarrassment or well-intentioned meddling of congregants. If I didn't feel the need to move away, perhaps far away, as soon as possible, I could have continued my work here; but I just can't. I am both sad and hopeful.

ðə   ðə   ðə

TEE-OFF TIME IS HERE

A story is told about an avid golfer who comes to his pastor and says, "You know how much I love to play golf. One of these days I am going to die and I would like to know when that happens if I will be able to play a round of golf with God himself. If you can grant me that knowledge I will give $250,000 to the church." Not wanting to pass up such a generous gift, the pastor replies that he must search out relevant passages in the Bible as well as pray for an answer. Two days later the pastor calls back and announces, "I have good news and bad news for you. The good news is that I prayed and prayed and read the Bible twice over, and I have it on good authority that when you die, indeed you will play the first round of golf with God himself. The bad news is that your tee-off time is Tuesday at 10:00 am!"

Our retirement "tee-off" time is either here or just around the corner. On that date and from then on you will be able to tee-off at any hour you so choose and need not worry about the congregation or who requests you for what tragedy or blessing. You will be at liberty to choose when, where, and *if* you want to participate in some function. However, it has been said, if the green looks greener on the next hole, it must be made of Astroturf. As happy as we are to have leisure time, there is more to your *heavenly* retirement than you might expect.

Interestingly, the dictionary definition of *retire* is to disappear, to go away or to withdraw, which was derived from the French, *retirer*, to go off into seclusion. Marc Freedman, in his wonderful book, *Encore: Finding Work That Matters in the Second Half of Life* (2007), suggests we think about retirement as ways of reinventing oneself and thus finding a new you. Maybe this retirement party might not be your final one. Perhaps there could be another one or even two ahead for you.

A brand new world is waiting out there for you to discover, yet be aware that there will be bumps and potholes in the road while you are finding it. The first time you fill out a form and mark your occupation as "retired," there may be a lump in your throat. If you get in touch with your feelings at that moment, you will probably find yourself questioning, *What value am I to society now?* When you were working and productive, you were a valuable member of the working class. Now you are eating up your savings. You feel like a consumer rather than a producer. In some ancient societies at this stage of life, they would put you in a boat and ship you out to sea. Sometime soon at an event you'll be asked what you do for a living. Notice how you may stumble on replying, *I'm retired.* You may hesitate because you worry what others will think of you as a retiree. Darcy L. Harris and Jessica Isenor identify that we are part of a world obsessed with doing and creating. We are busy, busy, busy, often not taking our full allotted vacation for we are too dedicated to our job. We are defined by our job and not by who we really are (Harris, 2011). Retirement is not uniformly celebrated. Some sociologists describe it as the "roleless role?" Union leader Walter Reuther once rather bleakly described retirees as "too old to work, too young to die" (as cited in Achenbaum, 2006).

Of course, some friends will envy you. You have attained their dream and have unlimited free time to play games, travel, read. On the other hand, you fear that some colleagues may regard you as old and no longer useful on the pulpit. They are relieved that you have vacated your position so they can take your place. You've heard some members of your community comment that the "elderly"— *your* generation—will bankrupt the Social Security system and it will be out of money when they reach retirement age. Deep down, they regard you as a drag on society, living too long and supported by the next generation. Companies and religious institutions seem to be eager to move older, high-priced employees off their rosters so as to reduce cost and improve their bottom line.

At one time, the aged were venerated and commanded respect. Once they were the source of wisdom about life, guiding and advising the younger generation about finances, marriage, and education. Once the younger generation thought that the fifth commandment spoke to them when it said, *Thou Shalt Honor Thy Father and Thy Mother.* When we were younger, we looked forward to being in that position of honor. As we grew older, we dreamed of retirement and everything it would bring us: leisure time, travel time, time for recreational activities. Common wisdom says that 70 is the new 50. We have taken this for granted because we have come to expect that modern medicine enables us to live a more active and longer life. I love the quip I read, *Inside of every older person is a younger person wondering what the heck happened.*

Society has changed. Today, knowledge no longer runs downhill but uphill. Parents and grandparents turn to 10 year olds to teach them how to use electronic devices. In turn, these digital natives mock us as we once did immigrants to the United States, for we are indeed digital immigrants who struggle to keep up with the constant development of new technology. The world is being run by 30 to 40 year olds who are taking management roles and often pushing elders into early retirement. They go on Google to find instantaneous answers that took us hours of research, leaving us to often to feel ignorant.

Didn't we push out our elders as well? In 1935, the concept of national insurance was adopted in the form of Social Security, with all of its medical benefits attached. This insurance was a leveling device that assured contributing members of society the necessary monthly income that has enabled us to retire at age 65. Ultimately this became an incentive for the older population to quit working, opening jobs for the next generation. This created an orderly movement in the workforce.

As a new generation of clergy assumes the pulpit, some of us are being summarily dismissed with the excuse that we cannot relate to younger congregants. We are being replaced with much younger clergy, some newly out of seminary, who are employed at a large savings to the congregation. With an eye fixed on hiring a more in-tune colleague, congregants are beginning to hint earlier and earlier for a change in the clergy. On the other hand, some of us are emotionally and physically spent and welcome the end of our career. Others wonder where all the years have gone, but still love the attention and playing an important role in this world. We feel that our life in the clergy has meaning.

Indeed, these days, this may not be your last retirement party but a temporary stop on your life's journey. Whether or not you liked your congregation, it provided you with stability and structure in your life. You knew what to do, you had a place to go every morning; you had an office, and you knew in which drawer to find things. You interacted with others. You knew your co-workers and congregants and all their quirks. But most do not realize that retirement throws off your equilibrium. It has a destabilizing effect, for we experience a loss of life roles (Neimeyer, 2006, p. 32). Even with jobs you are glad to leave, you must recognize that any time you miss the familiar, any time you cannot hang out with friends who made the job fun or tolerable, speak to the necessity of developing new routines. Closing the door on a major portion of your life means upheaval and a need for adjustment.

Dr. Paul Melrose, Director of Clinical Services at the Samaritan Counseling Center of SE Michigan, in a speech entitled "Some Thoughts on Retirement," reminds us that even though we go through this upheaval, we are still somebody. One of the advantages of aging and being retired is that we no longer have to please everyone. We are now free to speak our political and societal opinions without alienating some congregants. "Who you are has to do with the kind of person you are, the knowledge you have, the roles and relationships that bring out different parts of your personality. Your experience is unique and you have gained wisdom," he states (Melrose, 2011).

On the other hand, Rabbi Abraham Joshua Heschel, in his article, "To Grow In Wisdom" in the book, *The Insecurity of Freedom,* writes,

> Most of us are unprepared for old age. We know a great deal about what to do with things, even what to do with other people; we do not know what to do with ourselves. We know how to act in public; we do not know what to do in privacy. Old age involves the problem of what to do with privacy. (1972, p. 73)

For clergy, privacy is an interesting concept. In one sense, we have been alone most of our adult lives, living in a world where congregants had no concept of the pressure we were under. It was a 24/7 job of counseling, sermon preparation, administrative responsibilities, and life-cycle events, as well as trying to create a meaningful personal life. We found ourselves responding to the needs of our congregants day or night and simultaneously trying to meet the needs of our own families. It's not easy, as you well know. Our internal world has been private as well, as we felt unable to share much of our lives with others, even colleagues. With colleagues, it is either a case of one-upmanship or not trusting the other enough to reveal your or the congregation's weaknesses. Now, unaccustomed to sharing thoughts and with no job to talk about, life has new challenges. To succeed, we have to find ways to reinvent ourselves.

I kept a card given to me at a seminar, which reads, "We were told never to cross a bridge until we come to it, but this world is owned by individuals who have 'crossed bridges' in their imagination far ahead of the crowd." As Father Joseph Krupp, who works with retired priests, said to me, "We have to think about crossing the bridge earlier, for retirement is like a bridge and it better hook to somewhere on the other side." He advised, "People need to develop and to evaluate four separate plans for retirement: a financial plan, a medical plan, a recreational plan, and an activities plan, and we need to consider all four plans, perhaps simultaneously." In reality, most of us should emphasize our economic future earlier rather than later, for it is essential that we feel secure materially in these later years. Hopefully, you have already spent time with a financial counselor to prepare for when your cash flow slows down exponentially. We strongly encourage you to find a professional financial advisor who has experience with people planning for retirement, who does not have a product to sell, and who knows something about clergy housing rules. Unfortunately, many of us were told that God will provide, so we too often accepted a low salary, and now we learn that neither God nor the congregation provide very much economically. So, while we are waiting for the world to come, we may find ourselves in far reduced circumstances because we hadn't planned carefully enough for our future. Financial insecurity in retirement can be the greatest cause of stress and can make the "golden years" tarnish. As with many older adults, we are concerned about being a burden to our children, and we pray that our finances will not run out before we do.

Years ago when we applied for college, we considered not only the courses in a projected major, but other issues such as religious life on campus, fraternities/ sororities, and housing opportunities. So it is for retirement. We must not only do the financial work, but the psychological, emotional, and spiritual work as well. Just as you need a financial counselor, it would be a good idea to engage a "life coach," who understands the dynamics of the clergy retirement and who will encourage you to engage in all aspects of adjusting to retirement.

Retirement is Earned

Robert Kemper, in *Planning for Ministerial Retirement*, reminds us, "Retirement is an *earned financial subsidy*" (1988, p. 6; author's emphasis). When we enter this new phase, we cannot hold the attitude that we are living off the dole of others who are now funding our retirement through Social Security. Remember that paycheck after paycheck, you invested money with the government so that you would have a retirement income. Hopefully, part of your church's compensation plan was a contribution to your retirement account. You may now wish it were more or that you had set aside a larger amount each year, but nevertheless, the funds you are now receiving are *yours*, funds that you put away through *your* hard work and dedication. You and your family deserve this money and you are now free to spend it as you choose. May we remind you that you have no responsibility to leave an inheritance for your children? Recently, each of us and our wives have taken SKI vacations to rather exotic locations in South Africa and Asia. *SKI vacations to South Africa,* asked our friends? *We didn't know they had snow in South Africa or Cambodia. Yes,* we replied, these were a *"Spend the Kid's Inheritance"* vacations.

Now, several years since retirement, when I check off *retired* on my doctor's forms, I do not feel so bad. I realize that I have earned the title just as I earned the title of Rabbi Emeritus from my congregation. (Although someone once told me that emeritus comes from two Latin words: *E* from egress or exit and *Meritus* from *Thank God!*)

During this *earned next period* of one's life, the rhythms of life will change drastically. Throw away your watch! Time will be measured differently. Our previous world revolved around the weekends with final sermon preparations, services, pastoral visits, teaching obligations. While others had free time, you were working. Suddenly that rhythm is about to change. You will have free time anytime you choose. You are now one of the congregants. You will be off when everyone else is off. You can go out to eat the night before your Sabbath service and not worry about how your sermon will be received. You will not have night meetings unless you choose to attend one. It is hard enough to change your morning rhythm and to no longer need the alarm clock to awaken you at a specific time. No longer are you rushing to your office only to be confronted with a list of calls to make, letters and articles to write, and meetings with congregants. Now you can nap in the afternoon or choose from a plethora of continuing-education classes offered at the local university or just go to the gym to work out.

Even harder, if you have chosen to remain in the area, will be the anxiety of deciding whether or not to attend services at your old congregation, or any congregation. For the first time, attendance is optional. At first you will feel guilty if you miss a service, believing that others will judge you or criticize you. Then you may realize you are no longer beholden to other's opinions or judgments, and your income will not depend upon anyone's criticism of you. In this new era, you are the only one to whom you need to answer, unless you have a mate, of course. You will go to services because you are seeking a reunion with God and not because you are expected to be there. Rabbi Abraham Joshua Heschel tells us,

> The years of old age may enable us to attain the high values we failed to sense, the insights we have missed, wisdom we ignored. They are indeed formative years, rich in possibilities to unlearn the follies of a lifetime, to see through inbred self-deceptions, to deepen understanding and compassion, to widen the horizon of honesty, to refine the sense of fairness.
>
> One ought to enter old age the way one enters the senior year at a university, in exciting anticipation of consummation. Rich in perspective, experienced in failure, the person advanced in years is capable of shedding prejudices and the fever of vested interests. He does not see any more in every fellow man a person who stands in his way, and competitiveness may cease to be his way of thinking. (1972, p. 78)

Old age need not be a curse, although our aches and pains may make us feel as if it is. In this "encore" stage of life, we can do things that we never had time for in the past, enjoy new interests, or explore talents we put aside when we chose the clergy. We can read books that intrigue us rather than ones we had to read for the next sermon or class. We can finally stand for the morals and values that are personally most important to us and pursue how we can work on their behalf.

Robert Kemper (1988) reminds us that an enormous shift occurs in retirement:

> The shift from the circumstances, restraints, and conditions of work to a life freed from all of those encumbrances. This shift is why planning for retirement is essential, why if you define retirement as quitting work, you must recognize the necessity of defining new work for yourself, and why some ministers retire with satisfaction and some do not. (p. 10; see Chapter 6 on Meaning Making)

He reminds us poignantly and simply of the position we are in:

> One day I was the most important man in the building. The next day I was nothing. When you retire, you will feel stripped of the power, authority, status, and vocation that you have known for all the years you were a parish minister. At some point in the retirement process you will feel that you have been "defrocked," not by an ecclesiastical court, but simply by the process of retiring. (p. 19)

One respondent to our questionnaire felt that he was 'going from a 'Somebody' to a 'Nobody' because the people I met after retirement had no idea who I was, what my background was or the fact that I was good at anything!" Father Al Krupp asked, "What's left of Jack when Jack is no longer an active priest?"

Ah, Relief!

Whether you enjoyed your years in the clergy or not, retirement still sounds great. The rhythm of office work, clergy responsibilities, and the phone ringing with yet another call that will interrupt your family and personal plans will soon come to an end. Ah, the dream of engaging in recreational activities, of returning to a long put-aside hobby, of traveling or visiting family is finally going to come to fuition. But hold on! I once heard about a rabbi who was so upset that people were always interrupting his studies that he wished for peace and quiet without disturbance. God granted him his wish. It was wonderful for a week and then for a month, but soon he began to wonder if anyone still cared for him and why were people not coming to him for advice. Soon he found himself praying to God to let people back in his life for he could not live this way.

So it is as we approach retirement. Some of us are tired, burnt out, and looking for some relief. We need a sabbatical, some extended time off, a change of pace. If you have ever had the privilege of a sabbatical, you know how refreshing that can be. Then you can return to work feeling renewed and energized. This is the way we should think of the first 6 months of retirement—as a sabbatical. I tell mourners that in the first year of loss, they should not make any major decisions. I make a similar suggestion to those in the process of retiring. Do not make major decisions for the first 6–8 months, such as moving or choosing a new congregation. Instead, use this time as you would a sabbatical: travel, study, find a hobby, do the things that you have been dreaming of doing. Use this time to grieve for a change of rhythms (see Chapter 5) and allow yourself the privilege of experiencing them and not being afraid of them. Use this time for research and thoughts about new possibilities. But just as you would on sabbatical, set a date to return to your new job. New job, you say? I thought I was retired!

Marc Freedman (2007) reminds us that we are in the midst of fashioning a new stage of life between the traditional midlife years and careers, and true retirement and old age. Most of us are navigating uncharted territories. In the last generation, people referred to the "golden years" when they would run off to gated retirement communities where no one under 55 with children was allowed. These were often in the sunny south—Florida, Arizona, or California. But soon people found that they were not as happy as they thought they would be. Before long they discovered that the golden years became the *tarnished* years, and they missed something essential: intellectual challenge, social stimulation, and a sense of *purpose* in their lives (p. 102) With new medical procedures to keep us relatively healthy, at 65 we may think that we have only finished the first half of our adulthood (p. 113). Perhaps after our earned sabbatical, our next job will encompass a passion that we have long held. Maybe we should look upon this retirement as the first of perhaps several retirements and a bridge to a second career, or a new labor of love. As Albert Einstein (1914, radio broadcast) said, "Life is a gift, and if we agree to accept it, we must contribute in return. When we fail to contribute, we fail to adequately answer why we are here."

Reframing the Word "Retirement"

Since for some the word retirement carries a negative nuance, perhaps it would be best to think of this stage of life with other words. One person suggested that we call this stage "re-fire-ment." Some other suggestions could be "reactivate," "rededicate," "rediscover" (Halaas, 2005).

Father Krupp calls his directory of retired priests *Fraternity of Elders*. Some instead change the nomenclature *retired* after their name or *emeritus* and use the term *Clergy/Minister-at-Large* (Kemper, 1988, p. 95), or *Community Clergy*. At least it's not like a dead end street. We need to question what does God have for me to do now, rather than what has God taken away from me?

Let's Listen

Retirement is not a dirty word, even if some people make retirees feel worthless or worth less. Instead, some of the responders to our survey noted,

- I have more things to do now than ever. I play music in three or four venues. I teach as an adjunct professor which has caused me to expand my understanding of politics and religion, satisfying an old fantasy and bringing in extra money. Working on a project for publishing with a world renowned scholar is kinda nice too.

- I immediately stepped into a child-care situation with a four-month old grandchild who was soon followed by three more, so my wife and I did a lot of that. We were fortunate to find another church where we enjoyed the people and made some new friends, although it is not easy to find your way sometimes, going from being the pastor to being a retired pastor who is simply a church member now. Also, we had my elderly mother to look after for the past ten years—so purpose was there from the onset.

- We moved to Penney Retirement Community in FL, and I have plenty to do! I've made so many new friends, done a great deal of singing, preached a small amount (2–3 times a year, as I'd hoped), involved myself in a variety of service opportunities such as helping to "waiter" at meals for those in assisted living, team-teaching at a Bible study, attending classes put on by other residents, etc. I've tried to maintain a separation from the members of my former final church, and, for the most part, that has been successful. I'd strongly recommend that clergy contemplating retirement, but not equating that with being put out to pasture, investigate communities where there is an ethic of service to others, as here.

- I have a regular exercise program that doesn't get interrupted anymore. I loved the sense of freedom to seek God's will for my next "assignment." I have enjoyed my retirement with very little difficulty in making the adjustment.

- Actually, it was not so hard to find new meaning, since I had made some good efforts to plan for this time of my life. I had put together a whole file folder of plans and projects I wanted to get into, but I realized that it was important to take some weeks to just take it easy and get fully moved into the condo I had purchased. The adjustments came when I began implementing my plans. It took more than a year to work through these adjustments. Now, though, I am busy, my days are just full enough and things usually go smoothly. Also it took some time to get to know my neighbors, and I feel very much at home now in the small condo group.

Some responders felt sadly disappointed:

- I expected to be invited to contribute and or be consulted by the organization I left, but communication was cut off.
- Missing the church and the people in the church.
- Major adjustment was knowing that there was someone new leading the congregation I had created who did not seek out my advice on a regular basis or share what was happening unless I inquired. I was no longer part of any decision making process.
- The major problem in my retirement has been relationship with my successor. I had hoped for a positive relationship but it has been anything but positive.

The major cause is that I have found him to be rather incompetent and untrustworthy. I have been pained at the decline of the congregation under his leadership.

- I find I lack the discipline that my former schedule demanded of me. Consequently some of the things I had hoped to do in retirement, I have yet to do.
- I wondered what I should do with my spare time. I wanted more free time, but I now had too much. I was used to a routine and now I didn't need that routine but missed it. Saturday night preparation time felt meaningless now that I didn't have to prepare for worship. Sitting in a (different) church pew seemed strange. I had to get to know a new church family. They seemed to like me and my wife, but I didn't really know how to fit in.
- I went in many directions with little projects soon after retiring, but lacked sufficient focus and discipline to keep on task. There were many ways to volunteer, but nothing gave me the level of satisfaction that my former staff position had provided.

Many were left with quandaries:

- [I am] answering the question, "Does God have more for me to do in retirement than I am doing?" And this question still remains.
- I have experienced some guilt because my wife is still working and I am not. I feel that I should be doing more work around the house but I am content to read and do other things.
- At first the hardest thing was developing some kind of routine. Then it was finally figuring out that it was OK to NOT have a routine!
- A feeling of "wasting time" occasionally washes over me, but I soon drive it away by saying to myself: "This is what you've wanted. So go do something!"

SUMMARY

A new adventure is ahead of you. In your encore performance, how will you do? I leave you with the words from Martin Buber:

> Every person born into this world represents something new, something that never existed before, something original and unique. It is the duty of every person to know and consider that they are unique in their particular character and that there has never been anyone like them before; for if there had been someone like them, there would have been no need for them to come into the world. Every single person is a new thing in the world and is called upon to fulfill their particularity. (as cited in Diamond, 2002, p. 78)

You are different and special and you still have roles to play in this world with the days left to you. What are they? Only you in contemplation with God can decide. Listen and you will hear the "still small voice."

REFERENCES

Achenbaum, W. A. (2006, Spring). What is retirement for? *Wilson Quarterly, 30*(2), 50–56.

Diamond, J. (2002). *Narrative means for sober ends: Treating addiction and its aftermath.* New York, NY: Guilford.

Einstein, A. (1914). *Manifesto to the Europeans.* Radio Broadcast.

Freedman, M. (2007). *Encore: Finding work that matters in the second half of life.* New York, NY: Public Affairs.

Halaas, G. W. (2005). *Retirement and wholeness: Looking forward to the third age.* Herdon, VA: Alban Institute.

Harris, D. (Ed.). (2011). *Counting our losses: Reflecting on change, loss, and transition in everyday life.* New York, NY: Routledge/Taylor & Francis.

Heschel, A. J. (1972). *The insecurity of freedom.* New York, NY: Farrar, Strauss and Giroux.

Keller, H. (1929). *We bereaved.* New York: L. Fulenwider, Inc.

Kemper, R. (1988). *Planning for ministerial retirement.* New York, NY: Pilgrim.

Melrose, P. J. (2011, January 30). *Some thoughts on retirement.* Dr. Paul J. Melrose. Retrieved January 21, 2012, from www.paulmelrose.com/some-thoughts-on-retirement/

Neimeyer, R. A. (2006). *Lessons of loss: A guide to coping.* Memphis, TN: Center of the Study of Loss and Transition.

Schlitz, D. (1977). *The gambler* [song]. Nashville, TN: Sony/ATV Tunes.

CHAPTER 4

Saying Goodbye

The true meaning of life is to plant trees under whose shade you do not plan to sit.

Nelson Henderson (Henderson, 1982)

The great use of life is to spend it for something that will outlast us.

William James (Perry, 1935)

I am what survives of me.

Erik Erikson (Erickson, 1968, p. 141)

Every new beginning comes from some other beginning's end.

Seneca (Seneca)

RETIRED FOUNDER CLERGY

This is MY congregation! I founded it, created it, drew people together to create this community. Everything that is of value here has my imprint; its values and mission came from me. I even named it. But time has passed and my wife reminds me more and more each day just how much we (not just me!) have given of ourselves and the sacrifices we have made. Don't get me wrong, she shares my belief in God and is dedicated to my calling; but she is right. Unless I retire from active work in the congregation, our last years will slip away from us before we know it. We do deserve a rest and to come first for once; but I do feel both sad and guilty about leaving. This congregation is the child we never had; I birthed it, suckled it, and raised it to become a strong independent being. I am proud of the congregation and all those who have worked alongside me to bring it to this stage; but I am afraid at the thought of leaving. What if they can't carry on without me? What if they can?

ও৷   ও৷   ও৷

WHAT DO YOU WANT PEOPLE TO
REMEMBER ABOUT YOU?

A doctor, a teacher, and a rabbi were discussing what they would like people to say while standing in front of their coffin.

41

The doctor says, "I would like people to say that I was a good doctor, that I cared for my patients, that I was a good husband and a wonderful father."

The teacher says, "I hope people say I was a great teacher, that I cared for my students, that I was a good husband and a wonderful father.

The rabbi said, "I'd like people to stand before my coffin and say, 'Look! I think he's breathing!'"

How you would like people to remember you? What do you want them to say about you? What legacy will you leave behind? We all hope to be remembered as having had some impact on people's lives, of being the kind of pastor who cared for his congregation and brought hope and comfort in times of need, and who knew how to celebrate the joyous moments as well. Ultimately, we would like to be remembered for our achievements and not for our failures.

It is Hard to Say Goodbye

Saying goodbye for perhaps the last time is never easy. Do you remember your last days of high school and that final summer before going off to college, the army, or to seek your fortune? There were a lot of hugs, many tears, and a dull thud in each one's heart, knowing that perhaps this would be the last time you might see your friends. Even waiting until winter break to see your best friend seemed like an eternity. As summer wore down, there were late-night get-togethers and final elongated goodbyes as each one went off to their respective destinations.

Saying farewell is very hard to do. It represents change, and that is always disconcerting. Many of us know this experience of saying goodbye all too well, for in the past we have moved several times from one congregation to another. Certainly, it was unnerving to leave friends and congregants behind, but there was the excitement of moving on to a *Camelot* congregation. We were filled with hopeful anticipation of an upward career path with the financial reward that goes with it. Tearful goodbyes were the price we paid as we moved upward in our chosen profession. Not so this time! This, so to speak, is the end of the line, with a number of unsettling questions ahead. This time there will not be a new congregation awaiting us, nor does an increase in compensation lie ahead. In fact, unlike ever before, we worry about our financial future, and it places great stress on our mental state and on our spousal relationship.

In addition, reality gives us a knock on the head. Suddenly, we face the fact that we have grown old; that we are less physically able than we used to be; that we are tired of doing what we have done for years; that the work no longer excites us as it used to: and that we are just more tired—period! Then someone mentions that perhaps we need to begin thinking about making final arrangements and getting our will in order. Kaboom! Our psyche is shaken.

As we stand at the doorway of the congregation, preparing to leave for the last time, we tend to judge ourselves in a way that we never did before. Unlike when we left other congregations, looking forward to what awaited us, we now look back and reflect on our entire career and ask ourself, "What are congregants saying about us? What kind of pastor was I really? How good was my scholarship? Was I kind and caring, moral and ethical, honest and truthful? Was I a good spouse, an attentive and loving parent?"

Unlike any other time in our lives, this is a time for review and contemplation, when we confront both the past and the future. In many cases, we still feel healthy and able to contribute to the world, so we contemplate: What are the many things I have wanted to do, but never had the time to do? What will bring me joy and meaning in the years ahead? How can I still contribute my talents and abilities? How can I still be a force for good? In addition, we begin to think about our successor who will have the power to continue or replace everything we have built in the many years of service to the congregation. Even if we cannot watch this development ourselves, we will certainly hear about it from loyal congregants who still think of us as their clergy, and it will hurt when we learn that what we thought was an important congregational program has been tossed on the scrap heap of history.

Feelings

When it comes time to say goodbye, we need to listen to the words of Brian Hawkins and Carole Barone (2008),

> You will likely roll between feeling slighted and feeling irrelevant or even invisible. At this point, your identity is threatened, but you are not yet into retirement and cannot yet begin to redefine yourself. It is easy to over interpret actions during this stage, to take things personally, to perceive slights, and to become angry and frustrated. In all likelihood, this is just part of the grief, disorientation, and frustration that results as a loss of routine and influence. . . .
>
> The simple acts of deleting your signature line, changing your e-mail address, and turning in your keys are emotionally monumental. You are, in effect, wiping out your identity, your "being," as a professional.

A change of identity—never before have you experienced this emotion or this world.

As one pastor noted in our survey, how humbling and alienating it was to know that you no longer belong in a place where you were once the "center of action and the primary performer." Of course, add to that that the new pastor and the judicatory officials see you as undermining the growth of the church, so you have to give yourself some leeway in terms of your emotional and physiological roller coaster.

Want a humbling feeling! Read the poem by Saxon White Kessinger titled *The Indispensible Man* (Kessinger, 1959), in which he reminds us that you can swish your hand all you want in a bucket of water, but when you take it out the water returns in a minute to just the way it was. Thus, he relates, no human is indispensible.

Most pastors face a disruption of what has been described as *soul and role*. We do not simply do ministry, we are clergy 24/7. Our vocation is a matter of character, lifestyle, and self-definition, even if we have healthy family lives, relationships outside the church, and interests outside of our ministry (Epperly, 2010). In retirement, you can hide. You can hide by dropping Reverend, Rabbi, Father, or Imam from your introduction. You can move to another city and simply avoid telling people of your former profession or just not advertise it. You can hide by taking another job or choosing a different lifestyle. Those are conscious choices, but they cause us uneaseness.

For the first time in a long number of years, you get to make a conscious decision of what and when you want to do something. With no office to go to, where will you go every day—your neighborhood coffee shop, your home office, the library? Even in small congregations, you had a study. Ahead of you will be that discomforting feeling that you no longer have a place that is truly yours in which to retreat. Ugh! More feelings of chaos! From the time I first read Susanne Langer' remarks a person can adapt himself to anything his imagination can cope with, but he cannot deal with chaos, I have realized that grieving is the process of reclaiming balance from the chaos we have experienced.

In these final moments at the congregation and at this phase of life, there are a plethora of feelings and emotions that you have never experienced before. As prepared as we think we are, and as emotionally controlled as we attempt to be, we are, as at the loss of a loved one, never ready for that last goodbye. It will hurt. Allow it to do so and grieve for what has now ended.

Preparing Ourselves

We are all well aware of anticipatory grief, an awareness that a loved one or a pet is dying or a job or a marriage is coming to an end. In anticipation, you allow yourself to begin the grieving process so that when the end does come, you are not as shocked as you would have been if it happened suddenly or if you had put off facing reality.

We can do some preparatory work now that we have decided, or it was decided for us, that retirement is forthcoming. Often when working with hospice patients, doing a life review seems to relieve the stress of the dying process. applying beneficial exercise as we face retirement could remind us of what we have accomplished over the years and how much we have meant to so many people. You might find it helpful to sit in some quiet place and spend some time listing the high points of your professional life in no particular order, some of what made you feel most exhilarated and satisfied. What were your major accomplishments? What most inspired you? When did you feel you were performing at your personal all-time best (Anthony, 2007)? When a loved one dies, it is cathartic to go through the picture albums and tell the stories of the photos, where they were taken and who was there. It might be beneficial to go through old bulletins with family members and review what you accomplished during your years at the congregation. Talk about the wonderful experiences, the people whom you touched, and the special life-cycle events that you performed. Research shows that people are happier if they are grateful for the positive things in their lives rather than worrying about what might have been overlooked (Buettner, 2010).

In *Ten Commandments for Pastors Leaving a Congregation* (2006), Lawrence W. Farris proposes doing a review with members of the congregation who are active or insightful or who were there when you arrived. He suggests using some of these questions as a guide: How are we different today from how we were when you came? What accomplishments in my ministry are they most grateful for? What challenges have we together overcome and what did we learn from those situations? What do we wish we might have done had time and resources allowed. Farris indicates that it will be helpful for you and the congregation to gain a sense of accomplishment and for the members to assess where they have been and what they would like to accomplish with your successor. Farris goes on,

> It is sometimes said that the inability to change the past is the one limitation that God shares with us. The best we can do when it comes to leaving a congregation is to bring the past to as complete and whole a conclusion as possible so that all may rejoice in what has been good, learn from what has not, and move freely and faithfully forward into a promising future where God may be praised and served. (p. 90)

Ultimately, we want to ask ourselves this question: *Did I live my life conscious of the presence of God?* Translating this in another way, *Did I, as a minister and pastor, truly try to craft a life worthy to be being lived in the presence of God* (Geller, 2011)? We have to be the ultimate judge of ourselves and of what a clergyperson should do or be.

We all have a tendency to compare ourself to the accomplishments of our colleagues. We often demean ourselves by saying that we were not as great an orator or as impressive a scholar or as great a counselor as some fellow clergy we know. In reality, we all have our own particular talents, interests, and abilities. A Hassidic story tells us,

> Once, the great Hassidic leader, Zusya, came to his followers. His eyes were red with tears, and his face was pale with fear.
> "Zusya, what's the matter? You look frightened!"
> "The other day, I had a vision. In it, I learned the question that the angels will one day ask me about my life."
> The followers were puzzled. "Zusya, you are pious. You are scholarly and humble. You have helped so many of us. What question about your life could be so terrifying that you would be frightened to answer it?"
> Zusya turned his gaze to heaven. "I have learned that the angels will

not ask me, 'Why weren't you a Moses, leading your people out of slavery?'"

His followers persisted. "So, what will they ask you?"

"And I have learned," Zusya sighed, that the angels will not ask me, 'Why weren't you a Joshua, leading your people into the promised land?'"

One of his followers approached Zusya and placed his hands on Zusya's shoulders. Looking him in the eyes, the follower demanded, "But what will they ask you?"

"They will say to me, 'Zusya, there was only one thing that no power of heaven or earth could have prevented you from becoming.' They will say, 'Zusya, why weren't you Zusya?'" (Lipman, 1955)

There Are 50 Ways to Leave Your Lover

There are various ways to leave your congregation, both pleasant and unpleasant. Our ultimate advice is to never leave with words that you will later regret or that will leave a bad taste in the mouths of your former congregants, who will then feel assured that they will be better off without you.

Michael Anthony advises, "This is no time to get in your last shot at those who may have made your stay challenging. Be close to the Lord—you are God's representative. We cannot lose our grip on God's love and holiness" (2007, p. 101). Remember the many positives about being a clergy. We are trusted. Our congregants seek our advice. We are truly blessed for the opportunity to have made a difference in so many people's lives, to have a profession that allows us to do meaningful work in God's name. Don't let one or two irritated complainers undo all the good that you have done for others. Even though you might be tempted, don't air dirty laundry in public. The congregation doesn't need to know all the details of your relationships with other members. Remember that even smart people make mistakes. Use good judgement and have mercy on those who have offended you. Don't encourage divisiveness. Don't burn any bridges. Show class in your exiting. Be a *mensch*! (Yiddish for a human being) Proverbs reminds us, "He who guards his lips guards his life, but he who speaks rashly will come to ruin" (13:3 NIV). We are God's representative, and as God certainly has patience for His children, so should we as God's ambassadors. You do not want to be remembered for one moment of anger. Be gracious! Be thankful! Allow for goodbyes, for people need the chance to express their appreciation, and you need to hear it as well. Anthony continues,

> Even when forced to resign, you, as their pastor, would do well to give the church an opportunity to show their thankfulness for the ministry you have provided. It gives them, you, and your family a time to focus on the good memories and successes that are always there. (2007, p. 101)

Michael Anthony makes some thoughtful suggestions for writing a final letter to congregation. He encourages us to express some degree of appreciation and gratitude for their partnership in the ministry you have experienced together. Let them know that you have appreciated the opportunity to serve as their pastor and that you are thankful for the time you have had together. (2007, p. 120)

An important way to depart from the members of the congregation is to do so in a public ceremony. We can feign humility and protest that we do not want or need such a public display of affection, but in a study of priests who retired, we learn, "the general discomfort generated by the non-ritualized passage can contribute to an experience of malaise and trepidation" (Ladd, 2006, p. 92). Perhaps this is true for the congregation as well. Having a public ritualized ceremony is therefore very important. Ladd (2006) advises, "It may also be important that the retiree have some part in the planning thus having a sense of control in this area of retirement. . . . a 'quiet,' uncelebrated retirement may create intense psychological challenges."

When it comes to the farewell service, well-intentioned congregants might assume that what they want is also what you want. We suggest that the planning committee sit down with you. Tell them it is important to know some of the things that you would like or not like in terms of the ceremony. They might want to include your mate as a consultant and/or to be a part of the planning, for your partner is an important part of this process and is retiring as well (see chapter 8). Everyone needs to think broadly as to what elements would bring both the clergy and the congregation the greatest sense of closure. Perhaps you have attended ceremonies or receptions that you personally would find heartwarming or objectionable. Be sensitive to what the congregation might require so they can express their gratitude to you, which may be very different from your desire to leave quietly. Leave room in this negotiation for surprises and for others to plan what they want to do for you. This is a two-way street, and the concept should be a win-win outcome, even though it will be a bittersweet affair for both sides. Even though at a wedding there is a great deal of joy for the bride and groom, the parents also often feel an emptiness as they watch their beloved child leave their household forever. So this moment will be a happy/sad one. A career comes to an end, but new opportunities abound. Congregants also experience mixed feelings. They celebrate your retirement and wish you well, but also feel the loss of the one person they could go to for comfort, compassion, and their religious needs. Anxiety reigns! Who will replace their clergy? Will he or she be understanding? Someone to talk to? Inspire them with sermons? Bring inventive ideas to the table? Joy, sadness, and worry supplant the caring and compassion for their former clergyperson.

The Ceremony

In keeping with the aforementioned advice, this is not the occasion to express disappointment at what you had not been able to accomplish, but rather, as their spiritual leader, to thank and praise those who have supported and stood with you over the years. This should include the leadership (current and past), members of the congregation who particularly have shown devotion over the years, and your entire staff, including janitorial, co-clergy, and so on. Gratitude is always appreciated and will allow you to leave with a sense of endearment by your congregants. I love the following two prayers written by Naomi Levy, in her book, *Talking to God: Personal Prayers for Times of Joy, Sadness, Struggle, and Celebration* (2002). We can envision reciting this alone in the darkened sanctuary sometime shortly before that last farewell event. The second is a wonderful prayer that you might want to include in the service to be read in unison by the congregation.

A Prayer at Retirement

I am scared, God. Who am I without a title? Without a schedule? Without my job? Teach me, God. Show me who I am. Remind me that I am not my job, nor was I ever so.

Open my eyes to the beauty that surrounds me. Open my heart to the love. Open my arms to family members and friends I was always too busy to embrace. Open my mind to the vast world of knowledge that lies before me. Open my ears to the cries of those who desperately need my assistance.

Fill me with compassion, God. Let me transform these doubts of mine into acts of goodness and charity. Calm my fears, God. Remind me that I am vital, that I am needed, that I matter, that I am loved.

Teach me to embrace this precious freedom I have been granted. For the first time in a long time I can choose to spend my days as I wish, to explore whatever I wish, to travel wherever I wish.

Help me live this time wisely, God. Lead me on the path to meaning, to satisfaction, to joy, to peace. Stay with me, God. Let me know You are near. Amen, (p. 195)

A Retirement Blessing for the Congregation

Thank you for your insight, your guidance, your companionship, your
   integrity, and for all the sacrifices you made.
May God bless the path you take.
May God bless your future labors with success.
May your newly found freedom bring you great pleasure and deep
   satisfaction.
May God bless your body with health and your soul with joy.
May your work here continue to flourish in your absence.
May you continue to spread your kindness and wisdom upon us for many
   years to come.
May God watch over you and shield you from harm.
May all your prayers be answered. Amen. (p. 193)

We were also privileged to receive a service containing a "Ritual of Release for a Rabbi," which we like very much and can be altered to fit any congregation (Temple Sholom, 2010).

Congregation: A congregational family is constantly changing. It is important and right that we recognize these times of transition, of endings and new beginnings. On this night we mark a change in the spiritual leadership of our congregation as we say farewell to [name] whose time as our clergy has come to an end and prepare to welcome a new leader.

Congregation: As we move into the coming months and years, we vow to carry with us the spiritual legacy that we have gleaned from our time with [name]

Congregation: We will strive to imbue the new experiences that await us with a sense of the spiritual richness we have shared together with [name]

President: In that spirit, we say farewell to one who has served us with integrity and dedication.

Congregation: [Name], as our Leader, you have led us in worship and celebrated rituals that help give shape to the events of our lives. You have blessed our children, honored our teens, celebrated our anniversaries, and helped us remember those we lost. We hereby release you from these duties and responsibilities.

Clergy: I acknowledge release from my ritual role in the life of this congregation.

Congregation: You have cared for us in our times of need and celebrated our joys with us. You have accepted our shortcomings, offered us gentle guidance and listened to us with love. We hereby release you from these duties and responsibilities.

Clergy: I acknowledge release from my pastoral role in the life of this congregation.

Congregation: You have taught and learned with us—children, youth, and adults alike. We hereby release you from these duties and responsibilities.

Clergy: I acknowledge release from my educational role in the life of this congregation.

Congregation: You have led us in our works of justice and compassion, taking the teachings of our faith beyond these walls. You have spoken the truths you have seen, challenging and inspiring us to build a better world. We hereby release you from these duties and responsibilities.

Clergy: I acknowledge release from my prophetic role in the life of this congregation.

President: You have consistently honored the identity of this community and helped us keep it foremost in our thoughts. We are grateful for the many gifts you have shared with us as we journeyed together: your warmth, your compassion, your patience, and your understanding. We are also grateful to you for helping to set us on a path toward the realization of our vision for the future.

Congregation: We, the members of [name of congregation] of [name of city], now release you, [clergy name] from your covenant with us and ask God's blessing upon you. We accept that you now leave us as you retire from our congregation. Your influence on us, however, will not leave with you. We will remember with fondness the time you shared with us.

Clergy: I acknowledge release from my covenant with this congregation, and ask God's blessing upon you.

I thank this congregation—its leadership, those who have participated regularly in its services and programs, and all of you, its members for the love, kindness, warmth and support shown me during these [number of years] years. I thank you for accepting my leadership. I recall with joy the many things which we have been able to accomplish together and I recall with sadness the things we were not able to do. I ask your understanding and forgiveness for whatever mistakes I may have made and for the times when I did not live up to your expectations.

[Clergy remarks made here.]

Clergy: I believe that our parting, as well as our time together, is an expression of God's Presence among us. As we all serve as God's partner here on earth, I pray that our efforts together and the paths that each of us will now tread separately will lead us to a better future for all. Amen. (adapted)

To Whom to Say Goodbye

We suggest that you say goodbye to the staff who have worked beside you, including some who may no longer be with the congregation. Whether or not you like all of them and whether or not they all like you, it would be nice to do something special for them to mark this occasion. Be gracious to them! Don't expect them to do something special for you, but should they so choose, be gracious.

Farris suggests that during the final days you might want to make a special visit to congregants who are homebound or in nursing homes, people whom you have seen regularly. He comments,

> Yes, there will be another pastor, but for them that means undertaking the work of making themselves known yet again. These folks need to know that the pastor has valued his relationship with them, that they matter, and that they will be missed as individuals. Those being visited often welcome, indeed need, the opportunity to express their gratitude for the pastor's faithfulness in visitation. (2006, p. 30)

Particularly take some time to visit those who are dying, ones who may have counted on you to officiate at their funeral.

Listen

Some respondents commented about their final days in the congregation:

- I think once it was established the time I was planning to retire, the process went well. Small groups in homes at various dates gave people an opportunity to meet with me to say good-bye, share memories, etc. . . . and because it was a two and a half year period, there was time to process and grieve. Two weeks before I left, a farewell dinner at the church was held, which was very satisfying to me.
- I announced it first to the Board of Deacons, then the advisory board and then the entire congregation. It was received with mixed emotions and I, too, had the usual separation emotions that I had when I previously changed churches. I always had a sense of God leading me to each church and my retirement. This new step was just another leaving of old friends to make new friends in a new place.
- It was a great day with cards, well wishes, gifts (golf clubs and a cash gift), dinner, and program. It was a good day after fourteen years.
- This church had a strong leadership group who may have bullied some pastors out. . . . At the reception the church stood in a circle and each person thanked me and told me how my ministry had affected them. I told them how much I loved them. One woman at close of worship had wonderingly told me no pastor had ever blessed them when he left!
- The whole experience was very touching. They were careful to include my wife as my full partner—she was involved in the congregation and to an extent still is. They were happy we were staying in the community, even if we did travel a lot. There was one big surprise—they named the Temple Library for us and left us my parking space. There weren't any substantial material gifts. There didn't need to be. What was said and what we felt was far more valuable to me.
- It was entirely satisfactory. The final service was created by a few people and it reflected many of my values and interests. I was a bit anxious about what they would come up with since they kept it a secret from me. However, I was entirely satisfied and thought it was done quite well.

SUMMARY

Farris advises,

> In spite of how we sometimes speak, we know in our heart of hearts that no congregation is "ours." Congregations are not possessions, but partnerships between a pastor and a people. At most, pastors are the stewards of their congregations, those who have been entrusted with their care, well-being, and development. Remembering this important truth will allow us, in faith, to release a congregation with our blessing into other hands so that our own

hands might be free and open for a new experience of faithfulness in which our spiritual growth will unfold. It is not always easy to trust that work we began with a congregation will be continued and expanded upon by other, but trust we must. (2006, p. 90)

We need to think of our leaving the congregation in terms of the Hassidic story about the impending death a great teacher. When the hour came for Rabbi Elimelech to depart from the world, he placed his hands on the foreheads of his four disciples and gave them each a portion of his soul:

> To the Seer of Lublin, he gave the light of his eyes
> To the Maggid of Kosnitz, he gave his heart
> To Rabbi Mendel of Prustik, he gave his mind
> To the Rabbi of Apt, he gave the power of his tongue. (Elimelech, 2011)

What a beautiful story. We are to live so that when we are no longer in the congregation, there will be a light from our eyes worth someone's guarding, a heart that still beats in the thoughts of others, a mind worth recalling, and a tongue whose wisdom absence does not still.

REFERENCES

Anthony, M. J. (2007). *Moving on moving forward: A guide for pastors in transition.* Grand Rapids, MI: Zondervan.

Buettner, D. (2010). *Thrive: Finding happiness the blue zones way.* Washington, DC: National Geographic.

Elimelech, R. O. (2011). *Rabbi Elimelech of Lizensk.* Retrieved July 29, 2013 from Rabbi Elimelech of Lizensk: http://lizensk.com/biography-of-rabbe-elimetech-of-lizensk/

Epperly, B. G. (2010). *A time for last.* Durham, NC: Alban Institute. http://www.alban.org/

Erickson, E. (1968). *Identity: Youth and crisis.* New York, NY: W. W. Norton.

Farris, L. W. (2006). *Ten commandments for pastors leaving a congregation.* Grand Rapids, MI: William B. Eerdmans.

Geller, R. L. (2011, Spring). Not more than my place; Not less than my space. *Reform Judaism, 38.*

Hawkins, B. L., & Barone, C. (2008, October–December). Going . . . going . . . gone: Thoughts on retirement. *EDUCAUSE Quarterly, 31*(4). Retrieved from http://www.educause.edu/ero/article/going%C3%A2%E2%82%AC%C2%A6-going%C3%A2%E2%82%AC%C2%A6-gone-thoughts-retirement

Henderson, W. (1982). *Under whose shade.* Canada: Agricultural Institute of Canada.

Kessinger, S. W. (1959). *Indispensable man.* Retrieved August 13, 2013, from Appleseeds.org: http://www.appleseeds.org/indispen-man_saxon.htm

Ladd, K. L. (2006). Retirement issues for Roman Catholic priests: A theoretical and qualitative investigation. *Review of Religious Research, 48*(1), 82–104.

Langer, S. (1960). *Philosophy in a new key.* Cambridge, MA: Harvard University.

Levy, N. (2002). *Talking to God: Personal prayers for times of joy, sadness, struggle, and celebration.* New York, NY: Alfred A. Knopf.

Lipman, D. (1955). *The storytelling coach: How to listen, praise, and bring out people's best.* Atlanta, GA: August House.

Perry, R. B. (1935). *The thought and character of William James.* Nashville, TN: The Vanderbilt Library of American Philosophy.

Seneca. (n.d.). *World of quotes.* Retrieved January 5, 2014, from World of Quotes: http://www.worldofquotes.com/author/Seneca/1/index.html

Temple Sholom. (2010, June 18). *Ritual of release for Rabbi Richard Shapiro.* Cincinnati, Ohio.

http://dx.doi.org/10.2190/CLEC5

CHAPTER 5

Dangers to Watch Out For

Weeping may last for the night, but a shout of joy comes in the morning.

Psalm 30:5

One ought never to turn one's back on a threatened danger and try to run away from it. If you do that, you will double the danger. But if you meet it promptly and without flinching, you will reduce the danger by half. Never run away from anything. Never!

Winston Churchill

RETIREMENT AS AN ESCAPE— I'VE HAD ENOUGH

When my wife and I met with our financial advisor some years back, we had set age 67 as a tentative target date for my retirement. That would have meant a career of 40 years, which seemed like a nice, neat time to breakaway and financially seemed to make sense. But I don't think I can make it; I just can't last that long; I've had it! How many more sermons can I deliver? Over how many more births and deaths must I officiate? And if I have to attend too many more meetings, I think I'll explode. What makes it most difficult is that I feel I have less and less support each year. Due to budget cuts, we have fewer staff, and congregants complain about having such full lives that they just don't have time to volunteer the way they used to. I don't see how to make things better. I have to get out—as soon as I can!

ஐ   ஐ   ஐ

NEED A KIND WORD

A waitress approached me at a local deli and mentioned that I appeared very depressed. "I am," I told her. "Please bring me some scrambled eggs and a kind word." When she returned with the scrambled eggs, I asked her about the kind word. "Don't eat the eggs!" she quipped (Elinsky, 2002, p. 27).

We believe people need lots of kind words on their "change" journey. It is hard to imagine that there could be melancholy when for so many years we have dreamed of a life less frenzied, evenings at home, and uninterrupted weekends.

But being forewarned is being forearmed. As a thanatologist and a psychologist, we are well aware that when there is change, there is frequently grief work that must be done. When there is disruption in routine and the familiar, we often need time to retreat and find new balance. For some it will be a difficult period; for others it will not be as traumatic, but we still feel a sense of disharmony and remorse.

People grieve over many things: the death of relationships, lost opportunities, job changes, and loss of physical abilities. Even divorcees, who may believe they have rid themselves of "baggage," may discover that they lament for lost hopes and dreams and cringe at the thought of starting over again. Job loss causes one to question one's identity and sense of competence and thus affects self-esteem. Even if we might have chosen to retire, we may still go through periods of depression, guilt, anxiety, regret, and anger. It is possible that this cycle may worsen unless it is nipped in the bud. Often in our loneliness and depression we may increasingly withdraw from others, and our situation can seem more and more hopeless.

> In the extreme case, the unemployed person can conclude that others would be "better off without him." When we have invested substantial parts of our identity in our work over a long period, the result can sometimes be tragic, as reflected in the fact that unemployed men over the age of 60 are at greater risk of suicide than any other demographic group. (Koenig, 2002, pp. 33–34)

Listen to the words of Kathryn Patricelli, of the Mental Health Center of Denver:

> There seems to be a set of transitions that people need to complete before they become wholly adjusted to being retired. It is not at all uncommon for early retirement adaptations to give way to experiences of disenchantment, loss or loneliness, or for grief feelings to become intermixed with other positive feelings about retirement. (n.d.)

Retiring clergy face unique concerns due to the nature of our role. Our world is "role and soul." When one retires from a private company, one severs the connection between the person ("Who I am") and the job ("What I do"). The work of the clergy, however, is not readily put away. Professors, business executives, and mechanics may choose to no longer practice their professions. However, a priest, a minister, a rabbi, an imam do not cease to be clergy upon retirement. We continue to carry God with us. "This theological meshing of the role of the clergy with the person who takes on that designation may be the crux of the issue of retirement. The cessation of religious labor is, in important ways, antithetical to the theology of ordination" (Ladd, 2006, p. 90).

Depression

Yes, you have been through change many times before and even handled it well, but whether you realized it or not, it takes its toll. With change often comes grieving: grieving for the world that was, for dreams unfulfilled, for the sense of stability now gone. Grief brings an excess of radically fluctuating, often conflicting feelings and emotions. For instance, if I were to tell you that your favorite aunt died, one who practically raised you, you would feel distraught and upset. However, if I also told you that she left you a million dollars in her will, you might also be elated, a lot more secure, and even a little glad that she died. So it is when you retire. You are leaving the security of work, routine, meaning, and an income stream to engage in an uncertain and exciting world ahead. At the same time you will be overwhelmed with the worry: *What do I want to do in these encore years before I am too incapacitated to be active or too ill to contribute to others?*

This we know. Sometime during the first year you will feel moments of grief and sorrow for the people left behind (see Charts 1 and 2 at the end of this chapter on page 63). It should not be surprising if you experience some or all of the emotions associated with bereavement for a loved one, especially depression. Since each person's grief is as different as their fingerprints, it will be unique to you. We know that some mourners will go into their *cave* and try to do it alone, not letting anyone in. Others will be loquacious and will share readily with others. Some will deal with it quickly; others will fret for a long time. The best way to understand how you may deal with this loss is to investigate how you have handled loss in the past. There is no single way to deal with grief. The only bad way to handle it is by trying to avoid it.

Consider of the words of some of the priests in Ladd's 2006 study.

- I miss the prestige of being a priest.
- A challenge comes when you realize you are not as important to many people as you once were.
- I found retirement most difficult to go from a full day in the active ministry to an empty day. In the months that followed I sank into a deep depression which made hospitalization necessary.
- I found the holidays to be extremely difficult. Saying Mass in my own little chapel . . . lacked the joy and excitement of a parish celebration. . . . not being asked by a fellow priest to co-celebrate was very painful. I [have now] become very involved in [a Catholic organization helping children and the elderly].
- After retirement, I found it very necessary to have a schedule for the day. Just having a blank day brought on its own difficulties.
- The fact that we have nothing to do can be frustrating. So it behooves all who are facing retirement to plan their future lives so that they will be needed. We must make deliberate efforts to take care of an aging body with

proper diet and exercise and make ourselves available to help others. . . . It may require finding new interests that never crossed our minds. (pp. 90, 97)

It is important to review some of the signs of depression so that we will recognize if it should happen to us.

- Patterns of disrupted sleep. You either want to sleep all the time or can't get a good night's sleep.
- Weight loss or gain of 10 pounds within a month. You use food to deal with depression and gain weight, or you look at food and aren't hungry.
- Inability to concentrate
- Crying spells
- Lethargy
- Hopelessness
- Pervasive sadness
- Inability to enjoy usual activities hobbies, fun activities, and intimacy with a loved one
- Watching too much TV or spending too much time on the Internet to fill in the hours
- Alcohol use. Alcohol is often used in an attempt to drown out disappointment and disillusionment, and to alleviate boredom.
- Threatening suicide

A depressed person may use any or all of these defenses:

- Putting up walls
- Staying angry and not dealing with the anger effectively
- Keeping a closed mind
- Blaming everyone else and everything else for one's problems.
- Dwelling on past pain and resentments
- Avoiding people who care
- Giving others the silent treatment
- Isolating oneself
- Constantly using humor to avoid feelings
- Testing others to see how much one can get away with
- Complaining excessively about physical problems
- Denying that one has issues or problems

How does a person fight off depression? Understand that depression at this time is normal and that you are not doomed to suffer with it forever. Others will notice that you are giving off signs of depression. Believe them when they say you have changed and are not as joyful and outgoing as you once were. Don't defend yourself; instead, take action to counter it. Sometimes that means talking about your feelings with your doctor, who may offer some medication. Find a friend with whom you can share your innermost emotions and not feel rejected. Seek out a counselor who can get you over the hump and spend time addressing your feelings. Check out if there is a retired clergy group in your area or a counselor who might be willing to help you organize a clergy retreat or weekly meeting.

Research has demonstrated that elderly men who take early retirement have particular difficulty maintaining social relationships (Sugisawa, 1997). In one sense, we grow old because we fail to cultivate new links in the community. This tells us that when we retire, we must work at forming new friendships and social relationships. We need to remember that there are others just like you who are eager to meet new people. How does the expression go? To have a friend you must be a friend. All you have to do is approach someone with an extended hand, a smile, and a *Hi, I'm* ____. And where will you meet these new friends? You will find them anywhere you go: the coffee shop, a class, the gym, the golf course, and the new church you will attend. You might have to break the ice and invite them to lunch or coffee or to an athletic or cultural event. For your psychological and mental health, you cannot stand on ceremony and wait for others to ask you first.

We suggest that you do not forget your spiritual background. Explore! Return to that sense that God is with each one of us and helps us handle any ordeal. Open your Bible to Psalm 27 right now and hear the words in your soul. How many times have you preached about the ideas in the sacred words? Now it is time to follow your own good advice. An old saying states, "Faith is what helps us to face the music even when we don't like the tune." So don't dismiss your faith tradition that has brought you this far just because the music has now changed (see Chapter 7 Part I and II on Spirituality).

Elisabeth Kübler-Ross suggests, "We learn to get in touch with the silence within ourselves and know that everything in life has a purpose. There are no mistakes, no coincidences, all events are blessings given to us to learn from" (Kübler-Ross, 2013). We must have this sense of hope and trust in order to get through this next period of time.

Anger and Guilt

We believe that it is normal to have disappointment and even anger at sacred moments. For example, when I do premarital counseling, I discuss the disappointment that naturally occurs around the wedding. The couple whittles down their invitation list to carefully meet their budget. Even though they know not everyone can attend, I warn them that the first "no" response brings a sense of disappointment that this person could not or would not make the effort to be at their wedding. One remembers those who were present and makes a mental note of those who did not attend. Think of a time when you were grieving a loved one. I still remember people who attended my mother's funeral as well as those who never came to my home to console me during the mourning period.

Conversely, I remember those who visited and whose presence at our home was very comforting. That is the way it is with sacred moments.

These conflicting feelings held true at my final service and weekend farewell with the congregation. I was overwhelmed with the outpouring of warmth and support and wished I could have spoken to each and everyone at the reception. Yet, as I sat on the pulpit and scanned the congregation, I noticed that certain people who I had thought were my friends, or those with whom I had expended a great deal of time and energy, were absent. I know that I should count my blessings and be thankful for those who were present—and I am; but those who surprisingly absented themselves without even a note of regret left a pain in my soul. I share this story because I believe that we all go through a series of frustrations with individual congregants and with the congregation as a whole. It's an array of *should have/could have* feelings and, quite possibly, many disappointments. How many of us become a clergyperson not expecting to become wealthy, but we did expect the congregation to care for us in our old age, and suddenly we find that our pension is not adequate and the congregants do not seem to care. That is a very bitter pill to swallow (Carpenter, 2010).

You may become disappointed by the very people you thought genuinely cared for you. You might experience anger and resentment and feel used and forgotten. This will be followed by guilt feelings. Often we surmise that we did not work hard enough; that we did not call our congregants often enough; that somehow we failed. We may beat ourselves up for not being good enough. This will lead to anger at ourselves. How does that expression go? *Depression is anger turned inward.*

What can we do about all this anger? We can realize that we are human and that anger is within the realm of normalcy. It is like the widow who fumes at her deceased husband when she cannot find certain papers she needs for the IRS and shouts, "If you were going to die, at least you could have left me with a good filing system!"

One wonderful suggestion for handling anger and guilt toward those in the congregation is to write either individual letters or a community letter spilling out all the venom inside. It does not have to be well composed or with good grammar or even in complete sentences. Just write and keep writing until everything is down on paper. It may take days or even weeks to complete this. That is fine. Then place it in an envelope and take it to the cemetery or even your backyard and in a ritual that you have created, bury it or burn it. Allow yourself the privilege of sadness for that life and walk away doing a little dance of release as you open your heart to a whole new life.

Robert Kemper reminds us,

> The way to maintain a healthy attitude through the process of final disengagement is to have something to go to that you are highly enthusiastic about—a new home, a new life. Failure to end one life and start another will leave you open to expressions of anger about your loss. Vicious can be the lash of retired minister who did not really leave his or her church. (1988, p. 22)

The Big Letdown

Whether you planned to retire or were asked to retire, there will be distress in either experience. Until you really reach retirement, you can only imagine life without the daily world of work. There is a disorienting sense of bedlam with retirement. We have hopes and dreams that the congregation will come banging on our door, begging us to stay because they need us so badly and they will not be able to get along without us. So when you turn in your keys and the door hits you in the backside, you may find sorrow waiting for you there in the parking lot. Just know that this too is normal.

Retirement often represents a death of dreams. Gone are the days in which you will dream about new programs and activities for the congregation or organization. Never again will you be that creative force in your congregation that you once were; now you will just be a plain old member. It may be devastating for you to watch someone else take over and change some of your most creative ideas and implement a new vision of their own. The loss of dreams could cause any number of emotional reactions: anger, jealousy, resentment, sorrow. This grieving is normal if it only lasts for a short time. The important thing for the sake of your well-being is to find new meaning in new endeavors.

Yes, work can be a major source of gratification, self-esteem, and financial security, but it can also be the source of punishment, anger, frustration, and ambivalence. As indicated already, the loss of a job or retirement leaves a person bereft with contending with an overflow of new feelings and emotions. It is like waking up after your spouse has died and realizing just how much you now have to do yourself. This journey to your "encore" world will demand creative thinking to succeed.

Read some responses and anger expressed in our survey:

- In trying to negotiate a retirement contract, I found it very demeaning.
- The congregation did not want me to retire, but could not understand that even their *full time* salary was below denominational standards. They refused to believe that they could give more and show better stewardship.
- Forced out in favor of a young person. Could have sued, but declined.
- One denominational official seemed to blame me for my reaction to a congregational survey that had been taken.
- Board resented my retirement. Refused to help in any financial way even after 23 years of service. Refused emeritus title and status because "it might involve some future financial requirement."
- Board of Trustees declined to extend my contract one additional year.
- The leadership of the new merged congregation engineered their plan. My old congregation did not even vote on whether to retain me. Even though my six-year contract had been completed, I felt left out to dry. This was also during the recession and financial troubles faced by our denomination and its reorganization. There was no one to help me.

- I was somewhat unhappy with the process of retirement in the sense that our bishop was new and had no understanding of my 44 years of service to the Diocese.
- Manner in which retirement process came about due to one poisonous influence who made my final years miserable instead of the culmination of what had been a wonderful rabbinate (31 years in one congregation which I had fashioned), loss of status.

SUMMARY

Getting through this period of time is a journey of ups and downs. Most of them are perfectly normal and appropriate. We do not need to beat ourselves up when anger overwhelms us, sadness grabs us because we are feeling meaningless, or when we are feeling depressed on a particular day. Do not fight these feelings, instead recognize the emotions and acknowledge them verbally if you can with a spouse or trusted friend. Ultimately, the fight is not to let them become a consistent everyday occurrence. Instead, find ways to count the blessings you receive each and every day. Move forward step by step with the goal of filling your encore years with new adventures that will bring you joy and satisfaction.

REFERENCES

Carpenter, D. (2010, June 5). *Many clergy ill-prepared for retirement.* Retrieved January 21, 2011, from the Associated Press: http://usatoday30.usatoday.com/news/religion/2010-06-05-clergy-retire_N.htm

Elinsky, C. S. (2002). *Meisas.* Bloomington, IN: 1st Books.

Kemper, R. (1988). *Planning for ministerial retirement.* New York, NY: Pilgrim.

Koenig, H. G. (2002). *Purpose and power in retirement: New opportunities for meaning and significance.* Philadelphia, PA: Templeton Press.

Kübler-Ross, E. (2013). *Quotes by Elisabeth Kübler-Ross. Elisabeth Kübler-Ross Foundation.* Retrieved October 7, 2013, from http://www.ekrfoundation.org/quotes/

Ladd, K. L. (2006). Retirement issues for Roman Catholic priests: A theoretical and qualitative investigation. *Review of Religious Research, 48*(1), 82–104.

Merrill Lynch. (2013). *Americans' perspectives on new retirement realities and the longevity bonus: A 2013 Merrill Lynch retirement study, conducted in partnership with Age Wave.* New York, NY: Merrill Lynch/Bank of America.

Patricelli, K. (n.d.). Retirement and grief. *River Valley Counseling Center, Inc.* Retrieved December 21, 2012, from http://www.rvcc-inc.org/poc/view_doc.php?type=doc&id=10872&cn=359

Sugisawa, A. S. (1997). Effect of retirement on mental health and social well-being among elderly Japanese. *Japanese Journal of Public Health, 4,* 348–362.

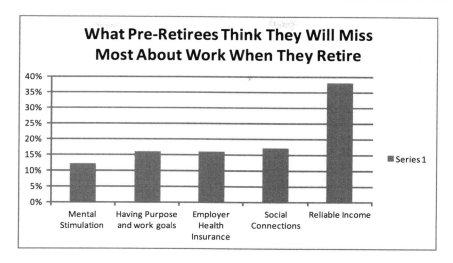

Chart 1
(Merrill Lynch, 2013, p. 6)

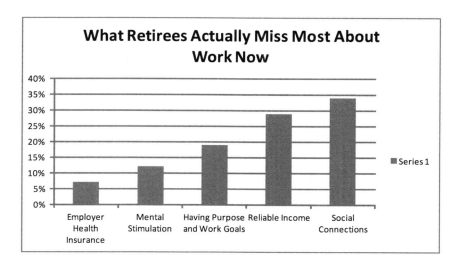

Chart 2
(Merrill Lynch, 2013, p. 6)

http://dx.doi.org/10.2190/CLEC6

CHAPTER 6

Thinking About New Meanings

You can either die while you are living or live while you are dying.

Daniel Roberts (2014)

Here is the test to find whether or not your mission on earth is finished. If you're alive, it isn't.

Richard Bach (1977)

LOOKING FORWARD TO RETIREMENT

I am one lucky gal! I have had a full life, successful career, and loving family. I almost feel guilty thinking about what will come next as my husband and I begin to plan for our lives after retirement. I'm scheduled to leave my congregation, where I have served for almost 15 years, just a year ahead of when he'll be retiring from the university. We are blessed with good health, given our ages and somewhat sedentary lifestyle, we have saved carefully throughout our working years, and our children are well established on their own. Now we get to engineer the next stage of our lives. For me, I am looking forward to having more control over my schedule and time to devote to my grandchildren, gardening, and reading just for pleasure. Sure, I may eventually look for some volunteer opportunities in our community, but not just yet. I must admit to feeling a bit self-indulgent when I view this coming year as all about me. But I deserve it and am not ashamed to say so!

ða   ða   ða

WHERE DID IT GO?

He's played golf every day since his retirement 20 years ago. One day he arrives home looking downcast.

"That's it," he tells his wife. "I'm giving up golf. My eyesight has gotten so bad. Once I've hit the ball, I can't see where it goes."

His wife sympathizes. "Arthur, sit down. I have a suggestion. Why don't you take my brother with you and give it one more try?"

"That's no good," sighs Arthur. "Your brother is 92. He can't help."

"He may be 92," says the wife, "but his eyesight is perfect."

So the next day, Arthur heads off to the golf course with his brother-in-law in tow. He tees up, takes a mighty swing, and squints down the fairway.

He turns to the brother-in-law. "Did you see the ball?"

"Of course, I did," says the brother-in-law. "I have perfect eyesight."

"Where did it go?" asks Arthur.

"Can't remember!"

Those two words sum up our greatest fear as we move into the encore period of our lives. We can deal with our eyesight diminishing by using a magnifying glass. We foresee using a walker when our balance deteriorates, but our anxiety is highest over the potential loss of memory. Already there have been moments when we beat ourselves up because we cannot find our keys or our glasses, or remember what we had for lunch yesterday. We worry that this is the first step on the road to permanent memory loss. I found it interesting that in Beth Howard's article, "Age-Proof Your Brain," she lists in 10 suggestions for remaining sharp that *discovering your mission in life can help you remain clear-headed.* She cites a Rush University Medical Center study in which participants who approached life with clear intentions and goals at the start of the study were less likely to develop Alzheimer's disease over the following 7 years (Howard, 2012).

Dostoyevsky described in *The Brothers Karamazov* what happens to a person when one doubts the purpose of life: "For the secret of man's being is not only to live, but to deliver something definite. Without a firm notion of what he is living for, man will not accept life and will rather destroy himself than remain on earth" (1999, p. 247).

We have an intuitive sense that God must have created retirement for a far greater reason than just being able to play golf or sit on a porch rocking back and forth or watching hours of television. Initially this might sound delightful, but within a short time we realize that our lives are slowly withering away from what we once were, and our intellectual needs that carried us through our "priesthood" are woefully unsatisfied. Seeing the world and traveling sounds great, but after a while we begin to hate unpacking and repacking our suitcases and all the places begin to look like somewhere we were before. There are only so many newspapers and books that one can read before becoming bleary-eyed. We find ourselves napping to escape boredom. Retirement should not become a second childhood where you play all the time. What then is our purpose in this period of our lives?

Jewish theologian Abraham Joshua Heschel wrote,

> Preoccupation with games and hobbies, the overemphasis on recreation, while certainly conducive to eliminating boredom temporarily, hardly contributes to inner strength. The effect is, rather, a pickled existence, preserved in brine with spices. . . . after all, to be retired does not mean to be retarded. (1972, p. 74)

Harold Koenig synthesizes Heschel's thoughts in a more modern way:

> Leisure roles have a difficult time replacing work as a source of self-esteem because they are typically not supported by societal norms (despite vigorous marketing efforts by leisure entrepreneurs over the past five decades). Furthermore, leisure as a legitimate source of self-esteem will likely become less and less valid in the future as our society (and the world) begins to feel the economic pinch caused by aging populations needing support and care. Consequently, the only kinds of leisure that are truly effective in providing identity are work substitutes that result in the production of something worthwhile. (2002, p. 44)

Work substitutes—now that sounds like a nasty idea for someone who is about to retire and who is looking forward to not working. However, finding meaning to the days ahead is going to be exertion for it does not come easily to us when seeking what brings us a sense of worthwhileness.

Rabbi Earl Grollman, a noted authority in the field of death and dying, further reminds us,

> The length of life has no bearing on the meaning of life. It is not the quantity of years that one accumulates which is of primary importance, but the kind of life one leads. . . . If life is meaningful, then quantity is not important. The real tragedy of death occurs when men are more concerned with how long they may live rather than with how they may live. . . . The two least important statistics of a man's life are placed upon his tombstone—when he was born and when he died. It is not the length of one's life—rather it is the breadth of his sympathies for others; it is the depth of his understanding of life's meaning; it is the height of his aspirations that are important. (1967, pp. 239–240)

Yes, it is not the length of our life that matters, but rather how we will write these last chapters in our Book of Life. We get to create and write this next chapter ourselves. In *Man's Search for Meaning* (1984), Viktor Frankl wrote that those in the concentration camps who had a friend to care for and who had some sense of meaning in life fared much better than those who thought they could make it on their own or who saw no reason for staying alive. I was fortunate to study with Frankl early in my career. One day, he scribbled on the blackboard the following formula: $S - M = D$. He went on for the next 20 minutes to explain that **S**uffering minus **M**eaning equals **D**espair. Writes Frankl, "According to logotherapy, the striving to find a meaning in one's life is the primary motivational force in man. That is why I speak of a will to meaning in contrast to the pleasure principle" (p. 153).

Maybe this is what gave Abram his meaning when he was 75 years old, as well as the prophets in the Hebrew testament their vigor when they each believed they had a purpose and their sadness when they lost it. Writes Professor Neal Krause, a professor in the School of Public Health in the Institute of Gerontology at the University of Michigan,

> That purpose was their calling. When they lost their purpose, no matter how much they had already accomplished, they often became depressed and useless. Consider the prophet Elijah who, after defeating the nine hundred prophets of Baal and Asherah, lost his sense of purpose and lay down to die. "He came to a broom tree, sat down under it and prayed that he might die. I have had enough, Lord," he said. "Take my life; I am no better than my ancestors" (I Kings 19:4). It was not until God himself appeared to Elijah and reminded him of his purpose that he straightened out. "What are you doing here, Elijah? Go back the way you came . . ." (I Kings 19:9, 15). Elijah then went back and anointed the new king of Israel. He had rediscovered his purpose with God's help. (Krause & Herzog, 1992)

Do not these Biblical quotes indicate that humans are meaning-seeking animals by nature and when we lose that sense of mission, we are ready for death? Viktor Frankl believes this to be so. He wrote of the man who believed that the Allies were coming on a certain date, but when they didn't, the man took to his bed and died shortly thereafter. Frankl also indicates that there are three main avenues from which one arrives at meaning in life:

> The first is by creating a life or doing a deed. The second is by experiencing something or encountering someone. In other words, meaning can be found not only in work, but also in love. Third: even the helpless victim of a hopeless situation facing a fate that cannot be changed may rise above himself, grow beyond himself, and by so doing, change himself. (1997, p. 170)

Our ultimate question at this moment of retirement should be *What does God have in mind for me now*, rather than *What has God taken away from me*? I love the story about a sage observing the construction of a famous church in Europe, who asked the workmen, "What are you doing?" One replied, "I'm earning a living." A second answered, "I'm doing my job; I'm a bricklayer." But a third said, "I'm building a great cathedral." His sense of participating in a higher purpose gave zest to his work and wings to his spirit. As clergy in retirement, each one of us needs to think that we are still working to build a cathedral to God, but now we may just be a worker and not the foreman of the project.

And the Old Shall Dream Dreams (Joel 2:28)

The reality that we are now old enough to retire comes as a shock for which most of us are unprepared. We look in the mirror and cannot believe that we are 65 years old or nearing it. I don't know about you, but I don't feel 65 (although I must admit that I'm not sure what 65 is supposed to feel like). We notice that our bodies are beginning to break down. It takes us longer to do certain things, like getting up from a chair. We have trouble bending down to pick up something off of the floor. My racquetball game has gone south and I have gone north. I can't get the shots that I used to easily make, and one of my partners said that I now move like a turtle. If life is defined exclusively in terms of functions and activities, then is it still worth living when these functions and activities are sharply curtailed? Some will say no and become depressed, retreating to the couch. Others know that "life is also comprised of a mountain of dreams as well as rivers of sorrow" (Heschel, 1972).

In this age of modern medicine and with the possibility of extended years of activities and good health, we have choices that our ancestors never had. You can become "aged" very quickly or you can revitalize yourself with new dreams. As Heschel indicates,

> The aged may be described as a person who does not dream anymore, devoid of ambition, and living in fear of losing his status. Regarding himself as a person who has outlived his usefulness, he feels as if he had to apologize for being alive. (1972, p. 73)

From this we understand that if one wants to age quickly, all one has to do is to live without dreams. Maybe that is why the prophet Joel prophesized of the time when the old shall dream dreams and the young shall see visions (Joel 2:28). To remain young, one must continue to dream. Thus, this new world we enter needs to be regarded not as an age of stagnation and play, but as an age of opportunities for inner growth and achieving the high values we longed for. What we want to strive for in these final years is not happiness, but meaning. Happiness is not a goal in itself; it is the byproduct of what we create. Our ambition should be in this time of diminishing physical capacity to utilize our mind and our spirit to its fullest, thus creating happiness in this new arena of life.

A growing body of evidence indicates that adults who seek meaning in their lives live longer and remain healthier in the face of stress than those whose sense of personal meaning is less clear (Krause & Herzog, 1992). Meaning systems are important aspects of adult living.

Perhaps clergy are fortunate to have been involved in organized religion for a lifetime, for in some ways we will fare better in retirement. In a study on priest retirement, when comparing the adjustment of retired clergy to retired professors, Acuff found that the clergy tended to score higher on a measure of purpose in life. He also found that religious involvement, regardless of profession, resulted in better adjustment, a finding consistent with research in the general population (Ladd, 2006, p. 90).

What does it mean to find meaning? Setting goals is a *component* of meaning-making but not its sum total. Viktor Frankl found purpose by uncovering not "what we expected from life, but rather what life expected from us" (1984, p. 85). This then is the essence of spiritual meaning, one that we clergy have experienced up until now as God's whisper to us. When we were young, the hush sound came closer to a shout. The billow was there as we wrestled with the Biblical texts trying to decide whether or not to enter the clergy. We obviously heard God loud and clear. Where is God's voice now when our phone no longer rings and our appointment calendars are empty?

Going Inside Oneself

Jacob had to sneak off from his two camps to the edge of the Jabbok River and wrestled with an angel to find his destiny. We all must wrestle within ourselves to discover new personal meanings. For clergy, wrestling is not new. We wrestled with angels during the agonizing quandary of whether or not to enter the clergy and whether we were worthy. Now, as this meaningful career comes to a close, like Jacob we are left to limp away. We have always been a decision-maker. In our pulpit or organizational job, we determined what social justice causes to take on, what topics to preach about, how best to counsel congregants and work with colleagues, when to devote time to family, and when our career had to supersede our personal life. We were the "lonely man," as the famed Rabbi Joseph B. Soloveitchik termed it (1964).

Now it is time to wrestle again with that *lonely person inside us*. What does God have in mind for us in our encore years? This is a hard question to answer and will require the most prolific struggle. Perhaps it is not just one but many missions that lie ahead, and we need to choose just a few, otherwise we will be overwhelmed and have no direction. Those that we do choose should be particularly meaningful to us and in keeping with our sense of holiness.

In the past we have been charged with various missions. We were God's messenger to congregants, fellow clergy, or an organization. We were nurtured by our parents and subsequently became their caregivers in their aging years. We were a spouse, a parent, a friend, a relative, a teacher, and a presence of some influence in the community. Just because we no longer have a pulpit or an organization to serve doesn't mean we can no longer continue to be the voice of protest, an advocate for the abandoned and alone, the poor who have no one else to speak on their behalf. Yes, at times we were the lonely voice and therefore sometimes not very popular, but we knew that it was the right thing to do. Great movements in history started when individuals who cared spoke out and changed the majority. If we had waited for the majority to change, we would still have slavery and segregated schools. The right thinking pattern has to be not that we have retired *from* something, but that we have retired *to* something. You may have retired from a job as a minister, but you need not retire from your values and purpose. We now ask ourselves how we can continue to work on behalf of these values and principles even in our retirement. You may no longer have a pulpit, but you still have a voice. In *The Essential Kabbalah*, Dr. Daniel Matt writes regarding the interpretation of God's command to Abram to "Go Forth" (Genesis 12:1).

> God said to Abram, "Go to your self, know your self, fulfill your self."
> This verse is addressed to every person. Search and discover the room of
> your soul, so that you can fulfill it and restore it to its source, its essence.
> The more you fulfill yourself, the closer you approach your authentic self.
> (Matt, 1996, p. 127)

To begin our quest for a meaningful life in retirement, a strategy might be to write down, in no particular order, what we felt passionate about during our ministry. What social action projects were of particular interest; what age group of people did we most enjoy working with? We might want to think back on all the organizations with which we have had dealings and underline those that come closest to our values and principles. One cannot sit back and wait for opportunity to come knocking at our door. There are myriad needs in our communities just begging for dedicated people to lend a hand. Sonja Lyubomirsky, a professor in the Department of Psychology at the University of California, Riverside and author of *The How of Happiness* (2007), tells us that "Genuinely happy people do not just sit around being content. They make things happen." If you want to be happy then we have to pursue a whole new world of new understanding new achievements and find new contentment. If one wants to be happy in this new period of life then one needs to find happy retirees and find out what they are doing and let them be a model (Buettner, 2010, p. 13).

It is not enough to decide that our mission will be to spend more time with our children. First of all we have to ask, Do they really want you to do more with them? They have developed their own lifestyle while we were busy with ours. Now we are asking them to adjust to a different role just because we have retired. Second, what does doing more with the family truly mean? What would bring us satisfaction if this dream were to come true? This is not a decision we can make on our own; we will need to share our ideas with the entire family to see if this is their vision as well. Third, we will also have to identify if this mission is really going to be sufficient to meet our spiritual, intellectual, and emotional needs. Our guess is that family will be like the icing on the cake, but there is so much more hiding beneath the frosting.

Perhaps we need to contemplate talking with a trusted friend, an understanding colleague, a coach, or a favorite therapist who we have recommended to others. We might also want to make an appointment with ourselves much as a retiring congregant might come to us seeking advice. We might want to vocalize and argue with ourselves as to what might work and not work for us. We might want to participate in the "empty chair" technique where we sit across from an empty chair and state what we want as if we were speaking to a counselor and then move to that chair and respond as we would if we were counseling that person. As we would with a congregant, address questions such as what are our favorite activities, what were the things in the workplace that we really enjoyed and which did we detest? What are our strengths and in which areas do we feel we need growth? Of course, we now have a choice. We can strengthen our growth areas and work on them so we feel more confident or we can simply say that they have unnerved us our entire life and we want to put them aside and concentrate on that with which we are most confident and enjoy the most. My wife often says that she has reached a point in her life that she does not have to finish a book if it does not interest her.

Richard Leider, author of *The Power of Purpose*, suggests that you take a personal inventory by using this formula: G + P + V = C (2010). His research suggests that to know your core sense of purpose, you first need to have a clear understanding of your core values—your Gifts (what you have to offer the world) together with your Passion and Values equals your Calling. Are you applying your GIFTS to something you feel PASSIONATE about in an environment that VALUES you? If so, Leider says, you're on purpose. You have reason to get up in the morning! (Buettner, 2010, p. 237).

In a study of older adults, investigators at the Institute of Social Research at the University of Michigan found that those who gave of themselves to others experienced significantly greater feelings of personal control and well-being than older adults who were more isolated (Krause & Herzog, 1992). Humans were created to be responsible for others. Cain revolted against this idea. *Am I my brother's keeper,* he asked God (Genesis 4:9)? God's answer to that question was an emphatic YES! Ultimately, what would you like to give of yourself? Just because an array of activities and hobbies is not on your palette does not mean that you cannot create from scratch a very desirable canvas for the future. You may end up giving less financially to a cause or project than you might have in the past, but now you can volunteer your time and share your wisdom. Perhaps you now need to look at volunteerism as a job that will provide you with a payback that is priceless.

As indicated in the beginning of this chapter, those who have goals and purpose can ward off dementia. We also know that people who maintain strong connections with friends, loved ones, and confidants and who give of themselves to others also have lower risks of just about every type of illness, including cancer, heart disease, and Alzheimer's (Gruen, 2008). Without such meaningful engagement, one can easily become depressed, subsequently marginalized by society, and ultimately lose physical and mental acuity and the capacity for independence. Landry recommends that older people do the following each day: exercise, try to learn something new in order to stimulate brain function (crossword puzzles, Sudoku, take classes at the local university, or go to the library regularly), and meet with or call friends. It is vital to do something meaningful! Join a book group or other special interest club, do volunteer work or resume an old hobby (Gruen, 2008).

According to the Center on Aging Studies at the University of Missouri-Kansas City, the key to successful aging is to maintain satisfaction and quality of life through your daily activities. These can be social or physical activities, hobbies, or volunteering. All of these are vital in giving meaning and purpose to the lives of elderly people (Gruen, 2008). Tom Sander, executive director of the Saguaro Seminar at Harvard University, which promotes social involvement, notes, "Civic engagement is the health club of the new millennium" (Hawkins & Barone, 2008).

According to a 10-year MacArthur Foundation study, social connections are the key to successful aging. The study found that lifestyle is more than twice as important as genes in determining whether individuals thrive late in life (Buettner, 2010).

We think that you might want to get started on your journey by using Rick Warren's *The Purpose Driven Life* or Richard Nelson Bolles's, *What Color is Your Parachute? for retirement.* There is also, *Don't Retire, REWIRE* by Jeri Sedlar and Rick Miners. On page 203 of *Living in the Blue Zone* (2008) there is a wonderful list that will guide you to new thoughts about the meaning of your life.

An Ethical Will

In the search for new meaning, it might be helpful to write an ethical will. An ethical will does not leave material inheritance to others, nor does it empower another to make medical decisions for you. Instead, it allows you to transmit to your children and grandchildren the values and ethics that have defined your life—arguably at least as important as the first two.

Rabbi Jack Reimer has preserved many examples of ethical wills in his book, *So Your Values Live On: Ethical Wills and How to Prepare Them* (1991), which is based on *Hebrew Ethical Wills* by Israel Abraham (1972). For more information regarding ethical wills, go to the website, www.ethicalwills.com. One outstanding ethical will I will never forget was written by the teacher and comedian Sam Levenson to his grandchildren. In it, he writes that he leaves them everything he owes: he owes his parents, this nation, and those who protect his safety. To them, he leaves a bunch of four letter words: help, give, care, feel, and love.

To assist one in writing an ethical will, one might begin with the words, *I write this to you, my children/spouse, etc., to share with you the history of my family and important events that happened to me along my journey of life. I also want you to know what religious principles and rituals have been most meaningful to me and which moral and ethical ideals have moved me deeply.* The will might also include personal history, mentioning those who were most influential in your life, as well as which events helped shape your thinking. What was the proudest moment of your life and what do you hope to be remembered for? The qualities that you most admire in other people should also be shared. The salutation could end with, "May the Almighty bless you with . . ."

You might also want to include advice you have received that has affected your life and that you would like to pass on. What has made your life worth living, as well as what regrets do you have and wish you could have changed? Of what in your life are you most proud? If you could live your life over, is there anything you would have done differently? What are some of your ideals and ideas that you would like your family and friends to most remember? List your five best qualities. List five things that you think need to be changed in your community and then list some things you would like to do to change them.

This is an opportunity to leave your family with an enduring sense of who you are, what you believe, and what you hold most dear. At the same time, it will cause you to focus on what you find most important in life that you now want to spend your time furthering.

Ideas for the Future

At this moment in life, there are innumerable opportunities that a retiree can now explore. One could learn a new skill and even get paid for it. On the website of Civic Ventures (www.encore.org) there are all kinds of ideas. How about becoming foster grandparents, reading for the blind, volunteering for a nonprofit that you enjoy and in whose work you believe, teaching a class, gathering together some friends and teaching them about a subject you love, or read and explore the Bible together. Or consider one-on-one contact such as tutoring, prison chaplaincy, hospice, mentoring a theology student, or auditing a university course.

Writes Harold Koenig,

> In a study of forty retirees, those who volunteered more than ten hours a week scored significantly higher on a "purpose in life" test than did those who volunteered ten or fewer hours per week. In that study, a significant negative correlation was found between degrees of purpose in life and proneness to boredom. Having a sense of purpose also predicts less worry about death and dying among older adults. This may have to do with the impact that purpose in life has on their sense of personal control and autonomy. (2002, p. 68)

Studies show that acquiring fresh skills later in life helps ward off depression and may reduce the likelihood of dementia.

We very much like the idea advanced by Harvard University offering people the opportunity to go back to school and use their background to create a program that will help others (see www.advancedleadership.harvard.edu). Of course, this concept is not limited to Harvard. One could create a similar program with a local college or university. For example, if one were interested in people having enough drinking water around the world, one could design a curriculum that would focus on this problem, using one's leadership skills and energy to create such a program. This is just one such idea, but using one's imagination coupled with one's life skills will enable a person to create new avenues. Remember, one does not know where involving oneself in such a new idea might take a person and who might then come knocking on one's door. By the way, when they do, don't forget to open it!

Risks

When we were young, we took a lot of risks, perhaps too many and foolish ones, but we were not afraid to test new thoughts and manners. Then we settled into a routine, and because of our life choices and responsibilities, we became nervous about taking risks, thinking we could lose our jobs or others would think ill of us. However, now that we are older, we can be bolder in our choices and begin to gauge people by different standards, such as how interesting or talented they are rather than by their financial status. Author David Brooks suggests, "Many more seniors regret the risks they didn't take than regret the ones they did" (2011). We are charmed by the title of a book, *When I Am An Old Woman, I Shall Wear Purple*, edited by Sandra Martz from the poem by Jenny Joseph (Martz, 1987). In it she claims that she shall wear it with a red hat that doesn't match and doesn't suit her.

One savvy retiree in David Brook's article writes, "Don't stay with people who, over time, grow apart from you. Move on" (2011). To leave others behind is a risk, for they may speak ill of you, but this is a time during which one needs to think about who lifts you up and not those who pull you down. This is indeed a risk, but it may also provide an opportunity, for you need to find what pleases you and aids in your growth.

You are entertaining a journey of continuous discovery. As the saying goes, "Yesterday is the past. The future is a mystery. Today is a gift. That's why it is called THE PRESENT!" None of us know what is in store for us in our golden years. It will take courage and flexibility, and you will eventually find your own balance. You have the power to make this new journey as meaningful, energizing, and enjoyable as you wish.

Responses

In our survey, the greatest adjustments people had to make were

- Deciding what to do with free time
- Finding new meaning
- Lacking an office outside of the home
- Making new friends
- Finding a good volunteer position
- Getting used to the new rhythm of time (72% answered affirmatively)

When it came to *meaning making*, people responded with these words:

- I am fortunate to have been pretty well rounded during my years of ministry. I have had other interests and have participated in doing other things. I think the real joy is to know that I really have a choice about what I say yes to. Most of my friends and family are still working so time with them is still limited.
- I now play trombone in a church brass quintet and a community orchestra. And I teach a young adult class.
- After three years I'm finally being content with the routine and the things I have developed.
- Luxury of doing what I want to do when I want to do it. Doing short-term projects which help the homeless in Portland, Traveling—both overseas—have son in Germany so did the continent and in US—go to national parks, bird sanctuaries etc.

- Life has opened up to historical research, playing a lot of music (I play in 3 groups and visit open mic nights), reinvesting in old friends, having time to ponder anew, being disciplined about personal health and, cooking more.
- Whole new vistas that have brought fulfillment beyond any planning could have done. I have been the Managing Editor of two significant publications and in January was designated as a Board of Director member to the denominational national Historical Society. A real coup for me.
- In a sense, I have "failed" retirement. I went back to work. But I only work three days a week, so I do have more time on my hands. I no longer feel like my church "owns me." In a sense, I don't care if my new church likes me or not—I can leave without it killing me financially. But they do like having me there and it's very fulfilling.
- A whole new sense of doing what I want to do. Discovered my artistic ability and started a small business caning and weaving chair seats. I also have been working for 9 seasons at a resort in town on the front desk. It has been fun having a secular job.
- Flying. I had been taking lessons off and on for several years. Finally got my license. Very gratifying (kind of unnerving, though—it's like "what's left to live for and daydream about?").
- Volunteer work includes working with homeless people which includes initiating retreats for them; spiritual direction for students at the University of Akron, and for others. Part of what this is involves a certain excitement in the mystery of the human person and in the discovery of the good and creativity in people. More than ever I enjoy long bike rides, hikes with my neighbor (and his beagle), and getting together with friends.
- Personal adjustment, working on yourself, all of this can be very exciting and challenging. And I took it as such. I still like the challenge of living graciously in my third-age. I don't have enough time to do all the things I want to do. One challenge is pace—learning to say no while choosing the best.

Response to Questions About Raison d'Être

- I remind myself that it is still early in my retirement and I need to give myself time to move into the next phase of my spiritual journey, but there is also that old sense of what was once called the "Protestant work ethic" that makes me feel that I "should" have found something by now. Some of life's dilemmas just never go away—someday I hope to learn that as a truth!!! God still has much to do to improve me!
- I am in a continual discernment process. I trust that in time new meaning/purpose will present itself. Right now I am still trying to embrace this health condition rather than fighting it.
- A combination of things including writing, studying astronomy, gardening more and being available for other clergy as a listening resource. I also hope

to travel more when my wife retires. These are all things I have always enjoyed.

- I work two days a week signing up low-income seniors for programs like food stamps which makes a real difference in their lives. I'm a docent at the art museum and on the board of an internationally renowned baroque orchestra. It is the best time in my life. I am finally fulfilled in all that I do.

- I believe God's Call to serve him is lifelong. We just have to allow ourselves to hear it and be open minded. For me meaning is found in relationships with family/friends/the church fellowship and doing good for others in whatever ways God gives me the ability and call to do so. I can see the future long term consequences of all sorts of actions, human and earthly. I think long term. I feel called to help feeding the hungry, help those who cannot help themselves, those Jesus was especially concerned for, and help keep our democratic way of life when it is healing and respectful of all people.

- The life of ministry is often filled with unrealized outcomes. We don't always get to see how our teaching and/or interventions affect people. I recently heard from a woman who is now a professor in Florida who was in my first youth group. She related how I had helped her through her mother's death. I barely remember the time! But years later, there was the fruit of seeds planted long ago. Now my raison d'etre is to leave something behind . . . writing, publishing, or playing for this moment which brings satisfaction.

- God has shown me my purpose for being at this stage in life: 1. Be a loving, caring spouse, parent, grandparent, in-law and friend. 2. Exercise an hour every day. 3. Volunteer at a nursing home I formerly served. 4. Do pulpit substitute work or be an interim pastor. 5. Keep mentally alert and fit for serving God.

- I have found that my meaning/purpose in life is more fluid. It is not governed by a board or committee; it is what may be needed of me or how I can help in a particular situation and my ability to go outside the religious community to be of service.

SUMMARY

In the Academy Award–winning movie *The Artist*, the main character, Jean Dujardin's George Valentin, wrestles with a universal question: *What does one do when the lights go out?* The reality is that you can either cry about it and make demands, or like Valentin, you can retool yourself. In the end he finds love and he learns to become a dancer. What will you do now that the spotlight of the pulpit has moved from you to someone else? How are you going to retool yourself? The answer, of course, is making new meaning in your life. Perhaps, for us as clergy, it is finding new ways to give back to a world that has provided us with amazing opportunities.

Albert Einstein wrote,

> Strange is our situation here upon earth. Each of us comes for a short visit, not knowing why, yet sometimes seeming to a divine purpose. From the standpoint of daily living, however, there is one thing we know: That man is here for the sake of other men above all, for those upon whose smile and well-being our own happiness depends, and also for the countless unknown souls with whose fate we are connected by a bond of sympathy. Many times a day, I realize how much my outer and inner life is built upon the labors of people, both living and dead, and how earnestly I must exert myself in order to give in return as much as I have received. (1931)

Finally, we close with these words from Gabriel Marcel, 1998: "Life is not a problem to be solved, but a mystery to be lived."

REFERENCES

Abraham, I. (1972). *Hebrew ethical wills.* Philadelphia, PA: Jewish Publication Society.

Bach, R. (1977). *Illusions: The adventures of a reluctant messiah.* New York, NY: Dell Publishing.

Bolles, R. N. (2010). *What color is your parachute? For retirement (Second Edition: Planning a prosperous, healthy, and happy future.* New York, NY: Ten Speed Press.

Buettner, D. (2008). *Living in the blue zone.* Washington, DC: National Geographic.

Buettner, D. (2010). *Thrive: Finding happiness the blue zones way.* Washington, DC: National Geographic.

Brooks, D. (2011, November 28). The life reports II. *New York Times.* Retrieved January 25, 2012, from http://www.nytimes.com/2011/11/29/opinion/brooks-the-life-reports-ii.html?emc=eta1

Dostoyevsky, F. (1999). *The brothers Karamozov.* New York, NY: Penguin.

Einstein, A. (1931). *Living philosophies.* New York, NY: Simon & Schuster.

Frankl, V. (1984). *Man's search for meaning.* New York, NY: Washington Square.

Frankl, V. (1997). *Man's search for meaning.* New York, NY: Beacon.

Grollman, E. (1967). *Explaining death to children.* Boston, MA: Beacon.

Gruen, J. (2008, December 18). *Active living is the key to successful aging.* Retrieved January 15, 2012, from Jewish Journal.Com. http://www.jewishjournal.com/50_Plus/article/active_living_is_the_key_to_successful_aging_20081217

Hawkins, B. L., & Barone, C. (2008, October–December). Going . . . going . . . gone: Thoughts on retirement. *EDUCAUSE Quarterly, 31*(4). Retrieved from http://www.educause.edu/ero/article/going%C3%A2%E2%82%AC%C2%A6-going%C3%A2%E2%82%AC%C2%A6-gone-thoughts-retirement

Heschel, A. J. (1972). *The insecurity of freedom.* New York, NY: Schocken.

Howard, B. (2012, February/March). Age-proof your brain: 10 easy ways to stay sharp forever. *AARP The Magazine,* 47–49.

Koenig, H. G. (2002). *Purpose and power in retirement: New opportunities for meaning and significance.* Philadelphia, PA: Templeton Press.

Krause, N., & Herzog, A. R. (1992). Providing support to others and well-being in later life. *Journal of Gerontology, 47*(5), 300–311.

Ladd, K. L. (2006). Retirement issues for Roman Catholic priests: A theoretical and qualitative investigation. *Review of Religious Research, 48*(1), 82–104.

Leider, R. (2010). *The power of purpose*. San Francisco, CA: Berrett-Koehler Publishing, Inc.

Lyubomirsky, S. (2007). *The how of happiness: A new approach to getting the life you want*. New York, NY: Penguin Press.

Marcel, G. (1998). *Gabriel Marcel's perspectives on the broken world*. Gabriel Marcel: Marquette University Press

Martz, S. (Ed.). (1987). *When I am an old woman I shall wear purple*. Watsonville, CA: Papier Mache.

Matt, D. (1996). *The essential Kabbalah*. San Francisco, CA: Harper San Francisco.

Reimer, J. (1991). *So that your values live on: Ethical wills and how to prepare them*. Woodstock, VT: Jewish Lights Publishing.

Sedlar, J., & Miners, R. (2007). *Don't retire, REWIRE*. New York, NY: Penguin Group (USA) Inc.

Soloveitchik, J. B. (1964). The community. *Tradition*, 12–13.

Warren, R. (2002). *The purpose driven life*. Grand Rapids, MI: Zondervan.

http://dx.doi.org/10.2190/CLEC7

CHAPTER 7

Finding Spirituality in the Next Stage of Life

PART I
Retirement as Spiritual Challenge and Opportunity

Linda Rabinowitch Thal

Spirituality is, first and foremost, a way of orienting to the world, a way of being and knowing, that emphasizes awe, wonder, and radical amazement at the glory of creation and the splendor of the universe. . . . Spirituality emphasizes the limits of our control, the need to learn to live in harmony with the rhythms of our planet of the universe.

Michael Lerner (1998)

Spirituality is a highly personal outlook about what is sacred to us, it is the expression of our most deeply held values, and it is that sense of higher purpose that guides our daily lives.

Dr. David Ariel (1995, p. 5)

Spirituality is about standing still and seeing where the world fits and balances.

SPIRITUALITY IN RETIREMENT?

I have been devoting significant time in anticipation of the logistics of my retirement but really haven't been focused on me—the inner me, that is. I was drawn into a life of religious service in part due to a desire to be closer to God and do holy work. After a long career as minister of several churches, I now appreciate how naïve I was during my years in the seminary. The reality was that much more of my work was relatively mundane and organizational than involved in spiritual engagement with my congregants, let alone myself. I found it hard to really pray while leading services and rarely made sufficient time for self-reflection. My spiritually, I regret, has stagnated. In retirement, I plan to rededicate myself to my spiritual search; but after so many years, will I be able to?

         ?▲   ?▲   ?▲

Moses said to the Holy One: Master of the Universe, if I must die [to vacate my post] for Joshua, let me be his disciple [in my remaining hours]. The Holy One replied. If that is what you wish to do, do it. . . . [When] the people said to Moses, "Moses our teacher, teach us Torah," he replied, "I no longer have the authority." They said, "We will not leave you." Then a divine voice came forth and commanded the people, "Be willing to learn from Joshua." With that, the people submitted to the command to sit and learn from Joshua's mouth. Joshua sat at the head, Moses at his right, and Aaron's sons at his left, while Joshua taught in Moses' presence. At that session, the tradition of wisdom was taken away from Moses and given to Joshua. When they went out, Moses walked at Joshua's left, and as they entered the Tent of Meeting, a pillar of cloud came down and formed a partition between the two. After the cloud parted, Moses went over to Joshua and asked, "What did the Word say to you?" Joshua replied, "When the Word used to reveal itself to you, did I know what it said to you?" In that instant, Moses cried out in anguish and said, "Rather a hundred deaths than a single pang of envy. Master of the universe, until now I sought life. But now my soul is surrendered to You" (Bialik & Ravnitzky, 1992, p. 103).

Like us, Moses desperately wanted to see his mission accomplished, even if he were not the one to complete it. He understood that he needed to step back and relinquish authority to his successor and even help the people transition to their new leader. The one thing that broke Moses's will to live was his fear of losing his relationship with God. He chose continued closeness to God over the possibility of diminished intimacy with the Divine.

Here is a retirement issue that may be all but unique for clergy, and it may not be at all apparent that this is the fear that lies beneath the discomfort or uncertainty we may be feeling about retirement. That fear can manifest in myriad ways:[1]

- As a seminarian, one of my most important experiences was being required to work out my personal theology. I found myself most attracted to [Martin] Buber's theology of relationship; that was where I found God most powerfully—in relationships. Knowing where to look for God had helped me through the death of my parents, and ultimately the death of my wife. But when it came to retirement, that theology seemed to crash. My relationships were so much thinner; I no longer had a steady flow of congregants coming for pastoral care; I was no longer central to people's celebration of births and grief over losses. Where was I supposed to find God then? It took me a long time to reestablish a relationship with God.

[1] Quotations from interviews conducted by the author.

- As I approached retirement, I was confident that God would show me what I was called to do next. I had always felt God's guidance in my life in a rather clear way. Suddenly, silence!
- When I retired, I discovered, to my surprise, that my personal prayer life was pretty barren. I had been leading prayer; I had been praying on behalf of others; I had found great satisfaction in teaching, leading and interpreting the liturgy, but now that those things weren't central to who I was, what was expected of me? I felt lost. I tried to remember how it was that prayer and ritual had originally drawn me to my vocation, but that seemed like light years away.
- One outcome of retirement for me has been reclaiming my own relationship with God. I hadn't realized how distant I had become from all the experiences and feelings that originally drew me to the ministry. I've discovered entirely new ways to pray; in fact, I understand prayer in a completely different way. Retirement has turned out to be a remarkably freeing experience.
- About six months after I retired, I felt like the world had gone flat. I made an appointment with a psychiatrist recommended by one of my colleagues, expecting to leave with a prescription for anti-depressants. Fortunately, the person I chose knew something about religious life. He said, "We could try you on medication, but I have a hunch that what you're describing isn't really depression." I left with a referral to a spiritual director.

It is one thing to counsel others through a crisis in faith, it is quite another to be in the midst of one's own. Often it's not at all clear to us that that is what we are dealing with. And crisis, emotional or spiritual, is certainly not the necessary or even usual outcome of retirement. But some sort of spiritual shift is indeed likely. It may be so subtle that we only notice it when, sometime later, we look back and realize that something about us has changed.

Leaving one's position of spiritual leadership does not mean leaving the service of God, but it may require new ways of relating to the Divine and of turning one's attention from nurturing the spiritual lives of congregants (the congregation) to further developing one's own.

Whether you are looking backward at the process of retirement that you have been through or forward in anticipation, this chapter is meant to help you notice, understand, and make wise choices about the ways retirement can be a life-enhancing opportunity for continued spiritual growth

DOING vs. BEING:
"WHAT ARE YOU GOING TO *DO* WHEN YOU RETIRE?"

It took a lot of trust to wait through that period of not knowing until something that seemed truly right became evident.

This is the question with which you will be bombarded as soon as you announce your retirement. You may have a very clear plan: I'm going to teach at the nearby community college, I am going to volunteer at the local food pantry, I am going to work on the campaign for low-cost housing, I am going to mentor ministerial students. Such responses are likely to be met by nodding heads and a satisfied glance. It is a comfort to friends, congregants, and families to feel that you have a well-formulated plan for this next phase of your life. They can relax and accept your decision because you'll be "okay."

But what if you don't have such a satisfying answer?

We live in a culture that defines us by what we do, that honors productivity, that applauds busyness. Undoubtedly you have been engaged in one of those conversations that sounds like competitive overscheduling and wondered whether a colleague's complaint about his tight calendar really amounts to bragging. All of this makes a reply like, "I'm looking forward to reading all the books I haven't read" or "I plan to take long walks in nature" or "I'm going to study—or meditate—more" or "I don't really know yet," quite suspect. Responding to the coming of age of the Baby Boom generation, the commercial discussion of retirement has shifted from leisure activity to encore careers.

On the one hand, this concern about what we will do when we retire makes sense in light of this generation's experience of approaching retirement age with the unprecedented expectation of 20 or even 30 years of good health before us. On the other hand, theologian Richard Rohr suggests that if we are on "the schedule of the soul," understimulation and greater introversion may be exactly what we need to process and integrate the insights and wisdom that our lives have given us (2011). Much of that unpacking, which is the natural developmental task of later life, requires silence and solitude. Abraham Joshua Heschel, speaking at a 1961 White House Council on Aging, noted,

> We know how to act in public; we do not know what to do in privacy. . . . age involves the problem of what to do with privacy. There are alleys in the soul where man walks alone, ways that do not lead to society, a world that shrinks from the public eye. (Heschel, 1972, p. 73)

It may look like you aren't *doing* anything. And that's just the point. You may just need this time to learn how to move from doing to being. That doesn't mean the end of an active life, but it means learning to be fully present to whatever arises in your life. You do know how to do this, because you've practiced *being* many times in your career as you've shifted from handling an overload of administrative tasks or a knotty problem with the congregational board to a hospital visit with someone who is dying. You've learned that it is not your reverent or polished words that matter here so much as your genuine presence. You know that sitting in silence by someone's bedside can be more healing than discussing the doctor's latest recommendation or bringing news from outside.

Such a visit is not about *doing* something; it is about *being with* someone. In such a setting, you are practiced at responding, moment by moment, to what is going on right now with the patient you are visiting rather than imposing any agenda you may have brought with you. Retirement may be a calling to learn to be this way with yourself. That may be hard to explain to those who want to know what you are doing with your new freedom, but it is legitimate to allow time to nurture your own soul if this is the direction to which you seem to be called.

So while it is ultimately important to find meaningful activity, retirement is also a time to explore one's own inner space, to resist the temptation to fill your calendar too quickly, to leave space open for hints of what comes next to ripen.

But How Does One Know?
Discernment vs. Decision Making

> As I approached retirement, I was confident that God would show me what I was called to do next. I had always felt God's guidance in my life in a rather clear way. Suddenly, silence.

This may be a time when we wish that God still used something so dramatic and visible as a cloud-by-day and pillar-of-fire-by-night to let us know when it is time to stay put and when it is time to move on, and in what direction we are meant to move. We wish that we too had Solomon's lev shomea—"the listening/understanding heart" for which he prayed when taking on religious leadership.

Depending on our tradition and context, we may be more or less familiar with the literature and conscious practice of discernment. A spiritual director at a seminary once confided in exasperation,

> They tell the graduating students who are interviewing for pulpits to think about urban vs. suburban or small town location, about how well they think they can work with this particular senior rabbi or the cantor, about the exact job description, about benefits. That's all fine and well, but nobody is telling them to pray!

Professor of theological studies Wilkie Au and Jungian analyst Noreen Au describe discernment as a process that involves "making decisions in a way that allows God to be a telling influence in our choices. The goal is to refine the acoustics of our heart so that we can better hear the Spirit's guidance" (Au & Au, 2006). Discernment is a commitment to stay connected to the divine, to constantly realign ourselves with what we, in our most prayerful moments, perceive to be the holy. The Aus note that "this requires cultivating the ability to stay with the discordant notes of our lives with alertness and sensitivity until we are able to grasp the theme of what God is about with us" (Au & Au, 2006). Thus, we need to perceive the melody hidden beneath what at first seem to be the disconnected, or even discordant, elements of our life and why we may need to practice solitude, silence, and slowness in anticipation, or in the early stages, of retirement.

Rabbi Howard Avruhm Addison, Professor of Jewish Spirituality at the Graduate Theological Foundation, suggests that discernment "involves a repeating cycle of prayer and intentionality, attention to external consequences and inner affect, 'trying on' provisional choices and testing results" (2006, p. 105). It is a process that you may discover began long ago. It may be a process that involves exploring and testing out alternative pathways. It is certainly a process that unfolds more in God's time than in ours. This is one of the things that makes discernment challenging and mysterious. God's time is often much slower (though occasionally much faster) than we are prepared to accept. There are periods of waiting when we can't really say what's going on with us. Something may indeed be gestating, but we aren't yet aware of it. We might call this time *b'midbar*—"wilderness time." The Israelites never knew when the pillar of cloud and of fire would lift or in what direction it would beckon them. During times like this, we learn to inhabit the space of not knowing. Perhaps Moses was being coy when he responded to Pharoah's offer to let the men go into the desert to pray but leave the women, children, and herds behind. But I suspect that Moses also knew he was speaking the truth when he claimed, "We won't know what we need until we get there" (Exodus 10:26). From this perspective, not knowing what you will do in retirement may be a manifestation of your willingness to relinquish some measure of willful control over the direction of your life and to stay open to the longings of your deeper self, which are also the desires of the One whom we wish to serve.[2]

Each of our religious traditions has its own texts and metaphors for talking about discernment. Catholics might look to Ignatius' Rules for Discernment or his 31-day Spiritual Exercises. Protestants may turn to Scripture; Jews may ponder the particular *tikkun* (repair/reparation/task) that their soul has been directed to perform during its earthly life. Sometimes it is simply helpful to meditate on the powerful verse in Deuteronomy 30:19: "I have put before you life and death, blessing and curse. Choose life," and to ask ourselves, "What is the life-enhancing direction in what I am considering? What would be most affirming of life and aliveness?"

Renewing Your Relationship with God

When I retired, I discovered, to my surprise, that my personal prayer life was pretty barren.

---

[2] For an elaboration of the difference between willingness and willfulness, see the first chapter of Gerald May's Care of Mind, Care of Spirit (2009).

Prayer and spiritual practices of all kinds are central ways of working on our relationship both with ourselves and with the Divine. One of the challenges of retirement may be a disintegration of the practices that have previously worked well for us. Sometimes this may happen because our practices were dependent on communal gatherings or on rhythms that are no longer providing the structure we need. Retirement may have precipitated a physical move away from the community with which we prayed and celebrated. Or we may feel that we need to back off from that community to give our successor space. We may find that we have lost the capacity to be led in prayer instead of being the leader. Even when our prayer and practice has not seemed to be dependent on the community, we may find that the old forms just aren't working for us in the ways they used to.

If congregational prayer and communal service have been your spiritual sustenance, you may need to actively work on reestablishing a more personal relationship with God. It may be that all you need to do is return to those practices, settings, and intentions that have felt God-filled in the past: walks in nature, solitary retreats, study of Scripture, centering prayer, meditation, music, journaling, volunteering for a charity. It may be, however, that you need to encounter God with fresh eyes or what Buddhists call "beginner's mind." That is more easily done with a practice that you have seldom or never used before. There are any number of practices, such as those just named, that can reopen portals to the divine and many books that describe them.

Hitbodedut (Aloneness)

> One outcome of retirement for me has been reclaiming my own relationship with God.

One such practice that is less generally known is *hitbodedut,* a powerful practice introduced by Rabbi Nachman of Brazlav, a 17th-century Hasidic master. Nachman was concerned with attaining intimacy with God as well as providing a potent process for discernment.

Hitbodedut means "self-seclusion" or "being alone with oneself." The essential practice is to isolate oneself—preferably outside, at night, but this is not essential—and to "pour out one's heart," in other words, to engage in a form of stream-of-consciousness "communication." The point is to let go of controlling our thought process by restricting ourselves to linear reasoning, polite or dignified forms, elevated subjects, or theological consistency. Indeed, some people think that this form of spiritual practice had an indirect influence on Freud's development of the analytic technique of free association. The goal is informality, intimacy, and lack of inhibition—the discovery and the sharing of one's truth in that moment.

Nachman encouraged his followers to feel free to speak to God of their most private thoughts, feelings, problems, and frustrations. No subject was too mundane. It was equally valuable to bring one's business or financial concerns to God as it was to plead for help controlling one's less admirable desires and character traits. One could cry out one's desire for closeness to the Divine or wail about God's seeming absence or even bemoan one's shattered faith. One may plead with God like a complaining and pestering child. Anything goes! Nachman even recognized that we may not know what we want or what we want to say. When that happens, he recommended simply repeating "*Ribbono shel olam*" (Master of the Universe) over and over again until, perhaps, more words—or tears—flowed (obviously, any other phrase that seems suitable to you would be equally useful). Similarly, he advocated engaging in a "silent scream" and "audible sighing."

Few of us can wander out into the forest at night, so any secluded place will do—your car, a large park, the backyard, the beach, the shower, the darkened sanctuary. Just keep talking. This is where your angst or your joy, your confusion or your clarity, your gratitude or your anger can be expressed. And this is one way to find out about the deep longings of your soul. While this may not be a daily practice, as Nachman suggested it should be, it is most revealing if it is not a one-time practice. Try it with some regularity, at least for a period of time. Over the weeks or months, both intimacy and clarity can develop, although I have also seen that it can have a powerful effect as a one-time experience.

Spiritual Direction

I left with a referral to a spiritual director.

Although spiritual direction is an ancient practice, many outside Catholic tradition had not heard of it until the last few decades when Protestants, and then Jews, began to seek and then offer some form of guidance or mentorship for religious growth and deepening. Unlike earlier forms of spiritual direction, the contemporary model is nonhierarchical and, despite its name, nondirective. The underlying assumption is that God is the real director, and the "director" is merely the facilitator of the central relationship, which is between God and the directee.

Many clergy find that having been in the position of religious "expert" for so long, they have not had opportunities to rethink their own religious ideas nor fully plumbed their own religious experience. Speaking one's own thoughts, beliefs, questions, doubts, and insecurities aloud to another, who can provide a safe space for exploration, vulnerability, and surprise, is often in itself revitalizing for one's sense of spiritual connection.

Both ordained clergy and lay people can offer spiritual direction. Clergy often see a lay director because it gives them some distance from colleagues with whom they ordinarily interact. Many clergy choose a director outside of their own religious tradition, while others are more comfortable with a director with whom they share common religious language and practice. More information about spiritual direction can be found on the Spiritual Directors International website: www.sdiworld.org.

Dark Night, Desert, and Descent

About six months after I retired, I felt like the world had gone flat.

While it is possible that the shift to retirement can trigger depression, it is also possible that what at first appears to be depression can actually be a positive step in your spiritual development. And it is possible that both depression and the spiritual stage called "dark night of the soul" may occur together.

The term "dark night of the soul" originated with Teresa of Avila and John of the Cross in the 16th century as they struggled to find ways to describe a confounding, often deeply unsettling, but ultimately positive process of spiritual deepening. During these times, it is likely that prayer and spiritual practices that have felt rich and satisfying suddenly feel arid and flat. One may feel somewhat "lost" and floundering. Dark nights are often talked about as if they were a stage, but a better concept is a state. That is because we may experience multiple dark nights, some long and intense, others short and mild, alternating with periods of religious highs, contentment, or just "normality." The language of Jewish spiritual dynamics speaks of *mochin d'katnut* and *mochin d'gadlut*—"restricted and expanded consciousness." The Hasidic masters acknowledged the dynamic of *yerida l'tzoreh aliyah*, "descent for the sake of ascent."

We know this familiar dynamic from other realms of life. Jean Piaget noted that the transitions from one stage of children's development to the next involve periods of disequilibrium (remember the "terrible twos!"); Thomas Kuhn, who coined the term "paradigm shift," described it as a "state of crisis," the point at which significant anomalies have accrued within a prevailing scientific paradigm which had not yet been replaced by a new theory. Rabbi Levi Yitzchak of Berdichev provided metaphors of consolation for such times, which his colleagues regarded as examples of *yesh mei ayin,* "existence arising out of nothingness." He asks that we imagine the transformation of an egg into a chicken or a seed into a plant. There must be some point at which there is neither a chicken nor an egg, at which time the seed has disintegrated but not yet become a plant. "Before a thing can become transformed into something else," he taught, "it must come to a level of Nothingness." It is this sense of Nothingness that gives rise to the notion of darkness.

Psychiatrist and spiritual director Gerald May described it this way:

> The dark night is a profoundly good thing. It is an ongoing spiritual process in which we are liberated from attachments and compulsions and empowered to live and love more freely. Sometimes this letting go of old ways is painful, occasionally even devastating. But this is not why the night is called "dark." The darkness of the night implies nothing sinister, only that the liberation takes place in hidden ways, beneath our knowledge and understanding. It happens mysteriously, in secret, and beyond our conscious control. For that reason it can be disturbing or even scary, but in the end

it always works to our benefit. . . . More than anything, I think the dark night of the soul gives meaning to life. (2005)

It may be of some comfort to remember that Mother Teresa, one of the most idolized religious figures of our time, privately confessed to have experienced an extended and severe period of religious aridity.

The whole time smiling—Sisters and people pass such remarks.—They think my faith, trust and love are filling my very being and that the intimacy with God and union to His will must be absorbing by heart.—Could they but know—and how my cheerfulness is the cloak by which I cover emptiness and misery. (Mother Teresa, 2009, p. 187)

It may also be helpful to remember that devotion and prayer can be offered from the place of spiritual discomfort. In such a period, Thomas Merton wrote,

My Lord God,
I have no idea where I am going,
I do not see the road ahead of me,
I cannot know for certain where it will end.
Nor do I really know myself,
And the fact that I think
I am following your will
Does not mean that I am actually doing so.
But I believe
That the desire to please you does in fact please you,
and I hope I have that desire
in all that I am doing. (1999)

It is important if you find yourself in a state that feels like what has been described to distinguish between dark night and depression. In periods of *katnut* or "dark night," one often has a sense that something fruitful may be happening in spite of the disconcerting confusion and uncertainty. Gerald May's excellent book, *Dark Night of the Soul* (2005), and his description of the differences between dark night and depression in *Care of Mind, Care of Spirit* (2009), are good places to start. As mentioned above, it is possible to experience both states simultaneously, so if you consult a therapist, it should be someone who understands and respects spiritual dynamics, and if you choose to meet with a spiritual director, which can be particularly helpful at such times, do raise the question of whether you may also be experiencing depression as well as a spiritual state of dark night.

What am I Going to Do in Retirement? Work on Myself!

Toward the end of his life, Rabbi Zusya's students noticed that he seemed distressed. Misreading their teacher, they asked, with great concern, "Are you afraid that when you die you will be asked why you were not more like Moses?" "No," replied Zusya, "I fear that the Holy One will say, "Zusya, why were you more like Zusya?"

Unlike the early stages of development demarcated by Piaget, the later stages of adult development, those that involve self-transcendence, are not givens. We do not naturally reach these stages simply by growing chronologically older. The Kotzker Rebbe, when asked to describe the essence of religion, answered that it was "to work on oneself."

In Galatians, Paul introduced the notion of the "fruits of the spirit," asserting that acceptance of "the Holy Spirit produces this kind of fruit in our lives: love, joy, peace, patience, kindness, goodness, faithfulness, gentleness, and self-control." In the Jewish Mussar tradition, emphasis is placed on the conscious cultivation of the characteristics of goodness, with the understanding that the process of soul refinement allows one to be more permeable to God's movement within us. What seems important is that these two dimensions of spirituality—inner work and relationship with God—are intimately linked, like the proverbial two sides of the coin.

Although as clergy, you have been working on soul refinement for many years, the work on oneself is never completed, as suggested by the pithy title of Jack Kornfield's book on the spiritual path, *After the Ecstasy* [of Enlightenment], *the Laundry*. In the book, he quotes a lama who returned to the United States after 12 years of Buddhist study and practice in India and Tibet.

> Old patterns came back surprisingly quickly. I got irritable, confused. I wasn't taking care of my body, I worried about money, about relationship. At the worst point I feared that I was losing what I had learned. Then I realized I couldn't live in some enlightened memory. What became clear is that spiritual practice is only what you're doing now. (2001, p. 176)

Regardless of the inner work we have already done, inner purification is the salient focus of this stage of life. The goal is somewhat paradoxical: to become one's most authentic self and at the same time to understand oneself as part of a whole much greater than the self.

Religious traditions offer many ways of working on oneself. Currently, mindfulness practice is receiving a great deal of attention. Centering prayer, adopted from the outlines provided in the *Cloud of Unknowing*, has also become popular beyond the Catholic circles in which it was developed (Keating, 1995, 2009). In Jewish circles, the practice of Mussar has experienced a major resurgence (Morinis, 2007).

"Working on oneself" is the true spiritual task of retirement, whether retirement takes on the appearance of an encore career, volunteering in the service of others, tending to grandchildren and family, traveling, writing, studying, or contemplation. Retirement, without so much of the clerical trimmings we have worn during our active ministry, is the opportunity to more fully discover, to become, and to enact who we are meant to be. We wish that it may it go well with you!

REFERENCES

Addison, H. A. (2006). *Berur: How do you know if it's God?* Woodstock, VT: Jewish Lights.

Au, W., & Au, N. C. (2006). *The discerning heart: Exploring the Christian path.* Mahwah, NJ: Paulist Press.

Bialik, H. N., & Ravnitzky, Y. H. (1992). *The book of legends, Sefer Ha-Aggadah.* New York, NY: Schocken.

Boorstein, S. (2002). *Pay attention, for goodness' sake: Practicing the perfections of the heart—The Buddhist path of kindness.* New York, NY: Ballantine.

Heschel, A. J. (1972). *The insecurity of freedom.* New York, NY: Schocken.

Keating, T. (1995). *Open mind, open heart: The contemplative dimension of the gospel.* New York, NY: Continuum

Keating, T. (2009). *Intimacy with God: An introduction to centering prayer.* New York, NY: Crossroad.

Kornfield, J. (2001). *After the ecstasy, the laundry: How the heart grows wise on the spiritual path.* New York, NY: Bantam.

May, G. (2005). *The dark night of the soul: A psychiatrist explores the connection between darkness and spiritual growth.* New York, NY: HarperOne.

May, G. (2009). *Care of mind, care of spirit.* New York, NY: HarperCollins.

Merton, T. (1999). *Thoughts in solitude.* New York, NY: Farrar, Straus and Giroux.

Morinis, A. (2007). *Everyday holiness: The Jewish spiritual path of Mussar.* Boston, MA: Trumpeter.

Mother Teresa. (2009). *Mother Teresa: Come be my light: The private writings of the "Saint of Calcutta,"* B. Kolodiejchuk (Ed.). New York, NY: Image.

Rohr, R. (2011). *Falling upward: A spirituality for the two halves of life.* New York, NY: Jossey-Bass/Wiley.

Saltzberg, S. (2013). *Lovingkindness; Faith; Love your enemies.* New York, NY: Ballantine.

PART II
Retirement—Exile or Promised Land?
In Search of a Spirituality for Retirement

How shall we sing the Lord's song in a strange land?

(Psalm 137. 4, KJV)

Bishop Patrick G. White, Retired Bishop of Bermuda

Epiphany at Tim Horton's

The idea for this reflection first came to me early in the morning at Tim Horton's (think Dunkin Donuts or Starbuck's). I had just retired and was beginning to feel the relief of a life of no obligations. At one of the gatherings the church had arranged to send me on my way into retirement, we had a couple of musicians who played through the event. At one point they played Jimmy Buffett's song with the line, "Wastin' away again in Margaritaville" (1977). I joked with those gathered that this was my idea of a good retirement.

Wastin' away at Tim Horton's was the best I could do for now, but that morning, suddenly and quite spontaneously, it occurred to me that I had now set my feet on the path that would lead to my departure from this world. I could put it more gently and say I realized I was now entering the last phase of my life. I had my first real "intimation of *mortality*."[3]

Now, this is not the kind of thing I normally think about early in the morning over a coffee. I was in the midst of my morning constitutional—a walk through the neighborhood and a coffee and muffin as a reward. I felt blindsided and unprepared for this uninvited intrusion. The chill of approaching winter was now being matched by another more spiritual chill.

Life is a Beach

Recently I came across a cartoon that illustrates some of what I mean. It is a drawing of an hourglass with the sand in the top of the glass halfway finished running through the narrow neck of the glass into the bottom half. On the surface of the sand remaining in the top half of the hourglass is the figure of a man lying on a beach towel, wearing a bathing suit and wearing sunglasses. Stuck in the sand beside him is a beach umbrella. Within arm's reach are a cocktail glass and a newspaper opened at the comic strips (this could just as easily be a woman).

Take away the hour glass and this is how many of us think of retirement either literally or figuratively (my fantasy about "Margaritaville"). It is time to "kick back and catch some rays," as the saying goes. Or travel. Or spend more time with the grandchildren. Or write that book we all think we have in us. All of these are very commendable. But the hour glass is a critical part of this experience as well. The sands of time do run out. The cartoonist has captured the irony, the fantasy, and the denial that accompany retirement.

Life After Life

I do not spend a lot of time thinking about end-of-life matters, at least not *my* end of life. True, as a clergyman I have often been called upon to think about it for others. And like many others, I have to think about an aging parent and

---

[3] To be honest, I thought this was the term the poet William Wordsworth had written but later discovered it was actually "intimations of *immortality*." I mention this for two reasons. First it is about failing memory, another casualty of aging. Second, because whether mortality or immortality, either term is relevant to my theme.

how and when her life might end. But this was now me, and I was surprised at how it felt. This felt more like exile than the Promised Land.

I do believe in an afterlife and I do hope to enjoy it. This is a consoling belief given the chill I was experiencing as I enter this last phase of my life. To come back to my intimation of mortality, I do not believe the sense of dread that chilled me that morning undermines or brings into question my hope for my prospects of a blissful eternity. I need to look elsewhere for what was starting to surface that morning.

So, What's My Problem?

One answer is a paradox. I realized I had both more time *and* less time in retirement. More free time to choose what I would or would not do. But less time in which to get it all done. I will not have forever, and now suddenly and unexpectedly it was beginning to *feel* that way.

I also need to mention at this point that another part of my morning constitutional and coffee at Tim's has been time for short scripture reading and writing in my journal. And so, more than just pondering this new awareness of my mortality, I also began to put some of my experience in writing.[4] What follows is an extended reflection on what I am calling my search for a spirituality that corresponds to the experience of retirement. My stance is that of an explorer rather than an expert. It might have begun as a journal entry, but it has developed far beyond that.

Spirituality

And so, what do I mean by "spirituality?" To me, spirituality encompasses all of what would be considered religious in our lives, including practices like prayer and worship, service within and without our faith communities, study and reflection. From one perspective, all these give form to our spirituality, but seen from another angle, our spirituality also informs and unites these as well. I believe we are fundamentally spiritual creatures seeking to understand our connections with and our alienation from something and someone greater than ourselves. For the believer, this sense of belonging to something that transcends our individual selves extends not only to all humankind but to our Creator as well. Spirituality runs deep, wide, and high.

---

[4] When I began to journal more intentionally about 10 years ago, I decided that I would not bind myself to a routine but just make entries as the spirit moved me. The subject matter is quite personal, probably about as deep and about as interesting as what you would find on Facebook. I am now on my sixth handwritten volume or roughly one every 2 years. My point is to say I have not followed a method but just put down my thoughts as I had time and inclination. And to this extent I would say it has worked for me.

I once tried to define spirituality as our *style* of being spiritual. And that would change depending on the context in which our beliefs were formed. It also implied that spirituality had a discernible public dimension as well as a private and inward one. And so, Catholics have one sense of spirituality, Protestants another, Jews still another, and Muslims yet another. This is to say nothing of the differences *within* faith groups. Some outward manifestations of spirituality only apply to clergy, others only to male or female believers, and some to all believers in a faith group. Signs of this spirituality extend to apparel like kippas/yarmulkas, beards, burkas, turbans, crosses worn as jewellery, rosary beads, and so on.

Most, if not all these, would carry naturally into retirement, although for some clergy, certain of the outward signs of office that are also expressions of our spirituality might be set aside. I think for instance of clergy from my tradition as an Anglican (Episcopalian) who spend their working lives wearing clerical shirts. (The joke is that some of us give the impression that we *sleep* in them.) Once they retire, some revert to what "society" wears. And with that goes an outward *indication* of spirituality but not spirituality itself. Our spirituality runs more deeply than clothes and more pervasively throughout virtually all that we "do" and "think" as a person who sees him/herself in the "light" of the divine.

Underground Rivers

My question then, is whether there is or is not a sense of spirituality that reflects and gives meaning to this last phase of our life. Is there a retirement spirituality that differs from our working-life spirituality? By way of answering this question, it occurs to me to look at those deeper experiences of life that run like underground rivers through our lives and can surface during times of crisis. These are the "what's it all about" questions that force themselves on us at the times of our greatest disappointments and at the major crossroads of our lives. But they may also surface unexpectedly when our guard is down.

Clergy time is much taken up with what has become known as "paying the rent"—attending meetings, visiting the sick, organizing and leading worship, just showing up on time *and* sticking around until everyone else has left! Among those who spend their time in the trenches leading and pastoring congregations (to say nothing of those at HQ), the tendency is to consign thinking deep thoughts to the philosophers, theologians, poets, academics, and artists. But there is a tension here for us.

On the one hand, we would all love to attend more to them, but the day-to-day demands of ministry often preclude that. We think we will get to them when we have time. On the other hand, we hear comments like that of the bishop who remarked that when he visited his clergy he could tell by the contents of the priest's library what year the cleric had "died." Hearing this encouraged me to continue to work at nurturing those deep roots I had begun to sink to at seminary. Despite my best intentions not to die in this way, it was a struggle and always at the mercy of more pressing pastoral and administrative tasks.

In retirement, the shell of "busyness" that insulated us from the big questions begins to thin out and break down. Part of what makes up that shell is a protection against too many thoughts about our mortality. At certain points, the thought of life coming to an end forces us to question whether it is all worth it. What will all our efforts amount to in the end? Will we have done the important things?

And so in retirement, stripped of our roles, our identities, our positions, and our work, we find ourselves vulnerable and in some sense less equipped to stem the tide of our, until now, submerged spiritual needs. In the words of the psalmist, we may well ask, "How shall we sing the Lord's song in a strange land?" Is retirement exile or the Promised Land?

What I am Not Talking About

Before going on, let me say this is not just about continuing to attend—church, temple, mosque—or praying more or reading the scriptures. These disciplines and practices over a lifetime of service are quite helpful in enabling us to interpret the course of our lives and set them in perspective. But they are also part of what we have used to create and maintain what we might call "a working-life spirituality."

We have all heard the comment from retirees, "I'm so busy I don't know how I ever found time for work." This is fine and may be in response to the surfacing of some of what I am calling the underground rivers. But I think spirituality is deeper than keeping busy or replacing one's former working life with a new voluntary "working life." It is not so much about finding things to *do* in retirement as it is about *understanding* what we do and who we are in the light of our divine origins.

In retirement, some clergy decide to finally make that trip to the Holy Land (or some other sacred place). Some take that religious retreat they just never had time for while working. Others embark upon new prayer disciplines and learn how to meditate. Still others take up yoga or go seriously green and embrace the doctrines of the ecology movements. These are closer to what I am talking about but still more like strategies to attend to an, until now, unrequited spiritual thirst.

Crossing the Border—Baggage and Luggage

One of the terms that has passed from the field of psychotherapy into our daily discourse is *baggage*. This is about those experiences from our past. Experiences that inhibit our ability to function, as fully and as freely as we would have liked, in the present. For example, if the circumstances that led up to one's retirement were not good or left one feeling disappointed, underappreciated, unprepared, cynical, or even downright angry, then that is baggage, and we can choose whether or not to drag it with us into retirement. This is to say nothing of those unhelpful baggage handlers who seem determined not to let us forget our sins and misdemeanors.

But there are other pieces of baggage we carry from years before retirement as well. They are the sum of our disappointments, failures, bad choices, and so on. They may also take the form of addictions. It is not easy to unload all of this stuff, but the truth is it would be better if we could just put some of it down and leave it behind.

I once read a story that speaks to this matter of baggage in spiritual terms. The author is Watchman Nee and it appears in his book *The Normal Christian Life* (1977). He relates the story of a man walking along the road carrying a large heavy backpack. Another man driving a horse and cart stops and asks the man with the backpack if he would like a lift. The man gratefully accepts, climbs into the cart, and stands at the front where he can talk to the driver. After they have traveled a short distance, the driver turns to his passenger and says, "You can take your pack off, you know. Let the cart carry it." The man feels a little silly and says, "I have just become so used to carrying my pack it felt like part of me." And so off comes the pack and the traveler gets double the relief.

Nee's point in telling this story was to illustrate the effect of God's grace on a new believer. But I think he tells a parable that can easily be applied to "old believers" like retired clergy who need to hear of this kind of relief as well. But it is worth asking how that good news, that experience of God's grace, might apply to this new and last phase of life. It is possible to look at the early time in retirement as stepping onto that wagon, taking the backpack off, and looking through it to see what we can leave on the cart before resuming our journey.

Baggage is one thing, but it is different than what I will call *luggage*. The difference between baggage and luggage is quite simply that luggage is the good stuff we bring with us into retirement. This is that accumulated expertise and wisdom we have developed along the way. It is those bits and pieces we bring along that will actually enable us to carry on into retirement with energy, commitment, and satisfaction. Some of it will have been packed away for some time, awaiting the opportunity to use it.

Another way to speak of this is to bring forward the things we have placed on the back burner while we did the necessary business of writing sermons, chairing meetings, visiting the sick, presiding at worship, and so on. (And again, for most clergy, there is the necessity of getting food on the table, getting the kids educated, and for some, paying down the mortgage.)

It isn't always easy to know which of the things we carry with us is baggage and which is luggage. The example that comes readily to mind is the personal libraries most of us build over our time in ministry. I have great affection for many of those books and some pride in the collection that I have amassed. But for very practical reasons, I have just had to let most of them go. My challenge is to decide which books might be the very thing I would want along to nourish my spirituality in retirement and which books I could just leave on the cart when I resume my journey. It is as difficult as losing weight and as painful as amputation. This does feel like exile. The bottom line however is that I need to travel lighter.

And so, the difference between baggage and luggage is not always between good stuff and bad stuff. Some of it is the difference between what we really need and, like the man in the cart, what we have just become used to carrying.

It would be nice of course if all this downsizing were neat and tidy, evolving along predictable lines. The truth is, it is not neat and it does not unfold predictably. Given the internal pressures to just keep busy and the awareness that we have both more time and less time in retirement, I believe there is a need for an *intentional* spirituality that matches these shifts. And so to the rivers.

RIVERS I HAVE KNOWN

Childhood Benediction

I begin way back in my earliest awareness as a child. It was in Bermuda, when my mother and father and I lived in the cottage on the grounds of the Bermudiana Hotel. The house sat on a rise looking across the large expanse of green lawn, which dipped down to the foot of the blue hotel with its corners edged in white. Just to the left in my field of vision stood a lone casuarena tree, a tall and sentinel-like tree standing some 35 meters in height.

One morning when I was 6 or 7 years old, I went out early just at sunrise. Although the horizon was blocked by the hotel and some other buildings, the soft light of the dawn suffused the scene before me—the lawn, sparkling beads of dew still on it, sloping away toward the darkened façade of the hotel and the casuarena already emerging from its silhouette in the growing light. There was something else as well. In part, it was that the scene was as if everything was new and that the world had just begun again as in the Garden of Eden. There was presence, but no figure and no voice; but I did feel comforted as if someone was smiling kindly on me and on the scene.

I do not know how long my awareness lasted, and I did not know what it meant at the time. But I do recall feeling that I belonged in the picture and was not just an observer. Even as I write this now 65 years later, I wonder what it was about that scene and my place in it that keeps me remembering it. But now I tie it into what I am saying when I talk about underground rivers. That experience was the spring, the source of a stream that has coursed through my life, sometimes seeming to disappear and sometimes surfacing.

This is one of the reasons also that, even though I am not by inclination an early riser, I still feel the time just after sunrise is a blessed time of the day. It is just as if it is all new, all just begun—a benediction. Some of that was within me during my morning walks and my reflection times at Tim Horton's. It is now the time I do my first meditation of the day. And it is a precious time.

I believe also that my intuition of the hospitality of nature is something that informs my lifelong interest in photography. (Even when nature is inhospitable, it nevertheless reveals an underlying or overarching order.) I find myself wanting to capture both the artistry inherent in the natural world and the elusive mystical quality that suggests a transcendent significance for even the tiniest wildflower. And so in retirement I will spend more time using this means of trying to capture something of God's good creation on film or on digital sensor. It is ultimately a spiritual exercise.

Brackish Stream

Another stream that has run throughout my life and also has its source for me in Bermuda has left a brackish taste in my mouth. And that is what it has felt like to have been born in a racially divided community. A succession of black women looked after me in that same hotel cottage on that same dew-sprayed lawn as my mother and father both went to work. I was told by my parents that it was OK for me to play with my black playmates, but it was not OK to bring them into the house.

I attended first a school that had both boys and girls but no black children. Later I attended a school for boys only, but again no black children were allowed. What bothers me now is that this is not the inheritance I would have wanted from my otherwise so beautiful birthplace or my otherwise so generous parents. The other thing that haunted me is the question, "Would I in time have resisted the current of racial discrimination had I remained and grown up in Bermuda?" It was a question that I would answer for myself later when I returned as an adult. As it was, I left at age 10 and moved to Canada. Canada has been both exile and Promised Land for me, but more of the latter.

One thing is certain and that is this brackish river has surfaced and resurfaced throughout my life. And its bad taste has been enough to fuel a deep longing in me for healing this wound in the body of our common humanity. It surfaced as I participated "in spirit" from Canada in the Civil Rights Movement in the United States. I did not march. I did not go to Alabama. One of the more concrete ways and yet still at arm's length was to learn to play the guitar and add my voice to the folk songs that embodied the movement to raze the barriers of discrimination in the United States. I stress this was more than an emotional identification but a matter of the spirit.

It wasn't enough. It wasn't much. But the river would not stay submerged. It has played a major role in forming my spirituality. It reaches beyond issues of justice and reparation to the deeper matters of human liberation. This brackish river continues to flow into my retirement for now. I wonder how to engage with integrity in my current context given the breaches these experiences represent with the world I believe God is calling us to create.

Interfaith Spirituality

In my quest, I have sought the roots of a spirituality that I believe we share at the level of our common humanity rather than one that divides us according to our specific faith groups and their histories (theologies, pieties, worship and prayer practices). I base this approach on the belief that being human, quite aside from any commitment to or upbringing in a religious tradition, entails a capacity for spirituality.

And so, when an Abraham, a Gautama (Buddha), a Moses, a Jesus, or a Muhammad appears, each evokes and refocuses a capacity and a longing already given. In the Judeo-Christian tradition, the metaphor that speaks to this reality for me is "image of God." We are created with a capacity to relate to the one whose ways are greater than our ways and whose thoughts are greater than our thoughts and to whom we are accountable. This is a belief we apply to all humanity.

The underground rivers I have described are like raw material from which we might refine spirituality for retirement. Our *capacity* for spirituality is something we have tapped into and taught others to tap into throughout our lives in ministry. We are not without resources as we engage in "redeeming the time" (Ephesians 5:16, KJV).

Looking Back to Tim Horton's

The trail that began with a sensation about mortality over a coffee, some scripture, and some notes in my journal has taken me some distance. One of the surprising turns was to be invited by Dan Roberts, whose book on retirement I reviewed for Baywood Publishing, to submit my reflections on my spirituality during retirement. This provided some impetus to take my thoughts where they wanted to go, as I said to begin with, more as an explorer than as an expert. This feels more like the Promised Land than exile.

I believe there is a common experience among those of us who face retirement. That is the challenge of maintaining our spiritual lives under quite different conditions than those under which we developed our spiritualities while still "in harness." I believe that along with the capacities for reason and imagination, we have, as human beings, an inherent capacity for spirituality. In fact I would go so far as to say that without that capacity, we are not fully human. And just as we can suppress or leave undeveloped our ability to reason and to imagine, we can also do the same for our spiritual nature.

CONCLUSION

Spirituality is about our awareness of ourselves bearing a divine imprint. Endowed as we are by our creator with a capacity to find meaning and significance for ourselves, we find that meaning and significance across the whole fabric of our lives and not just in certain strands, like what we did for a living. Retirement draws a line in the sand between our working lives and what comes next. Is it to be exile or the Promised Land? Spirituality suffuses it all, informs it all, and questions it all in the light of the One who beckons us into wholeness, out of exile into the Promised Land.

REFERENCES

Ariel, D. (1995). *What do Jews believe?: The spiritual foundation of Judaism.* New York, NY: Schocken Books.
Buffett, J. (1977). *Margaritaville* [song]. Coral Reefer Music.
Lerner, M. (1998). Spirituality in America. *Tikkun Magazine.*
Nee, W. (1977). *The normal Christian life.* Wheaton, IL: Tyndale House.

PART III

For the People
in Your Life
(Chapters You Will Want
to Share)

CHAPTER 8

Listening and Sharing with Spouses (To be Read by Both You and Your Spouse)

He who answers before listening—
That is his folly and his shame . . .
The heart of the discerning acquires knowledge;
The ears of the wise seek it out.

Proverbs 18:13, 15

Throughout our lives, we grow by giving up. We give up some of our deepest attachments to others. We give up certain cherished parts of ourselves. We must confront, in the dreams we dream, as well as in our intimate relationships, all that we never will have and never will be. Passionate investment leaves us vulnerable to loss. . . . And sometimes, no matter how clever we are, we must lose.

Darcy Harris (2011)

SPOUSE LOOKS BACK AND AHEAD

Throughout the years, I often thought being a clergy spouse was difficult—unreasonable expectations on me, protecting my family's privacy, advocating for my husband in the face of congregant attacks, being his sounding board. Religion had always been part of my life growing up, but never actually at the core. I had never even thought about the possibility of becoming a clergyperson myself. (Perhaps that was somewhat generational in that women were just beginning to assume congregational leadership roles at the time I was completing college.) In fact, I had never contemplated the thought of being a clergy wife. But then I met this wonderful man whom I not only loved and with whom I wanted to create a family, but also someone who genuinely inspired me religiously. In the blush of early love, it seemed easy to commit myself to being his wife in all that would require given his path to ordination. But looking back now, I was naïve; I didn't know what life ahead would be.

Now, as my husband is preparing to retire, I have been reflecting on the past 30 years—both the wonderful times and the challenging. I now am not sure whether I would have done it again if I more fully understood what it would have meant to my

105

children and my own life. But here we are at the brink of a new stage of life, and I feel it is my turn to set our direction in order to have more of my unmet needs and interests met. I feel a strange combination of excitement, resentment, guilt, and anxiety at the prospect, and need help in figuring out how to make this a constructive conversation with him. It will be difficult to plan for and manage through the changes that lie ahead on unfamiliar paths, but I am optimistic that this may bring us even closer together.

ᘒ   ᘒ   ᘒ

LISTENING TO OUR MATE

There are two gates in heaven for men.

One gate reads: "For all those men whose wife rules the house."

The other gate reads: "For all those men who rule the house."

Saint Peter sees that the line for the first gate is a mile long. The second line, however, contains only one person—an old man standing all alone. Saint Peter rushes over to him and asks, "How is it that you are in this line and managed to rule your household when there is a line a mile long over there?" The old man looks at the other line and replies, "I don't know! My wife told me to stand over here."

At times, in order to make a wise decision, we need to listen more to our mate.[1] Often we don't attend as carefully as we should to the voice of our spouses. In the daily excitement in the life of the ministry, we often forget the sacrifices that our spouse makes every day on our behalf and on behalf of the congregation. We too often take them for granted and perhaps do not praise them sufficiently or give thanks to God for the blessing of having them in our lives. When it comes to the final service for our retirement, the center of attention is usually reserved for us alone, while our spouses are often either overlooked, pushed to the background, or their role is simply mentioned casually. Is this not reminiscent of the many times they never received credit for the support they provided? Think of all the contributions they have made not only to our success but to the success of the congregation—the smile they wore when listening to congregants complain about you; the compassion they exemplified as they listened to sad stories of a life trauma; the setups and teardowns they participated in when no other volunteer was available, their chipping in to buy things or make things; editing sermons—the list goes on. In a survey by *Just Between Us*, a magazine for clergy spouses, *loneliness* was rated by pastor's wives as their number one problem (Zoba, 1997). Another study by United Methodist ministers in Minnesota showed similar results. Linda Hileman writes in her article, "The Unique Needs of Protestant Clergy

---

[1] The use of the words mate, spouse, etc. refers to either male or female or a significant other or a partner. The intent of the chapter is to make one aware of the psychological underpinnings that are occurring in a couple's life. In places where we use one gender and your mate is of the other, please mentally substitute the correct one.

Families: Implications for Marriage and Family Counseling," that one pastor's spouse expressed it this way: "The loneliest feeling in the world can be sitting in a pew by yourself in a sanctuary full of people where your spouse is preaching" (Hileman, 2008).

We often forget that just as we are going through an emotional trauma when our active ministry ends, our spouse is suffering alongside us. Your spouse married you and not the congregation, but sacrificed for your sake. She is empathizing with the sorrow you are experiencing and would love to protect you from it. As the congregation goes through premourning in anticipation of your departure, negative comments that cover up their anxiety can be hurtful to both of you, but your spouse just has to smile and bear the unintentional sting. Often she may secretly harbor anger toward the congregation in these parting days, feeling that you are not being given enough credit for all the hours invested or for the years you have neglected family on their behalf. Worst of all, they have no one to share it with, particularly you, for fear of upsetting you further (see below).

This is a time of transition for both of you. Unlike other professions, the world of the clergy involves an entire family. Just as certain conduct was expected from you, your spouse was expected to dress appropriately for every event and act as the host or hostess. She always was expected to approach everyone with a smile and friendly greeting. Often she was expected to bake brownies, teach Sunday school, lead Bible study groups, clean, babysit, sing in the choir, play piano, be an active member of the women's or men's group, sit on the finance committee, redo the website, direct Christmas plays, visit the sick, do secretarial work, be at services, greet others at the reception, and generally act as an unpaid assistant to the pastor. So when you retire from the ministry, so does your spouse.

Writes Robert Kemper,

> The deference, honor and respect she received as a minister's wife may have come from the wrong reasons and may have been inadequate, but in time, they became important to her. She, too, will miss the role she had known in the congregation. Like the minister, she will experience the symptoms of grief in her loss. She, too, may say, "Yesterday I was the most important woman in the building. Today I am nothing." (1988, p. 36)

Your mate, too, needs to be recognized and honored as well during the final ceremonies. If the congregation gives you a gift, perhaps your spouse should receive something as well, acknowledging her contribution to the congregation. Such acknowledgment and recognition may help your spouse come to terms with the end of this chapter in both your lives.

Transition of your spouse means

- They go from being a Very Important Person—often considered as an assistant clergy by the congregation—to a nonexistent role. They may have to suppress their former role so as not to step on the toes of the new minister's spouse.

- The warm community that has cared for both of you is now focused on making room for a new clergy family. You both will now be treated differently as you share their attention. This new situation will hurt, and for some more deeply than others.
- The spiritual home you both once knew may no longer exist. You both will be challenged to find a new comfortable house of prayer, but your mate will no longer have his favorite minister on the pulpit. This takes a lot of adjustment.
- You may have to move from your home (especially if you have been living in a parish house) to a different one—yet another upheaval at an already difficult time.
- Some denominations require retiring clergy to refrain from contact with their former congregation and its members, thus leaving them bereft of longtime friends. This too can create a state of chaos. To whom does a retired clergy or spouse turn for comfort, help, and advice? One minister expressed that he and his wife had no children and were originally from another country. With no family close by, the congregation had become that extended family. They were forced to ignore the rules of their diocese regarding private friendships.
- You and your spouse are in the midst of a *Catch 22*. Unlike other critical times in your marriage, you had each other as a confidant. Since you both are undergoing this transition, you may likely hesitate to turn to the other for fear of adding to her stress and/or upsetting her. If you are upset with how your final days are going, do you or do you not share this with your spouse? You may fear distressing them or alienating them from congregants who are not being particularly kind. When your spouse is upset by how you are being treated, does she tell you, with the risk of making you more distressed?

It is imperative to tune into the emotional and psychological ordeal that your spouse is enduring during this time. According to author David Goetz in his article, "The Pastor's Family Safe at Home," pastors often have a difficult time relating to their spouses' struggles because they feel a sense of satisfaction from the ministry and may not understand the spouses' negative feelings (Goetz, 1992). Linda Hileman's husband, a United Methodist pastor and marriage and family therapist, believes a larger, more hidden issue may be that the pastor does not want to admit that the spouse is suffering because of the pastor's job. He may fear being pressured to leave the ministry. "This inability to articulate their feelings of dissatisfaction leads clergy spouses to become guarded and closed off to the help that can be available" (Hileman, 2008). Once such a pattern is formed, it is not easy to change.

- You may need to develop new patterns of communication and interaction, and you will need to work on this area of concern for quite some time.

- You may need to put the issue of dissatisfaction on the table and open it for discussion—not only as it relates to your current situation but also if you face decisions about taking a part-time assignment at another congregation.

Many of us retire because we are emotionally fatigued and "burnt out." Our joy in service to others gave us a sense of meaning in life, so we were able to push the exhaustion aside. However, our spouses, who likewise are burned out, fatigued, and stressed, may not have enjoyed the sense of completion of a mission and may not have gotten the positive feedback that we have. During the years of active ministry, we probably did not pay attention to the hours our mates dealt with their loneliness while we were at evening meetings or were called away by a needy congregant.

If this transition requires recuperation from stress and mourning, then it becomes imperative for the two of you to deal with the issues.

- We suggest that you talk openly about the grief process and the stress you are both experiencing. We sincerely believe that people talk their way through grief, and the more one is open to vocalizing their emotions, the more able they will be to handle their anguish. "Blessed are those who mourn, for they shall be comforted," said Jesus (Matthew 5:4). Most of us are afraid to share our feelings because we do not want to cause pain to our loved ones. We can see that they are hurting for us, and we would like to protect them from this upset, so we try to bear the pain in silence. In reality, this is a bad idea. Everyone in the family can sense that something is wrong and may assume that somehow they are the cause and their offers to help have been rejected.
- We suggest that the two of you take turns being the *listener*. As a listener, you should know that there is no way you can fix or take away the other's pain. You can mitigate it by allowing your mate to share, emote, and express their anger and upset. As a listener, one must avoid defensiveness and not offer suggestions, fix-it solutions, or advice, or make excuses. Your role is to set the atmosphere for your partner to speak and feel comfortable knowing that you care enough to hear their pain. In turn, another appointment needs to be established where the *listener* becomes the *sharer*. At this point, each becomes more of a communicating couple, and grieving is allowed and sharing is encouraged.

A wonderful poem highlights this idea:

When I ask you to listen to me
And you start giving me advice,
You have not done what I asked.
When I ask you to listen to me
And you begin to tell me why I shouldn't feel that way,

You are trampling on my feelings.

When I ask you to listen to me
And you feel you have to do something to solve my problem,
You have failed me, strange as that may seem.

Listen! All I ask is that you listen!
Don't talk or do—just hear me.

When you accept as a simple fact
That I feel what I feel, no matter how irrational
Then I can quit trying to convince you
And get about this business of understanding
What's behind this irrational feeling.
And when that's clear, the answers are obvious
And I don't need advice.

Perhaps that's why prayer works, sometimes,
Because God is mute
And doesn't give advice or try to fix things.
God just listens and lets you work it out for yourself.
So, please listen, and just hear me.
And if you want to talk
Wait a minute for your turn
And I will listen to you.

Anonymous[2]

A Sense of Control Aids the Transition

How does one grab a sense of control when everything seems to be tumbling down? One way is to seize control by talking through all the issues that will need to be faced in this next period of life. Writes Carol Darling,

> Planning in advance of retirement helps people develop reasonable expectations about their prospects for the future (Jensen-Scott, 1993; Longino & Lipman, 1981). This foreknowledge can contribute to the formation of better attitudes toward retirement and more successful dealing with the emotional adjustment involved in the withdrawal from the role of worker (Kasschau, 1974). Early planning is perhaps most important because of the simple need to prepare financially. (2004, p. 86)

This is also a time to discuss what new rhythms are going to have to be established and how both of you can get a "sabbatical" until new routines can be established. Writes Robert Kemper,

---

[2] This poem was written by a mental health consumer who was institutionalized over a number of years in Queensland. He wishes to remain anonymous.

The essence of retirement living is finding substitute rhythms for those imposed upon us by work. The great shock of retirement will be the absence of these rhythms. The shock of their absence may be the first and only time we will fully realize their enormous power and impact on our lives. If it is true, as said earlier, that retirement is the "the self-regulated life," the rhythms we find in retirement are the self-regulations. (1988, p. 27)

You and your spouse can begin to seize control by

- Going to see a financial advisor. To use your time wisely with the advisor, you will need to make out a realistic budget before the appointment. The rough budget needs to include some of your dreams as well as the realities of everyday life. Discussing and writing down how each one imagines this next period will be spent, will help you begin to focus on how to allocate finances. If you look forward to travel, you will need to set aside the resources to do so. You also need to write down your joint concepts for leaving an inheritance to your children and contributions to causes in which you believe. Take time to review your wills, durable power of attorney for health care, and thoughts about organ donation. Discuss your fears about running out of money before you run out of years. Financial issues are by far the most stressful of all the issues facing retirement. The earlier they are discussed and the more fully they are faced, the less will be the anxiety and the more cooperative each will be in being part of the solution. Budget, Budget, Budget needs to be the motto for a stress free retirement.
- Meeting with a funeral director to make pre-need funeral arrangements, and consider putting money aside in trust to pay for the funeral. Difficult though it may be, determine where you would like to be buried and explore your feelings about the kind of funeral you want. Then write it down and make sure trusted family members have copies. We suggest that you not impose instructions from the grave that might leave the family with a difficult decision. You might want to read the book, *The Other Talk*, by Tim Prosch (2014), which will encourage you and suggest ways to have such a conversation with your family. You will also want to share Chapter 9 in this book written for children of retired clergy, which will encourage them to engage you in such a conversation.

New Rhythms

You and your spouse should begin thinking about openly discussing how you will spend your time—together *and* apart. One couple in the congregation divorced after 40 years of marriage; after her husband's retirement, she could not get used to having him around when she used to be alone. She was able to manage their conflicts because she had her space. Now, after retirement, she just wanted him to find some things to do and give her back her *alone* time. The husband rightly felt that their house was his home too, but he could not find enough places to go and/or things to do to satisfy her schedule. Eventually he moved out and they divorced. Researchers have found that over half the woman studied reported problems of impingement because husbands were spending more time at home (Vinick & Ekerdt, 1989). We suggest that you be sensitive to this issue and try to prevent these feelings and the resentment it entails. If, for example, you have been sharing a home computer, this might be a good time to purchase a second one. Renegotiate the shared responsibilities of household chores. Who will clean, pay bills, arrange family functions, cook, and plan excursions? As you redefine yourself, even if you find other employment, volunteer activities, or chose to do nothing but play, you must mutually determine and agree upon your lifestyle, both in and outside the home. What "used to be" is now is a new beginning.

As a couple, you might want to discuss the concept of making new friends. How will you do that during this next period of time? Who were the friends you enjoyed in the past and what were their qualities that made them friends? Since making younger friends are a way of keeping you young and vibrant, how might you deliberately set out to do that?

Complicating the situation, your spouse may be working outside the home after you retire. What are your expectations when your spouse is hard at work? How much of the household responsibility was yours when you were working? Does there need to be a reshuffling of household tasks? Address these issues from the beginning of this major change in lifestyle and remember that flexibility is key. For example, be mindful that although you may have spent your day at a slow pace, your working spouse may come home exhausted. You may want to go out after dinner and your spouse may be too tired. Next to flexibility comes compassion and understanding of the each other's needs. When your spouse finally does retire, you can use all the lessons you have learned in this book to help them grieve the loss of the world she left behind. This will be another difficult stress point in the life of a couple.

One of the most difficult questions must be addressed carefully and thoughtfully: *Do you move from your current home and if so, do you stay in the same city or move elsewhere?* Other than dealing with a death, one of the most stressful events in life is moving. You will need to consider and understand all of the ramifications. Those living in a parsonage will be forced to vacate the house, and the question looms as to where to relocate. We advise the newly widowed not to make any major decisions for at least a year if possible. With retirement too, there is enough stress and adjustment that one does not need the added pressure of relocation. One does not need the tension of closing the door on family memories while simultaneously coping with the loss of a lifelong vocation and finding a new sense of self. While it is exciting to think about new beginnings in a different city (with perhaps a better climate or closer to extended family), your excitement may cause you to gloss over the practical matters of a move that cause real stress. It is lonely while making new friends. It is difficult to find your way around a new city. It is discombobulating not knowing whom to call for help with plumbing, electrical work, or any other area of domestic concern. Psychiatrists Thomas Holmes and Richard Rahe investigated the relationship between social readjustment, stress, and susceptibility to illness and found a definite connection (Holmes & Rahe, 1967). You must give yourself time to adjust to one set of changes before you bargain for another. (See below for the adjustment that one spouse had to make in finding a new identity in a new location.) Moving runs the risk that one spouse may adjust to the new world but the other may not be able to do so, and then what. Of course, if you simply move to a new house in the same city, there may be significant adjustments but not a total disruption to your lives, for you have a history with doctors, plumbers, and such.

Understanding Disenfranchised Grief

You and your spouse may feel a great sense of relief when all the retirement hoopla is over, but you will wake up that next Sabbath morning having to make a choice. In the beginning, it will likely feel terrific for the two of you. You don't need to write yet another sermon or get to church or synagogue early to prepare or put on a smile even though your back may be killing you! Your spouse can make plans for Saturday evenings. You both may feel like you are on vacation. You don't have to rush and be there at a certain hour. You don't have to be *on* as soon as you walk in the building. You can both go to services or the two of you can sleep late. But somewhere down the line you will both hit the proverbial wall. The two of you will miss the good parts of congregational life: the holiday celebrations; the life-cycle events; the opportunities to lead, teach, and learn; the sense of being needed; your colleagues and staff; the congregants. That is when you will feel a sense of loss, and the grieving process will most likely truly begin for both of you or for one or the other of you.

Unfortunately, it is highly unlikely that anyone around you will understand this grief. After all, the two of you are supposed to be happy now that you can just play whenever you want and are free to travel to visit family or see the world. Few will comprehend, support, or even acknowledge that you might be grieving, that you and your family are in pain and are suffering. In the field of thanatology, this is called Disenfranchised Grief—grief that is experienced when a loss cannot be openly acknowledged, socially sanctioned, or publicly mourned (Doka, 1989). So, besides the adjustment to retirement, there comes loneliness and a feeling that no one understands or cares about you anymore. As a clergy family, you have often felt embraced by the congregation; suddenly there may be a feeling of being deserted. It may seem that when your family needs friends the most, no one outside a very few in your immediate circle comprehends your lamenting a life that no longer exists. As authors, we want to share with you the concept of *disenfranchised grief* so that should it occur in your world, each member of the family will be able to understand that this is real grief. While you had a final service with the congregation (your funeral, so to speak), there is no sympathy from others who expect you to feel only relief and joy. This is disenfranchised grief.

Some Issues Expressed by Clergy Couples

Many of the couples we interviewed faced the concern of finding a new, comfortable place to worship. For many, their home congregation did not feel the same as when they were on the pulpit. The sense of spirituality that each felt when they were the leaders was gone and they felt a huge chasm. For those required to depart from their home congregation for at least a period of time, trying to find a new spiritual home was difficult. Many clergy and their spouses reported that visiting various congregations left them feeling more isolated than before. For many of these retirees, this was the first time they did not belong to a congregation at all. Spouses reported that even driving by the old building and seeing former members entering for services was like a stab in the heart.

As clergy, we often have difficulty withdrawing from the spotlight and the excitement of speaking before others. Thus, we often search for an interim or a weekend opportunity to not only supplement our income but as a chance to get back on the pulpit again. One minister titled himself a *Recovering Presbyterian Minister*. Sometimes, with the lure of the adrenalin rush, we fail to consult our spouse regarding their true feelings of once again having to put on a smile and risking rejection by a new group of people. We never speculate that this could possibly be a negative experience for either one of you. This is exactly what happened to one minister with whom we spoke. He was told that he didn't know how to preach by a group of insensitive congregants. Then his spouse was left to pick up the crushed pieces. When a possible opportunity presents itself, and even beforehand, we suggest you have a heart-to-heart conversation concerning both of your desires and needs and the risks involved. One minister warned, "Be careful what you get yourself talked into!"

One clergyman said that it took 3–5 years to restructure his time so that he had a routine. Grieving takes time, and one should not expect to go directly into retirement without an adjustment period.

Understanding Your Spouse's Feelings

In the following stories by the wives of a bishop and of a rabbi, you can sense the fears, devotion, and commitment to a mate, and the adjustments that each made as spouses of active or retired clergy. Although these are women's stories, they could easily come from a male who is married to a clergyperson, for he too must help his partner fulfill the dream of serving God. Interestingly enough, a female clergy related that there is male bias, for the congregation does not expect as much from the husband of a clergyperson as they do from the wife. Men thus have to be that much more sensitive to their wives' experiences and be aware of their struggle adjusting to retirement.

Phoebe Griswold shared difficulties when she wrote,

When I married Frank, he was then an assistant priest in an affluent suburban congregation. I, on the other hand, was an early childhood education teacher who knew nothing about being a priest's wife. Nonetheless, I did have a faith that told me there was something for me in the life of the church. Soon after we were married, I left my job because I felt I wasn't being a good wife. The moment of discovery happened when I discovered wet socks that Frank had washed dripping in the bathroom. Taking care of laundry was my job, I thought. Next, we moved to a small rural congregation where our two daughters were born. I enjoyed the role of rector's wife, taught church school and participated in women's activities, as well as in community environmental projects. Yet, I stayed on the edge of Bible study and prayer groups. I can distinctly recall refusing invitations to go off on retreats. I could feel the apprehension within myself. What if I were to get there and discover no God for me, no inner voice in the silence? I had no idea how to discover or be discovered by a personal God, One who transcends my busy activities of family, church and community, but One who also was at work within those mundane worlds. I prided myself on being a master of busyness! I could cook more creampuff swans for the women's lunches, bake more cakes to give away and glue more cotton balls on the Christmas crèche sheep than anyone thought possible. I was a good parish priest's wife. I listened carefully to what Frank had to say and could even make helpful sermon criticisms. The congregation flourished, thanks in part to my efforts to help the community grow by getting people together. I had created connections between people and built lasting relationships for mutual friendship and support. The Christian community was strong and happy.

Then we moved a second time to a larger, more urban congregation. There I was miserable because I left behind so many of the activities that had previously given me an identity. I was lonely and empty, as was revealed to me in a dream—a dream that described where I was, but which also pushed me forward. Here I had an experience that became one of the most formative insights of my life. I dreamed that I was standing at the entrance of our church home. I was ushering people in and out. I noticed bookshelves standing all around the room, all of which were empty. It was a library—with no books. At the same time I heard a baby crying upstairs. This dream so haunted me that finally I asked an extraordinarily intuitive member of our congregation to help me understand it. After she heard the dream she asked, "What do you keep on bookshelves?" "Books!" I retorted. Then she said one of the most devastating things anyone has said to me. "But you have no story to tell, do you? And why is the baby crying?" I reached back into the dream. "Oh yes," I replied. "The baby is hungry. I haven't given the child any meat, just fruit and vegetables." The immediate lessons of the dream are obvious. I had become my husband's best pupil, but I did not know what I myself really thought. The images of the dream were tailor-made for me.

I knew about feeding my own babies, but I did not know how to feed a growing need within myself. Someone had placed a lesson deep within me that was focused on my own growth. An inner voice caring for my life's wholeness had spoken while I slept.

[When Frank became a Bishop], in making this move I experienced the sadness that comes from loss of a community. In a parish you see people again and again; you learn to live for each other. But what happens when you have no parish or church home? I have a metaphor for what it felt like to go from parish priest's wife to bishop's wife. A bird takes off in flight, but because it has no feet it can never land on earth again. Instead, it must learn to find the air currents that would keep it afloat. I could not find a home in the same way. For me this felt like an adventure—to set forth with only a wing and a prayer.

In the new diocese things were very unsettled. Early on I set off many landmines when I tried to be part of the workings of the church. People who were at odds with my husband would project their anger onto me. I did not want to bring these conflicts home. So I chose to work outside the life of the diocese.

We are an extraordinarily hard-working group who takes our vows seriously—both our baptismal and marriage vows. We are a group that sees our marriage vow as the ground for shaping a vocation. We share similar struggles around the conflict of family and church, and suffer the difficulty of making choices when both ask for our attention at the same time. We know the feelings of isolation and loneliness that come from the solitary nature of our unique position within the community. We also know what it means to be invisible, unrecognized for the work we do. We know, time after time, what it means to be taken out of a familiar life and then be forced to create another from scratch. We know what it means to be handed a position that comes with no written job description, but nonetheless carries many unspoken expectations. We know what it means to bring children up in the Christian faith and hope that they will hold on to that faith as "preacher's kids." We know what it means to walk the fuzzy lines between spouse and church community, trying to be ourselves and find our own faith. We know the difficulty of making a life with an authority that has been derived from our spouses, but which must be eventually earned by us. We know something about the face of evil as it appears in the church's efforts to do good.

Time and time again I must walk into a room knowing no one and stand vulnerable to whatever may happen to him or to me. I remember sitting in a congregation while members of the parish grilled him with questions. Behind him was a crucifix and I saw the analogy immediately as Frank stood to receive and hold their anger as our Lord did on the cross. (Griswold, 1999)

Barbara Klein tells of her painful adjustment to a new life in a new city close to her children. In a private letter, she shared the difficult task of finding a new identity.

As soon as our first grandbaby was born in March of 2004, my husband David announced to his synagogue board that he would be retiring after the

High Holy Days and moving to Boston to be a Saba (grandfather) to Ela. He was about to turn 70 years old and could have stayed in his Louisiana congregation as long as he wished. We had been there for 15 years and he had become an integral part of the city's secular and religious communities. The congregation expected this, having watched him for years playing with babies in the congregation. They understood.

David and I had decided when our daughter became pregnant, that we would both retire and move to Boston. We had dreamed of "grand parenting" and now it would become a reality.

During our 15 years in Monroe, I worked for the youth division of a regional amateur theatre teaching, choreographing, and doing all of the public relations and marketing for the complex. It was easy to work closely with the media and I loved it. When the theatre director or actors couldn't be on TV or radio, I went on for them. Eventually, I left the theatre and went out on my own, calling my business Art and Soul and writing a monthly column for a regional magazine. I put programs together for schools, and did marketing for a regional honors ballet company. That included doing all the publicity for a five-state regional festival held in our city and hosted by our ballet company.

As the rabbi's wife, I served as Sisterhood program chairman for a few years, baked when needed and did whatever I was asked. We created a city-wide program with all of the neighborhood churches creating displays, presentations, and booklets on our life-cycle and seasonal holiday celebrations. This won national recognition from Sisterhood in the Reform Movement.

Our lives were rich and filled with challenging projects. We felt much loved and we loved our community. Just prior to our departure, the congregation threw us a magnificent reception, inviting everyone we had befriended and all of our colleagues. Our children from New York and Boston joined us, even speaking about our family from the pulpit.

As thrilled as we were to be living near our kids and especially our grandbaby, taking leave of Monroe was extremely difficult. I loved our home where we had hosted many visiting artists for dance and theatre companies, as well as national figures in the larger Jewish community who came to present programs to our congregation. A dear friend, who happened to be a decorator, and her husband, an artist and a house painter, had generously helped us turn our home into a beautiful, comfortable place I didn't want to leave. Congregants and our Baptist Minister of the Arts (also a nationally renowned floral designer) annually decorated our Sukkah (the hut built for the Feast of Tabernacles) where we hosted dinners and luncheons for our seniors, confirmands, and young singles throughout the holiday.

The move to Boston necessitated major downsizing. Every piece of furniture had family history, making it difficult for me to sell much of it. But, that was nothing compared to my husband giving away at least 60% of his library that included valuable books from his father's (also a Reform rabbi) library.

We found a darling apartment in a two-family house in Newton, sold our Monroe home very quickly, moved our furnishings into the new place and returned to Monroe to finish out our contract, living in a B&B for three months; not comfortable, but actually a good transition space. After our departure from Monroe, a very hard day for me, we drove to New Orleans, one of our favorite places, and on to Atlanta where our Baptist minister friend and his family now lived. We took the scenic route up to Boston, taking our time and arrived just days before the legendary snowfalls of 2004–2005 began.

David immediately began interacting with colleagues he knew well. They provided him with teaching positions that he loved. Our colleagues and our children encompassed our social circle. I had no colleagues in Boston and felt disoriented. My daughter, CEO of a non-profit organization, suggested that I make out the same kind of to-do list that I did daily while working. That helped a bit. Our week was anchored by childcare two days a week. We began our tradition of Shabbat dinners with the kids. My daughter and her husband have had very high profiles in the Jewish community. I loved being introduced as my daughter's mother, being treated exceptionally kindly by the many who know her, but that didn't help my feeling of identity loss. I felt depressed and tried to find a volunteer position in the performing arts community, deciding that I wanted to work in the professional arena rather than amateur. It took a good year and a half to become active with Celebrity Series, the premier presenting organization in Boston. I loved being in the atmosphere of the professionals working there, but have only stuffed envelopes, a job I used to delegate to seniors in Monroe. Still, the other volunteers love the arts and I had "my people" around me once again. I sensed that coming from the South tagged me as "small town amateur" even though the reality was that I did everything the big guys did, but on a smaller scale. I still miss conversations and brainstorm sessions about "the business" of presenting the performing arts.

The first few years I felt miserable and complained a lot, I'm afraid. I love to meet up with women friends, but the very few I had lived at least an hour away. My daughter did her best to cheer me up. Now that I think back, I must have behaved like a spoiled child. I don't know how David or my daughter put up with me. I'm usually a cheerful, energetic person, but this change was just too difficult. I suppose I should add here that I brought my 92-year-old mother from a Monroe nursing home to one in Boston where she passed a year later, adding to the emotional stress.

David reconnected with Brandeis University, his alma mater, and began teaching Bible at BOLLI (Life-long Learning Institute). This has given him enormous pleasure. He also teaches Hebrew and Bible to a musician, a colleague of our younger daughter who is a Jewish Kiddie Rocker based in NYC, and he continues studying with a Catholic priest and scholar from Louisiana via Skype. He has also been writing and has had several articles accepted for publication. So his retirement has been fantastic.

Slowly but surely, I discovered wonderful activities such as free forums at the JFK Library, readings by famous authors (many my favorite), at independent bookstores, dance classes for adults.

Interestingly, we never joined a congregation in Boston. We thought we would enjoy sampling the great variety that exists in our area, and we did—some. Listening to my husband in the pulpit for forty-plus years surprisingly made it difficult for me to listen to others read the same prayers. My husband got excited about one congregation, but it was too far to make an easy commute. What we have enjoyed immensely, have been Shabbat dinners with our children and grandchildren . . . A few weeks ago we attended a Friday night service and when it came time to say Kaddish for the departed, I suddenly yearned to be part of a group that supported us when we remembered a departed member of our own family. For the first time, we are talking seriously about the need to join a Jewish community—a congregation. We seem to be entering yet another stage of life.

My husband and I give daily thanks for the blessing of good health. We enjoy traveling in the US and abroad when we have the funds. We will be moving to Brooklyn, New York in September as our son-in-law took a wonderful new job in Manhattan and since our daughter also will continue to work full-time, our services as Grandma and Saba will still be needed. This move will be easier for me. I'm ready to sell more furniture, china, and whatever we need to strip away from our lives. David will have to give up his beloved tools, the spacious section of the house he uses as a study, and his teaching at BOLLI. But, I know he will find plenty of more than satisfying projects in our new location. As one of our rabbinic wives said to me about this next move, "Changes like this keep our blood flowing."

Anonymous

Listen

Let us listen to some of those who responded to our questionnaire:

- Felt depressed and angry that denominational leaders would look down upon our being present at significant events in our former church like funerals, weddings, and holiday events.
- The major adjustment has been a good one for my wife in that she no longer carries so many church responsibilities. It has been a bit strange for her, but it has also been a good time of rest for her until the time we find a new church to participate in.
- My untimely retirement brought partner to decision to retire earlier than planned.
- We both saw this as a new adventure.
- Delighted not to live in a parsonage any longer and could own our own home. Missed the choir very much, but nothing else. Glad to be able to return to the choir where he had community. Probably worried about me because it took me time to adjust to retirement.
- My wife never did like moving, but never did it create a problem. It was the idea of possibly losing friends and then having to work at making new friends.

- She's a very balanced person, and retirement did take some getting used to, but so far it's been a blessing. We're in the Sun Belt, and when Season is on it gets very busy, just as it did before retirement. We've pretty much kept our lifestyle intact, with the addition of travel to see the kids and grandkids. Before retirement, no one expected us to be at their school for Grandparents Day—now they do. We're not complaining.
- She also retired and has not found a way to continue her professional interests as I have in teaching. She had no readymade circle of friends and associates. Harder to meet people.
- My spouse had expected to continue working for a few years after I retired. Lucky for me and unlucky for her as her job had been terminated. She did mourn that loss, but I did not. I had hoped we could spend more time together. And we have.
- Occasionally I have the urge to try to allocate my time, but we have worked that through pretty well.

Lots of Good Adjustments

- We agreed on one basic guideline: we had married for love but not for lunch! In the initial period of about three months, we took care to leave the house during the lunch hour a couple of times a week. This gave space and time to do our own thing. None of this is even thought about, since our schedules are filled with meaningful activities that accomplish the same thing.
- She works part time for H&R Block, and that interferes with our time during the months of Jan.–April. She is a hard worker and working at home is not quite enough. She may change jobs, but only to fit her own desires. We seem to have good support from one another in the decisions we make, individually and together.

Suggestions

- Listen in anticipation of the anxiety of facing the unknown. Be patient with yourself and your partner. This is not the note of *Time heals all ills*, as much as it is the recognition that both persons are passing through a stage—as an individual and as a couple. Give yourself freedom to explore avenues that will be new. Make no unilateral decisions! If offered what appears to be an *opportunity*, tell the inquirer that you will get back to them after sleeping on it. That means, *I'm taking time to talk it over with my spouse.*
- Be sensitive to each other's emotions during those early adjustment months. It is a different change than that which takes place when moving from one church to another. We chose to look at it as an adventure, and that it has been, but one in which our love for one another has grown and has been enriched by the change.

- Spent a lot of time thinking things through. No matter how much prep, there are still things unexpected. When a man retires, he's immediately considered an old man by others.
- I think all of us who retire need to find our own way through retirement. One thing that helped my wife and me was to go to the Midwest Career Development Center to meet with a counselor, who talked with us about the issues we would face related to retirement. We did this a year prior to my retirement. We also met with a financial advisor from our denomination who knew how my pension would work and who helped guide us through the financial concerns related to retirement. So, as we faced retirement, we had already talked out many of the concerns that we would face.
- Keep open, caring communication lines. Expect conflict as adjustments are made and recognize that it is OK. Choose a new activity to share with partner as a sign of a new stage in life. We learned to square dance and enjoyed it greatly.
- Lots of talking even with a therapist to assist.
- Keep communication open and go with the flow. You are each still the same person you were before retirement.
- Think carefully about what you want to do after retirement. Do you want to be active in any way? Is it OK to just retire, never more to preach, lead studies, and such? We had to think of each other and allow for that person to make up their mind. Sometimes that did not allow for the person to do what he or she really wanted to do. There was the feeling that one had to give in as well.
- We attended a retirement seminar that helped us prepare. Also I went to an Alban Institute *Ending it Well* retreat.
- Communicate, communicate, communicate! Do not assume that your partner knows what you are up to on a daily basis. Do not assume your partner wants to charge off into a new life.
- Talk it out together. Seek to make this final quarter of your lives as meaningful and satisfying as possible.
- Don't camp out at home, and recognize that YOUR retirement decisions deserve her significant input.
- Discuss well ahead of time. Make decisions together. Understand that life will not be the same and surprises need to be mutually addressed. Hang loose.
- Be sensitive to his/her spiritual needs and wishes. Look forward to doing fun things together. Don't try to share computers or office space. Keep some separateness, each having your own life.
- Talk to others who've done it. There's no substitute for experience. Just as we couldn't imagine what rabbinical life would be like when we were in school, one can't envision retirement until one is in it. Realize that what others do isn't necessarily what you have to do. They don't give grades for this.
- Have a great time. Change the word retirement to *refirement* and start your new life with gusto!!!

- It really depends on what the partner does. For a working professional spouse like mine, the task is to remember that professional life goes on for her, with all its demands and stresses, and I need to accommodate around this fact.

SUMMARY

How are we to get through this next period of time? Don't forget the lessons you learned when you confronted difficulties as a family. People who can see the benefits of the situation in the face of adversity and can put a positive spin on their situation cope far better (Harris, 2011, p. 106). We know that those who engage their spirituality are often better able to reframe their situation in a more positive way (Harris, 2011, p. 106). Please note that most people transition into retirement successfully as they have done in other stages of life and have no increase in health-related problems (Darling, 2004). As indicated in other chapters, good health, adequate financial resources, meaningful activities, and social involvement all contribute to successful adjustment in this next period of time. Of course, as much continuity and as little chaos as possible are important aspects in one's successful adjustment.

We hope that you have become aware that retirement presents a critical moment for all those involved in your life. Yes, there is a whole new world awaiting you with countless possibilities, but to get to that new world filled with meaning there will likely be a few bumpy roads along the way to traverse with the very mate that got you this far. The intent of this chapter was to raise awareness as to what your spouse is equally going through when the once-stable world that she knew is turned upside down. We hope that we have made it clear that your spouse is equally enduring a "retirement" of her own and undergoing all the emotional decisions that confront you at the same time you are going through it. As authors, it reminds us of the loss of a child in a family where all the members of the family are mourning at the same time and find it difficult to be a comforter to the other since so much energy is taken up in the grieving process. The trick in such a situation is to avoid making comparisons, not to ask why you are not mourning like I am but to just allow the other to express their sorrow. We hope this chapter has made you a little more sensitive to the emotional upheaval of your spouse and has given you some techniques on how to approach her at this disjointed time.

REFERENCES

Darling, C. A. (2004, October 18). Understanding stress and quality of life for clergy and clergy spouses. *Stress and Health, 20,* 261–277. Retrieved from www.interscience.wiley.com

Doka, K. J. (1989). *Disenfranchised grief: Recognizing hidden sorrow.* Lexington, MA: Lexington.

Goetz, D. (1992). The pastor's family safe at home? *Leadership, 13,* 38–44.

Griswold, P. W. (1999, Winter). Living the theology of a bishop's spouse: Experience, experiment and adventure. *Anglican Theological Review, 81*(1), 83–94.

Harris, D. (Ed.). (2011). *Counting our losses: Reflecting on change, loss, and transition in everyday life.* New York, NY: Routledge/Taylor & Francis.

Hileman, L. (2008). The unique needs of protestant clergy families: Implications for marriage and family counseling. *Journal of Spirituality in Mental Health, 10*(2), 119–144.

Holmes, T. H., & Rahe, R. H. (1967). The social readjustment rating scale. *Journal of Psychosomatic Research, 11,* 213–218.

Kemper, R. (1988). *Planning for ministerial retirement.* New York, NY: Pilgrim.

Prosch, T. (2014). *The other talk: A guide to talking with your adult children about the rest of your life.* New York, NY: McGraw-Hill.

Vinick, B., & Ekerdt, D. J. (1989). Retirement and the family. *Generations, 13*(2), 53–56.

Zoba, W. M. (1997, April 7). What pastor's wives wish their churches knew. *Christianity Today,* 20–26.

http://dx.doi.org/10.2190/CLEC9

CHAPTER 9

For Children of Retired Clergy

It is said preachers' kids are the worst. It must have been a preacher's kid who said this first.

Gary E. Brownlee

Each goodbye is a rehearsal for death
mourned Tristram Shandy in Laurence Sterne' eighteenth-century novel,
The Life and Opinions of Tristam Shandy, Gentleman (1769–1767)

FLYING HIGH

I am flying across the country to participate in a celebration of my father's lifelong career leading his congregation. I am having so many different emotions as I reflect on the many memories of growing up as his son. I know none of us gets to choose our parents' careers, but for so many years, I absolutely hated being the pastor's kid! It seemed like everyone had so many assumptions about me and expectations about how I was to behave. It felt like I had an entire community of parents watching and correcting me. Moreover, except for a very small group of close friends I was able to make at school, most treated me as if I was different and avoided spending time with me unless they had to. I also resented feeling as if he put the congregation ahead of me when he was so busy that he couldn't come to all my games the way some of the other Dads did.

However, after moving away for college and making my own home across the country, I have definitely gained perspective. As hard as it was to be his son, I really am proud of him! Not everyone's father is so well known and respected by so many people in their town. And although I was often reminded about confidentiality, I couldn't help but to do just that, overhear how he helped so many people in the congregation. While I never contemplated becoming a religious leader, I now realize what a positive role model he has been for me and can only hope that when I retire, others will have as much good to say about me as they will about him this weekend. I guess it's time for me to tell him all of this; I need to make sure to find time this weekend!

ào   ào   ào

125

WHAT PLEASURE YOU BRING YOUR PARENTS

IT IS HARD TO BE A PK (preachers kid), BUT ONE CANNOT UNDO THE PAST

A woman announces to her friend that her daughter is getting married next month to a world-renowned architect.

"Wait a minute," replied her friend. "Is that the same daughter who was married to the world-renowned symphony conductor?

"Yes, that is the same daughter," the woman responds proudly.

"And is that the same daughter who was married to the world-famous surgeon?"

"Yep, that's the very same daughter!" she responded with pride.

Slapping her cheek with her hand, she exclaims with glee, "*So much happiness from one daughter!*"

Yes, parents do get immeasurable joy from their children and take much pride in their accomplishments and achievement, for their attainment is a reflection of their parenting skills and completing the most important job that God has given them to do. As parents, they took this gift from God, the baby who was entrusted to them, supported them financially and emotionally, transmitted morals and values to them, and led them to become a valued member of society.

However your parents pride as a clergy person may exceed the ordinary delight that any parent has. As a PK you well knew that there were certain expectations of you that other children did not have. Your parents expected you to *behave properly at all times*. They took great pleasure when you acted appropriately and were mortified when you did not set the example expected of a PK. They were pleased when you greeted bereaved congregants and showed proper empathy even though you were a child. Your parents were delighted when you helped around the church setting up seating in the social hall, babysitting, or running youth services. They swelled with pride when they called on you to read a passage at the service or to be a leader in the youth group and you did it with grace.

On the other hand, you probably wanted to be a normal teenager like your friends. You felt burdened when any of the aforementioned were thrust upon you. You were held to a higher standard and if you acted out, there seemed to be harsher consequences for your actions. An adult PK tells of her experience in high school, "Other kids would stop talking and telling jokes when I came in the room. I would hear 'Shhhhh, she's the preacher's daughter!' It can be very isolating" (Hileman, 2008, p. 124), I required my sons to go through the high school department at our congregation, for I felt my children had to set an example for others. In my mind, I could hear other children protesting, "The rabbi's son doesn't have to go to the high school program, so why should I?" So my sons attended with chips on their shoulders and a sour attitude. I remember standing next to each of them filled with pleasure as they participated in the graduation ceremony and I was able to bless them. For me, it was a great moment, although I am not sure it was for them. Years later, I heard their anger over being forced to attend because I demanded it.

There is no doubt that being a PK is very difficult. Bruce Hardy reports that 73% of clergy children whom he surveyed commented on living in a fishbowl (2001, p. 546). There are churches in which the child of a pastor is expected to know the Bible from front to back. Others are told that they should gladly mow the lawn for the privilege of living in the parsonage.

Does any of this sound familiar? Did you ever feel excluded because someone was upset with your clergy parent and told their child not to have anything to do with you? How about the confusion and anger when told that your parent's contract was not being renewed? How did you feel when the bishop transferred your parent and you had to move to a new city? Now your schooling and your social life were going to be disrupted. It can be a demanding and different life as a PK. But the past cannot be undone. As you will read below, there were certain advantages to being in the world of religious life.

Being an Asset to Your Parent (Listen to Their Loss of Identity, Financial Concerns, Open Doors of Communication About Final Wishes)

As your parents approach retirement, this is the time to think of how you can be the greatest asset to them in this stage of their lives. Chapter 5 will provide you with some insights on some of the psychological ups and downs of retirement. Realize that with retirement comes a sense of loss: loss of status; loss of purpose, meaning, and identity; loss of the security of a daily routine and a sense of order; loss of friends, colleagues, and congregants. With loss comes grieving. The best thing you can do is allow them to talk. You can help them by being there to listen and acknowledging that there may be good reason to be depressed and to grieve.

Though there are few studies regarding the children of clergy, much to everyone's surprise, PKs said they would raise their children in the faith (Strange, 2001). Perhaps this demonstrates that their resentment as PKs does not really run deep. On the other hand, a majority said they would never consider going into a church-related ministry as a career. What does that tell you?

What is surprising is that a large majority of the PKs disagreed with the statement that their family had financial difficulties. Is this testimony to the adaptability of families or the naïveté of children growing up (Strange, 2001)? Probably if we were to suggest what your parents' greatest concern right now is, it would be financial worries. They fear that even with Social Security they will not have enough money to meet their normal daily living expenses, let alone if a major illness occurs.

It is very possible that your parents may have been tight lipped during your childhood about what they did and did not have. Most of us grew up oblivious to the cost of living and raising a family. Even now as adults with growing families ourselves, we are only concerned with our own finances. We do not show an interest in our parents' financial situation as long as they seem to be managing adequately. We certainly do not want them to think that we are only interested in our inheritance! In most cases, it is only when our parents become widowed or when health issues arise that we step in and become concerned with their financial stability.

Retirement presents a wonderful opportunity for you, their child, to open new doors of communication. You can indicate that you care by simply letting them know that you realize finances must be a major concern and that you might be able to help them seek good money management. Ask if they have talked with a financial advisor. If not, encourage them to do so. Please remind them not to choose an advisor who is selling a particular product or advocating for a certain company, for they have their own self-interests in mind. Encourage them to consult with the advisor for their denominational pension fund. Ask if they have updated their important documents recently, such as their wills, insurance beneficiaries, durable powers of attorney for health care, and living wills. Discuss recording an Ethical Will (for a fuller description of this, see Chapter 6; for resources, see Appendix I) that reflects their value and dreams for you, their children, and grandchildren. Talk to them about what organizations are important to them and charitable gifts they would like made from their estates.

This is a natural opportunity to talk about what they envision for their funerals. Where they would like to be buried. If they desire to be cremated, what is their request for the disposal of the ashes? Reflect back to them how you and your siblings feel about cremation. Regarding the funeral, you might want to know which clergy should officiate and what music or readings should be included. Of course, you need not discuss all of these emotionally laden topics at once. Take this opportunity to open an ongoing frank dialogue with them about their encore years and how you can help fulfill their wishes. Should you meet any resistance in having such a dialogue, you might want to give them the book *The Other Talk* by Tim Prosch (2014), which encourages them to have this conversation.

Understanding the Adjustment (Helping Parents to Ground Themselves in the "New World," Parenting the Parent, Sharing Your Own Growth)

As a child, you took for granted that your parents were in charge and knew what was best for all of you. In their advancing years, emotional upheavals demand adjustment as your parents grieve the past and experience melancholy. The encore years are not just fun and games, but also a time to reevaluate life's meaning and purpose. You cannot assume that they have new direction just because they decided to retire. Your parents have a right to a sabbatical when they can enjoy leisure, travel, and engage in new recreational activities. However, they may not have planned how to fill their time after their sabbatical without the daily rhythm and demands of a career. They may be unsettled or even disoriented about what their new roles may be. They may be unsure of where to live and what their new lifestyle will be. Just remember that *new* can often be both exciting and traumatic. You can be of enormous support just by listening to your parents as they strive to ground themselves. It may surprise you how much they will appreciate your invitation to discuss their concerns and plans and to know that you are interested in them. They may even appreciate your insights and suggestions as long as you are thoughtful to present these without being demanding or condescending; just think about when you were a child and the tables were reversed!

At some point, you will probably start worrying about them as they once worried about you. More a part of aging than of retirement, there will most likely be a struggle between older parents and adult children as to who is dependent upon whom (Kemper, 1988). They will want to remain independent and make their own decisions, but more and more they will need you for physical and medical help. The ultimate question for you will be, *How does one parent a parent without becoming the parent?* Just as you would like them to treat you as an adult, you will have to do likewise. Spend more time listening than speaking; bite your tongue and avoid giving advice unless it is requested. To show you are interested without being overbearing, ask questions and then listen without trying to fix their lives or direct them as to what they *should* do. Remember how validated and respected you felt when your parents treated you this way. Encourage them to think about alternatives. Help them figure out what they want to accomplish during retirement and how they might get there. Support their discovering new talents and interests, even if these curiosities seem to be counter to everything they once represented.

As you browse through other chapters of this book, you will learn that beneath the surface of a supposedly carefree retirement lies emotional upsets that seems counterintuitive. It might be helpful to share how their retirement is affecting you as well. If you are a member of your parent's congregation, it may be tough to worship there when your parent is not on the pulpit. If you live somewhere else, you might share how hard it was to move away from the congregation where you grew up and to find a new one. Ask your parents to share their joys and sadness concerning their final days in the congregation and how they are dealing with the finality of it all.

This is a perfect time as well to share the advantages you experienced growing up in this clergy household there certainly were some. You can recount stories of interesting people you met, the feeling of belonging to a broad congregational "family" your friends did not share, wisdom you gained, meaningful social-action opportunities, developing a deep sense of spirituality, values you saw emulated. You might express gratitude for the pride you felt in your parent who was pastor of the congregation. You might want to look through some of their mementos and photos and organize them into a scrapbook, not only for them, but for the grandchildren (present and future) as well. Ask them to share some of their proudest moments in the congregation and share some of yours as well. Your goal is to create an atmosphere in which your parents feel comfortable to share their honest feelings with you and for you likewise to share with them.

Relocating (Thinking About Where Your Parents Should Live, Discussing New Rhythms of Life)

We suggest that you *not* encourage your parents to relocate quickly unless they are living in a parsonage and are required to do so. Retirement is tough, but moving at the same time is even worse. It requires deciding what to take and what to sell, what to throw away and what to keep. It will be the shuttering of a significant part of their lives, including a host of wonderful memories. We are not suggesting that they never relocate, but all in good time, perhaps a year down the road.

Ask yourself, *How do you, as their child(ren), feel about them moving closer to you or farther away from you?* This may be the most difficult of questions. When a parent moves close by, it represents wonderful opportunities for new family time and deepening relationships. On the other hand, it will certainly change your lifestyle, for you will now have the added responsibility of involvement with your parents. At times, you may find yourself reverting to your role as a child and feeling accountable to them. Perhaps they will advise you how to act and dress and even what relative to invite to a family function. To be sure, having them close by will be a godsend should you need additional childcare or personal support or if they become ill, for you can make sure they find the correct medical facilities. However, there is a potential for suffocation, so think about this issue very carefully. Discuss the ramifications with your spouse and ask for input from your children and others who will be affected.

We have no good suggestions as to how to tell your parents that perhaps they would be happier living elsewhere, should you decide it might be best that they not live near you. You must be honest with them should they indicate that they would like to move closer to you. An alternative would be to propose a schedule of mutual visits and be sure to include them in all the significant life events, even if you have to pay for their trip. You know best what conditions will be so that you can best interact with your parent(s) now that you are an adult.

Aside from talking about their plans for relocation, you can also help your parents deal with the new rhythms of family life now that the ministry does not tie them down. You can remind them about the activities they enjoyed in the past and encourage them to renew those interests. You can help them to explore a completely new array of hobbies, adult education, and volunteer opportunities. Again, listen and guide rather than instruct. Offer to do some legwork for them should they desire or need help.

Since this is the first time your parent is not beholden to the congregation, this might be an occasion to unburden yourself concerning the resentment you may have repressed for years. However, do it in a thoughtful way to minimize their defensiveness. Although you might feel relieved to get this off your chest, they might likely feel guilty and remorseful. Give them a chance to apologize or to be startled for they did not know you felt that way. You must bear in mind that although your parents now know your feelings, they cannot go back and change history. The best that your parents can do is change the future and be more attentive to you and your needs.

Take this opportunity to discuss about how they view their own relationship changing in the days ahead, especially if one of them is not yet retired. Ask what they envision an their biggest concerns about retirement. Talk about changing family roles and being open to renegotiating them. You might also want to hear their thoughts about seeking work at other congregations as an interim clergy or filling in on occasions. Since being a clergy spouse is much more difficult than one might imagine, ask both parents their feelings of again having to put on a smile and pitch in. Ask how stressful it is to hear whispered comments in the pew that might not be complimentary, especially knowing the effort that went into the sermon or development of the program. Whereas the clergy might get ego strokes from being back on the pulpit, there are real risks associated with returning. There is the great risk of rejection by the next congregation, and a spouse could be left having to pick up the pieces of a deeply bruised ego. All of this could make for a wonderful family discussion and something that you as a PK can feel proud that you helped facilitate with your parents.

As you can sense from the aforementioned issues, the life of a retiree is vastly different from any of the previous stages of young adulthood, career building, parenthood, or maintaining one's balance in the work world. This new stage is unlike any that preceded it and demands new skills and the continued development of meaning making. It is not a "do-nothing-sit-back-kick-off-your-shoes-and-relax time." Instead, it is a wonderful opportunity for a retiree to choose and participate in the things that are the most enjoyable and meaningful instead of only those that one is obligated to do. It is an opportunity to develop talents and interests. It is an opportunity to spend significant time making a difference in the world. Moreover, you, their child, can help tremendously in easing the entrance into and journey along the way in your parents' stage of life.

SUMMARY

Retirement represents an opportunity to begin the relationship with your parents anew. You can help them through a very stressful time in their lives. You can be a wonderful listener as they design their futures, and a great help in suggesting the varied options for their potential. You can also take this opportunity to raise questions about legal matters associated with the eventual ends of their lives. Finally, as their child, you can use this next stage of their lives to begin a more mature adult relationship with them during their encore years.

A List of Reminders

1. Being a PK is very difficult.
2. The past is the past and cannot be undone.
3. Retirement presents a wonderful opportunity for any child to open new doors of communication. Some conversations:
   a. Time off for sabbatical
   b. Helping to fill time with meaningful activities
   c. Financial concerns: pension, Social Security, worries, finding a financial advisor
   d. Where to live, relocating
   e. Important documents: will, healthcare power of attorney, insurance, living will
   f. Funeral plans

REFERENCES

Hardy, B. (2001, Fall). Pastor care with clergy children. *Review and Expositor, 98*, 545–557.

Hileman, L. (2008). The unique needs of protestant clergy families: Implications for marriage and family counseling. *Journal of Spirituality in Mental Health, 10*(2), 119–144.

Kemper, R. (1988). *Planning for ministerial retirement.* New York, NY: Pilgrim.

Prosch, T. (2014). *The other talk: A guide to talking with your adult children about the rest of your life.* New York, NY: McGraw-Hill.

Strange, K. S. (2001). Evaluations of clergy children versus non-clergy children: Does a negative stereotype exist? *Pastoral Psychology, 50*(1), 53–60.

http://dx.doi.org/10.2190/CLEC10

CHAPTER 10

Clergy Transition:
Engaging the Congregation

CHANGE IS HARD—
A CONGREGANT'S PERSPECTIVE ON
CLERGY TRANSITION

This is hard! I have so many conflicting feelings and thoughts at this moment that I'm finding it difficult to sort them out! I love, yes love, our pastor. No, not in the inappropriate way that we read about all too often these days in the papers, but as my spiritual leader and deep personal friend. He was the first clergyperson who I both admired and felt genuinely cared for me. I have learned so much from him by attending his classes, hearing his sermons, and experiencing the example he has offered us by the way he lives his life. Now he will be leaving! Damn; I will miss him! But I feel guilty and selfish thinking this way. He has worked so hard for so long that I truly believe he deserves a break—time to enjoy life with his family and friends without the constant sense of responsibility for so many others. I know this is right, but I hate the feeling of impending loss. Rationally, I know our congregational leaders will carefully search for his successor, but I am afraid that I won't be able to accept the change. After all, it just won't be the same!

୬ଈ   ୬ଈ   ୬ଈ

A HEALTHY TRANSITION FOR EVERYONE

It's time to broaden the perspective of clergy transition beyond just the clergy and consider the impact upon the congregation, its staff, lay leaders, and congregants. It is time to think about how everyone can make this transition as healthy and as smooth as possible. Engaging everyone in this process will provide a constructive opportunity for people to understand the needs and emotions of a clergy who is retiring as well as the family, congregants and colleagues. We strongly suggest that as many staff and laity as possible share this chapter; and we have included targeted recommendations for each of these critical parties to this complex process. (Although this section is written for those

133

in congregations, many of the ideas are easily applicable to organizational institutions.)

Congregations, like most other organizations, have a life of their own. They can best be understood as living organisms that go through many of the same developmental stages and have similar emotional reactions as the members of which they are composed (Weese & Crabtree, 2004). Although some congregants seek stimulation and seem to thrive on variability in their lives, others are less resilient and prefer steadiness and predictability. Change is difficult whether it is "good" or "bad"; it is an unsettling disruption and therefore experienced as stressful by many.

Even when expressed in rational terms, almost all resistance to organizational change is emotional. Some of the congregation's most critical members will be among those genuinely upset by the departure of their clergy and may act out their discomfort in a variety of ways. Others, concerned about losing their valued spiritual leader and friend, may sense the planned departure as betrayal (Mead, 2005) and express their grief, loss, and vulnerability in ways that may surprise and disappoint the retiring clergy. In any case, William Bridges' classic work (2003) on transitions reminds us that the emotional reactions to transitions are mitigated and subsequent results enhanced when those involved reorient themselves by letting go and allowing time for repatterning before starting a new beginning. At the same time, it is important to recognize how a clergy transition can offer all concerned (i.e., the clergy, his family, lay leaders and other congregational staff) the opportunity to learn, grow, and change (Bookman & Kahn, 2007). "Transitions are at once wounds—gashes in the congregational body—and opportunities for growth—moments in congregational histories that offer choice about what the congregation can and will be" (Bookman & Kahn, 2007).

The more thought clergy give to aiding their congregation in preparation for their retirement, the healthier that transition will be for all parties involved. Some clergy resist this notion in the belief that as they approach this very personal stage of their own career and life, it is time to focus on themselves. Some express years of pent-up frustration with comments like "It's time to take care of me; if I don't, nobody else will." While this may be true in some circumstances, it seems that this is a sad way to end a career dedicated to serving others. This is therefore an essential moment for lay leaders and staff to guide the congregation in considering the needs and emotional stress being faced by their clergy and family.

Since lay leadership of most congregations turns over every few years, the clergy's retirement is likely to be very unfamiliar ground, particularly if the leaders haven't already planed their own retirements. The clergy may find himself in an uncomfortable position. While preparing to cope with a personal sense of loss, financial concerns, and finding meaning in the next stage of life, he must take a leadership role in the congregation's advanced planning for this major transition. Some believe it is almost as important for a congregation and its clergy to develop a clergy transition plan in advance as it is to develop a meaningful strategic plan (Weese & Crabtree, 2004). The common element here is *planning*, without which individuals and organizations lack a sense of direction and stability. The goal is a *healthy transition*, which enables a congregation to move forward into the next phase of its development with a new leader appropriate to those developmental tasks and with a minimum of spiritual, programmatic, material, and human losses during the transition (Weese & Crabtree, 2004). A healthy transition will also aid the retiring clergy to manage his own emotional reactions and approach the next stage of life with a sense of accomplishment and inner peace.

For the congregation, Mead (2005) posits a set of "developmental tasks" as it journeys between clergy. These five nonsequential tasks include

- Coming to terms with the congregation's history;
- Discovering a new identity, a new sense of mission;
- Helping the congregation's internal leadership to grow and change;
- Rediscovering (and enhancing) linkages to the denomination;
- Establishing a new commitment between people and the new pastor to engage in their mission together. (p. 18)

Among the strategies offered by Weese and Crabtree (2004), the following will facilitate healthy transitions:

- Consult with denominational organizations and other resources such as private consultants about proven strategies for healthy transition of clergy. (See Appendix I for books on this topic that will be helpful for clergy and the congregation's lay leaders.)
- Create a transition plan in advance if possible. While this activity should be led by lay leaders, clergy input is essential. Nonetheless, retiring clergy must be careful not to dominate the process with their personal needs.
- Engaging an interim clergy for a specified period of time (typically one year) is becoming more popular in synagogues and churches. This specially trained clergyperson can provide a time of rest between long-term clergy during which emotions may be calmed and the congregation can engage in thoughtful reexamination of its mission and values. Interims are particularly helpful when the transition is unexpected, the departing clergy's tenure has been particularly long, or when he was the founding clergy of the congregation. When the clergy's departure has been long expected and there is a clear transition plan, an Interim may be less critical.
- A process for sharing critical information between retiring and succeeding clergy is essential. This is not a blueprint for how to handle every aspect or program of the congregation but an exchange of sensitive information about

congregants and staff, unique traditions or customs, and local resources that have been particularly helpful.

- Just as the retiring clergy needs to express confidence and optimism about his successor, the incoming clergy needs to publicly honor his predecessor and the congregation's history.

UNDERSTANDING THE RETIRING CLERGY

Lay leaders, even those who have been exceptional partners with their clergy in congregational work, may be unaware of the multitude of the clergy's feelings and needs as they prepare to retire and face the next stage of life. Unless the clergy have been particularly revealing about their joys, frustrations, hopes, and fears about their future, how can the lay leaders comprehend? Without crossing professional boundaries and compromising their privacy, we encourage clergy to be prepared to selectively share some of the emotional issues we've addressed throughout this book.

Below are some of the most common and relevant issues that might help lay leaders to better understand what their retiring clergy is going through:

- Planning for one's retirement will be a different experience if it is totally voluntary as opposed to involuntary due to issues of health, performance, or the congregation's financial stability.
- Leaving a congregation in which one has invested so much of himself ("breathed life into") has been likened to leaving a child you have birthed and raised.
- Depending on the particular congregation, a certain degree of influence, control, and prestige came along with the title and work of its clergy. For some, these are difficult to give up and can result in a significant sense of loss.
- While moving ahead may be exciting, it brings along a degree of uncertainty that can be very unsettling. Loss of financial security, a familiar routine, and some long-standing relationships can be upsetting to anticipate and difficult to adjust to when the time arrives.
- Perhaps the greatest fear is potential loss of meaning in one's life when so much of it has been defined by very personal work that has been valued by the community.
- In addition to the personal losses and fears associated with retirement, clergy are often concerned and therefore focused on the impact of this change on their families—particularly their spouse (see Chapter 8).

Recommendations for Lay Leaders

- Honor your clergy and respect the difficult decision he has made to transition to the next stage of life. Inquire about his plans, dreams, and concerns and how you and the community may be supportive. It may be a struggle to avoid focusing on how this decision will impact you and the congregation, but this is the time to be generous of spirit.

- Encourage your clergy to seek counsel and support from denominational resources, experienced professionals, and colleagues who are also preparing to go through this transition or have recently retired.
- After hearing your clergy's decision to retire and time to process this information, it is important to develop a rather specific plan.
  - If you have had a good relationship with the clergy, build on the strength of that partnership to plan together. If not, appoint an appropriate congregant who can do so on behalf of the congregation (Mead, 2005)
  - Although sooner is better, more than 2 years in advance of retirement is likely to be too long and result in a sense of limbo, which can be demoralizing and derailing for both staff and congregants (Mead, 2005) and unintentionally send out the wrong message to the community at-large.
  - The plan should be written and address critical details such as dates (end of duties, moving from office and parsonage, termination of benefits, etc.), any continued compensation and benefits (such as conference attendance and administrative support), use of earned vacation time, extent of role in the successor search process, status, and possible title as "Emeritus" as well as any responsibilities and benefits associated with that status.
  - Discuss with clergy their plans to responsibly terminate relationships with counselees and congregants in nursing homes and hospitals. Determine how information about these particularly needy congregants will be shared with his successor.
  - Somewhat less critical, but still important, is to discuss and agree upon plans to honor the service and mark the farewell of the clergy and his family. A properly planned farewell service will be appreciated by your retiring clergy and his family. Congregants will benefit by marking their community's significant transition in a ritualistic manner (see Chapter 4). Here it is most appropriate to engage a committee of congregants and to consult with the clergy's spouse
  - To free your clergy to contemplate and plan for his personal future, lay leaders should not withdraw from congregational life and responsibilities. This is the time for leaders to step up and demonstrate their commitment to the congregation and its future.
  - Encourage clergy to meet with the successor (if possible) for a professional debriefing and agree upon what materials, resources, etc. will be left or handed off.

UNDERSTANDING CONGREGATIONAL LEADERS

Congregational lay leaders are often unprepared to guide the congregation through a transition of their clergy. Since frequent turnover of lay leaders is typical in congregations, very few of the current leadership were actively involved in selecting and integrating of the current clergy when they first joined this community. With a lifetime of service to your, and perhaps other, congregations, your clergy is therefore the resident expert in matters of this transition. While it may feel awkward, the retiring clergy may need to initially educate the lay leadership about the process of transition, including how he would like to be treated— personally, socially, and financially. Unexpressed desires and needs often result in disappointment and resentment. At the same time, unless there has been advanced planning for this transition that specifies roles of all parties, the retiring clergy must begin to let go and make room for others to assume leadership. Finding the ideal balance will be a challenge. The following list of recommendations will help guide your congregation or organization during this critical stage in its life.

Recommendations for Retiring Clergy[1]

- Meet personally with the president/senior leader of the congregation and the lay leader assigned to be your professional liaison (if it is not the president) to tell them of your intentions to retire and begin very preliminary discussions of details. No one in the congregation should know of your plans before this discussion, and all subsequent communication should be consistent with the agreed-upon plan. Family members, colleagues, and your closest friends need to be reminded about the confidentiality and sensitivity of these discussions.
- Encourage appropriate lay leaders to seek input from the denomination and other reliable resources regarding preferable approaches to clergy transition. This may be unfamiliar territory for your congregational leadership, but many others have gone through this before and there is no reason for your congregation to reinvent the wheel. It will be helpful for involved leaders to read this book and the included references. As they gain insight into how this process may affect you and your family, they will be better prepared to include your needs in their planning.
- Meet with appropriate lay leaders to negotiate terms of your retirement. These might include compensation, benefits, title, office space, administrative support, and duties, if any. Some clergy prefer to be represented by legal counsel or an independent representative in these negotiations.
- Meet personally with the rest of the congregational staff as soon as possible but before making a public announcement to the congregation. Share your preliminary retirement plans and any preliminary decisions made by the lay leadership about the congregation's future.

[1] And valuable for lay leaders too!

- Meet with appropriate lay leaders to clarify your role in selecting your successor. Plan for transition of authority and responsibilities, logistics of your physical move, and farewell event. As mentioned in Chapter 8, it will be important to consider your spouse's and children's feelings and needs in these matters. If appropriate, include your spouse in some of these discussions with lay leaders.

UNDERSTANDING THE REMAINING STAFF

Depending on the size of the congregation or organization, retiring clergy have likely worked with and possibly supervised others—clergy, educators, programming professionals, administrative or support staff. The retiring clergy's relationship with each co-worker will understandably vary based on roles, personalities, and customs of their work environment. Likewise, their personal reactions may vary. Some co-workers will be very pleased for their colleague and supportive; others may be envious that he is at this stage of life and they are not. Some colleagues may be anxious about how this retirement will change things and may impact their job security while others may see this as an opportunity for career advancement. Even though the retiring clergy has announced his planned departure, he is still a leader within this community. The more sensitive he can be to the needs of the staff, the healthier this transition will be for all. While it is not unreasonable to expect support from one's co-workers, one shouldn't be overly disappointed if it isn't forthcoming. As mentioned above, it may be a good idea for the retiring clergy to have an open discussion with individual staff about his needs and wishes at this time to minimize disappointment and resentment later.

Recommendations for Retiring Clergy[2]

- Counsel lay leadership about the emotional impact of your retirement on the remaining staff. It would be understandable for them to be so focused on finding your successor and even on you that they might ignore the rest of the staff. For as long as you are still its spiritual leader, being the voice protecting others will help ensure the congregation's successful functioning.
- After your retirement has been announced, meet with staff members individually to answer their questions and gain a sense of their attitude about this transition and outlook for the future. Where questions are raised that you can't answer, encourage staff members to speak with the appropriate lay leader.
- Be prepared to counsel and support those staff who are anxious and rein in those who may be acting out.

[2] And valuable for lay leaders too!

- Once your successor has been chosen, be positive about his abilities and confident about the future of the congregation.
- Prior to the end of your engagement, be absolutely clear with staff about boundaries—limitations of your new roles, responsibilities, and authority. If you are not clear yourself about such boundaries, you can't expect staff or congregants to be. The result will be not only confusion but also disruption.

Recommendations for Lay Leaders

- As much as possible, include staff prior to making a public announcement.
- Reassure staff of the congregation's desire for their continued service/ employment.
- Share the transition plan and timeline.
- Specify any anticipated changes in their professional role during the transition and possibly thereafter.
- Clarify what, if any, role they may be asked to play in the search process.
- Solicit their support throughout the stages of transition and express appreciation for their participation.
- Invite their participation in farewell activities.

UNDERSTANDING CONGREGANTS

Congregations are communities of individuals and as such include a wide variety of viewpoints, needs, and personalities. For some, the departure of the spiritual leader who has been instrumental in their lives is virtually unimaginable. For others, clergy define the congregation, and they are impacted deeply— sometimes negatively—when the congregation transitions to another clergy- person. Some congregants will need to know with some degree of clarity whether the retiring clergy will be remaining in the community and available to continue to counsel and support them, and if not, to whom they may turn in times of need. Here again, clear communication is critical to remaining staff, congregants, and the clergy's successor.

Not all congregants will be upset about the announced clergy departure; some will be indifferent and others (hopefully very few) will be pleased by the thought of new clergy. Some will focus on the future and others will be concerned about how the departing clergy and their family are being treated as their tenure ends. The spectrum of congregant reactions adds another dimension to the tension associated with their clergy's retirement and the search process for a successor. All will be served best when reassured about the security of the congregation's future and reminded that a congregation is more than any one person—even its clergy!

In *A Change of Pastors*, Mead (2005) writes,

> It's not about the pastor who is leaving or the one who is coming. It's not even about you (congregants) who are stuck with having a lot of new jobs to

do. It's about how you build from what has been the strength and integrity of one period of ministry into a new relationship in which a new ministry takes off for all of you. (p. 14)

Weese and Crabtree (2004, p. 16) offer the following principles to support congregants through pastoral transitions. Some are for the retiring clergy and others more for the successor:

- Honor thy predecessor/successor: Whether you are the retiring or arriving clergy, discourage people from talking about previous clergy; this locks them into the past (whether positive or negative) which keeps them from focusing positively on the future. The retiring clergy must speak with confidence about his/her successor and express optimism about the future.
- Build on health: Neither quicksand nor mud provide a strong foundation on which a structure can be built organizationally any more than physically. Rather, reflecting on the positive experiences of the congregation's past, its strengths and successes, sets the foundation for its continued vitality. You may want to explore the approach of organizational development called *Appreciative Inquiry* for more insight and strategies for this approach.
- Respect the past and build for the future: All of the work that you did and accomplishments you facilitated in this congregation need not end nor be forgotten when your tenure ends, but neither should they dominate the congregation's future. New clergy leadership can often provide the opportunity for needed changes within the congregation—particularly those that were not obvious to you or the previous lay leadership. The goal here is to build on the past successes while embracing new ideas to revitalize the congregation. Don't think "either _____ or_____" but rather "both _____ and ___"!
- The future is opportunity: Leaders need a vision and a plan to move an organization forward. They also need the acceptance of those who came before them so congregants will be open to the possibilities of doing things differently. Whether you remain in the community or not, communication with congregants and staff needs to be as optimistic and accepting as possible if you want your successor and the congregation to succeed.
- Create capacity: Congregations can never have too many committed qualified leaders and volunteers; they are the source of direction and energy as they work collaboratively with clergy and staff. If you have been successful in building a cadre of leaders and a culture of engagement in your congregation, this will be one of the most significant gifts you can bequeath your successor. If not, think about this as a priority during your last year(s) at the congregation; it would be a legacy for years to come.
- Fight the demons: Dysfunctional elements within an organization tend to emerge as a strong established leader begins to recede. Be on the lookout for congregants acting out and be prepared to step in to constructively address

their underlying issues and redirect them into positive forces for the future. Confronting fears is more effective than trying to avoid them. They don't go away on their own; but instead they fester and spread. Ironically, the departing clergy is in the best position within the congregation to model how to constructively move through this transition; in this regard, your work is not complete even once you've left.

Recommendations for Presidents and Lay Leaders

Although anticipation and planning for the transition of clergy leadership for the congregation or organization may feel all-consuming, remember that you and your fellow lay leaders are not the only ones anticipating this significant change.

- Make yourself available for congregants to share their concerns, complaints, and wishes. This is one of the most important times for you to reinforce relationships within the congregation and to build community.
- Work with a representative committee to plan multiple opportunities so all factions of the congregation will be able to say farewell, express their appreciation, and even mourn the loss of their spiritual leader. Consider the needs of the retiring clergy, his family, and the culture of the congregation. These moments may include events such as worship services, parties, or a collection of personal messages in a scrapbook or memory box.
- Direct and thoughtful communication is vital to the transition and may also counteract negativity. Make a formal announcement rather than allowing people to learn through the congregational rumor mill.
- Share at least the highlights of the transition process and timelines.
- Describe opportunities for expressions of appreciation and farewell and participation in search and transition planning.
- Reassure members that the congregation's core values and quality of services provided will be maintained, particularly during an interim period of transition.

Recommendations for Retiring Clergy

Allow yourself time to reflect on your years of service as you begin to plan for the future and identify your needs and desires as you face the end of your role with this congregation or organization. As mentioned above, it will be far more beneficial for all concerned if you can be clear and communicate your wishes.

- Even though you may be a private person and may prefer to leave silently in the night, you and your congregants deserve the opportunity to say goodbye.
- Within the bounds of confidentiality and professionalism, do not hesitate to also share your reflections of your shared moments and highlights with this congregation. You need the opportunity to tell your story, and congregants will benefit from reliving and learning about the past. Just as

important for congregants is your modeling respectful honest sharing of memories— happy and sad.
* Save time to say farewells, particularly to those who have become dependent on your attention and counsel. These are the congregants who your successor will particularly need to learn about. In certain cases, make referral to professional resources where they may receive consistent support in the community.

UNDERSTANDING THE SUCCESSOR CLERGY

After years of personal and professional investment in a congregation, the most impactful legacy retiring clergy may leave is laying the groundwork for the new clergy to succeed. Clearly, this will be easier for some in some circumstances than others; but even when leaving with some disappointment or resentment, this is a time to be the best one can be and rise above personal emotions.

Some recommendations above and in Chapter 13 on Encouraging the Other certainly apply here. Most important are the retiring clergy's genuine expression of optimism about the congregation's future and confidence in the successor's ability to help it thrive, as well as a private offer to debrief with one's successor. See Appendix I for Weese and Crabtree's checklist for doing so. Because some of this information is very confidential or sensitive, some retiring clergy are hesitant to share it. In such circumstances, a face-to-face meeting or telephone conversation would be preferable to avoiding exchange of such valuable information in writing. There is the possibility that one's successor may not be interested in hearing your perspectives; and although we view that as an unfortunate mistake, you can only offer and remain available to consult in the future.

SUMMARY

Congregations are complex systems with a multitude of interdependent elements. When dealing with significant change, such as the retirement of clergy, all players must be considered. Though retirement seems a rather personal decision, its impact extends beyond the clergy and his family, much as a pebble tossed in a pond creates rings of concentric ripples. The needs of lay leaders, other staff, and congregants all must be factored into the planning, and their potential roles in the success of the transition should not be ignored. Each player approaches this change with a unique perspective and comes with his own gifts to help fuel the congregation along on its journey.

The process of transition can be as complex as the number of various participants. As a whole, the congregation must engage in three essential aspects: *reflecting* (who are we, where have we come from, and what are our values and beliefs?), *planning* (where are we going and how will we get there?), and *communicating* (informing members, staff, and community of key decisions and plans). Considering and including all those who will be impacted by this transition will enhance its outcome.

REFERENCES

Bookman, T., & Kahn, W. (2007). *This house we build: Lessons for healthy synagogues and the people who dwell there.* Herndon, VA: Alban Institute.

Bridges, W. (2003). *Managing transitions: Making the most of change* (2nd ed.). Boston, MA: DaCapo.

Mead, L. B. (2005). *A change of pastors . . . And how it affects change in the congregation.* Herndon, VA: Alban Institute.

Weese, C., & Crabtree, J. R. (2004). *The elephant in the boardroom: Speaking the unspoken about pastoral transitions.* San Francisco, CA: Jossey-Bass Leadership Network Publications.

http://dx.doi.org/10.2190/CLEC11

CHAPTER 11

The Responsibilities Leaders of Religious Organizations Have to Their Retirees (To be Shared With Organizational Leaders)

> Cast me not off in the time of old age; When my strength faileth, forsake me not.
>
> Psalm 71:9 JPS

CONTINUITY

Sister Regina was committed to her order's mission of teaching. She taught in several parish elementary schools throughout her extended lifetime. However, the day came when she no longer had the stamina, patience, or focus to teach a class full of young active children. This was a painful realization for her to accept, but it was made more palatable when the Mother Superior offered her the opportunity to stay in the convent as a contributing member of the community rather than move to their order's Mother House. Regina assumed a new but active role. She gave individual piano lessons to several motivated parish children, substituted during Mass when the organist was ill or on vacation, and prepared lunch in the convent on schooldays for those teaching. This provided her with opportunity to stay engaged in the life of the school, and she was grateful to be able to serve as a source of community history for the parish.

SENDING LIFEBOATS

Along the Mississippi Delta, there was a very religious and ethical man who would pray three times a day and observe every holiday to its fullest. When a flood came, the man decided to remain in his home, much to the consternation of his friends who encouraged him to leave with them. He was sure that God would deliver him from death because he was so dedicated to God.

145

As the waters rose and entered his house, he climbed to the second floor. Along came a dinghy with three men in it. They urged him to get in the boat, but the man refused, "I'll be okay. God will save me!" he responded. The waters rose even more and soon the man found himself on the third floor of the house. Again a row boat came and its occupants pleaded with him to get in. "No, go on," said the man, "I'm a religious man, I've observed all the laws. I'm sure God will save me." The waters roared and the man soon found himself up on the peak of his roof praying mightily. A speedboat came along and the driver urged him to grab a life preserver. "Go save my neighbors. God will surely answer my prayers and save me, I am sure of it," he argued.

Shortly thereafter the waters overwhelmed the man and he drowned. When he got to heaven, he angrily confronted God. "Why would you take my life? I have been religious and ethical all my life, and I have obeyed everything You demanded." God replied, "My son, I did try to save you: three times I sent a lifeboat for you!"

What lifeboats are we, the leaders of judicatories, sending to the very people who have served the congregations in our dioceses for years? Do we have any obligation to those who have finished their careers and are now in the "greener pastures" of retirement? We might argue that we have enough on our plates keeping up with all the active clergy and meeting the demands of the congregational leaders who are clamoring for our attention. What use is a retired clergy person who has health issues, who is slowing down, who has lost their dramatic flair, and is becoming a little forgetful? What use are clergy who are swimming upstream against a current of change? What use are retired clergy who are gone from the parish? Why should we continue to serve them?

We hear the words of Leviticus concerning God's commandment to care for the widow and the orphan, the poor and the stranger, the lowest people on the rungs of society. Are these not our retirees who have gone from a job of prestige to that of common parishioner? As clergy leaders, what obligation do we have to anyone in our congregations who is suffering mental distress? Can we not hear the cry in the Book of Psalms: "Cast me not off in the time of old age; when my strength faileth, forsake me not" (71:9). Just throwing a retired clergy to the wolves is not fulfilling either the aforementioned plea or our obligation to those in the throes of a life change.

In the storm above, God directed the men in the lifeboats to risk their lives to save the religious man on the roof. Certainly God would make it our responsibility, as elected officials, not to abandon those who have devoted their lives to God and their congregations now that they have reached senior status.

The Hurts

Touching words of various priests in the study Kevin Ladd conducted of retired priests reveal the great pain that they experience during their retirement years:

My greatest ill feeling is that the Bishop and Diocesan committees don't talk with me anymore. Being put out to pasture is one thing, but no longer being considered as part of the farm is another. I think experience occasionally needs to be called upon. As priests, we still need to be acknowledged and accepted before our funeral Masses. (Ladd, 2006, p. 96)

Another recites,

I found retirement most difficult to go from a full day in the active ministry to an empty day. In the months that followed I sank into a deep depression which made hospitalization necessary. I found the holidays to be extremely difficult. Saying Mass in my own little chapel . . . lacked the joy and excitement of a parish celebration. . . . not being asked by a fellow priest to co-celebrate was very painful. (Ladd, 2006, p. 97)

Others put forth these resentments:

Most of the time I feel quite useless. [Among the priests in my retirement residence] there are a number of walking wounded.

[I retired so I would not] be a burden to a parish in my last few years.

One of the problems of retirement is the sense and feeling of no longer being needed.

We had to drastically limit marriages and funerals because it cut across the duties of the parish clergy who in most cases wanted to safeguard their standing with the people. It's surprising how jealous some parish clergy can be!!!

[Sometimes] people treat you differently [for instance] at a religious goods store where they know you won't be buying much anymore.

I guess it is the loss of being needed which was the hardest to take. I wish there was a political action committee for retired clergy.

I think Bishops should remember their retired priests, maybe having an annual dinner instead of totally forgetting them as if they were on the same list as the dead priests of the diocese.

Retirement is absurd. (Ladd, 2006, p. 97)

Not only priests feel lonely and abandoned by the very people in the dioceses who they thought were their friends—every clergy retires. "Where are they?" one minister asked in our survey. "Where are they, our fellow leaders, who purported to care about our careers and our families? Weeks and months have gone by and there is no reaching out just to find out how I am faring during my time of transition. It would have been nice."

Others report how enjoyable it is when there is an occasion to get together with fellow clergy and just share memories.

Although retirement is considered to be a process, little is written about the effect it has on us as clergypersons. Nobody writes about our experiences and feelings of abandonment, worthlessness, and depression once retirement has commenced and we are no longer in front of a congregation. Combine this with various other fears (i.e., change in residence, anxiety about aging, health concerns, finances) and this process influences the rest of our lives. Just as seeing to the mental health of our most active clergy is a responsibility of the adjudicating organization, so we as authors believe that the well-being of its retirees should also be the concern of the leadership.

What Needs to be Done

Many people transition easily into the retired lifestyle, but that does not mean that the journey is not fraught with potholes and detours. Instead of allowing our fellow clergy to drift off without a map, as judicatories we need to conduct a yearly seminar for those approaching retirement age. Planning in advance helps clergy better understand the emotional and practical challenges ahead and develop reasonable expectations about the future. This foreknowledge can contribute to the formation of realistic attitudes toward retirement. More importantly, reflection and planning will lead to healthier emotional adjustment to withdrawal from the role of God's servant and community leader. In addition, it will force people to face the reality of financial planning.

To counter possible feelings of abandonment, clerical organizations should establish a means for those who have retired to come together for fellowship. The atmosphere should encourage sharing honest feelings with colleagues. A conference, meeting, or social gathering can provide a safe opportunity to listen, not to judge and not give advice, but simply to allow colleagues to share what is happening and how they are reacting to it. Sometimes just putting words to a feeling is enough to be helpful, and hearing that others are experiencing their own struggles can be liberating.

The image of the cowboy of the Old West who just pulls up his boots and goes on need not be our model. Our ideal should be one of compassion and concern. Sharing is a way to break off parts of the grief we are experiencing and send it packing. Retirees leave behind a piece of themselves and are entering a new world without the *me* they once knew. Retirement brings wide emotional swings, from a sense of relief and opportunity to bouts of sorrow, anger, frustration, loss of meaning, and feelings of incompetence. These are all common and normal emotions when one ceases work in a lifelong vocation and must find new meaning in life. We as authors believe it is both an opportunity and duty of diocesan leaders to assist retirees during these moments of upheaval, just as we would if a colleague had a disaster occur to his home or family. We have noted that in some Catholic dioceses someone is assigned to just such a responsibility. For example, in Cleveland, Ohio, Father Joseph Krupp works with fellow retired priests. He keeps their names in a little notebook and calls them on a regular basis. He calls this directory his "Fraternity of Elders." What a great service.

Father Krupp suggested that clergy organizations need to put together a "skills bank," which can facilitate ways to utilize the talents of their retirees. He feels that dioceses should have retiring clergy fill out a skills and interests assessment as if applying for a new job. The Diocese should then find ways to utilize their gifts.

In communities where there are enough retired clergy, leaders could organize weekly or monthly meetings and invite clergy, maybe even those of other faiths, to join and study together. Invited speakers could discuss issues pertinent to retirement, for example, financial planning, insurance, travel, health issues, and so on. Judicatories could consider hiring a "life coach," social worker, or psychologist who understands the dynamics of the clergy retirement. If there are not funds to do so, identify "coaches" who are sensitive to the clergy and encourage them to run groups on their own. A judicatory could publicize such groups or coaches and their availability. Writes Rabbi David Wolpe, "What loss cries for is not to be fixed or to be explained, but to be shared, and eventually, to find its way to meaning" (Wolpe, 1999, p. 15).

A yearly social event is another way to acknowledge to retired clergy that they have not been forgotten. For example, both the Central Conference of American Rabbis and the Rabbinical Assembly have organized and staffed subregional groups dedicated to keeping retirees involved. Annual conventions enable retirees and their spouses to come together to learn, share, and schmooze with old friends and new ones. Milestones are celebrated, and officials from the hierarchy update the attendees on current issues and developments in the movement. Such conventions build community and give members the feeling that they are not forgotten. Those who attend return year after year and rave about the opportunity to reconnect with fellow clergy.

In addition, retired clergy who want to remain active and maintain an income stream can be of great benefit to congregations undergoing leadership transitions. Judicatories might want to encourage and conduct an Interim Ministries program. By working with the Interim Ministry Network (http://www.imnedu.org/), both congregation and clergy gain by having a trained minister to help them during their transition. The clergy would have a mission for a year while figuring out exactly what he/she wants to do during retirement, and the congregation will make a smoother transition to its next permanent clergy.

Reality Hits

Change is difficult for everyone involved. The tendency for those who are still working is to jealously look upon retirement as a dream world. Popular culture identifies retirement as a time to do what one wants, when one wants, with responsibilities to no one except oneself, all while getting paid (through Social Security and a pension) to do "nothing." In a certain sense, this is true, for the retiree does get to make choices unencumbered by career-focused demands. We remind you that the transition is difficult (see Chapter 5), for one goes from a meaningful world of activity and involvement to a world in which one must create new meaning, find new importance, and develop ways to fill the many empty hours. It is a world filled with health issues, new aches and pains, and worries about finances and mortality.

We truly understand that as officials of a religious movement, you have the responsibility of finding and supporting the new pastor who takes over for the retiree and to facilitate as smooth a transition within the congregation as possible. But we strongly encourage you to include stewarding retired clergy as one of your responsibilities and include those who have retired recently, or not so recently, in a meaningful way. An occasional get-together will go a long way in helping the retiree still feel remembered and important. We simply remind you that it's not so easy to retire, and making this transition just a little bit less stressful will be blessing to you and them.

REFERENCES

Ladd, K. L. (2006). Retirement issues for Roman Catholic priests: A theoretical and qualitative investigation. *Review of Religious Research, 48*(1), 82–104.

Wolpe, D. (1999). *Making loss matter: Creating meaning in difficult times.* New York, NY: Riverhead Books.

http://dx.doi.org/10.2190/CLEC12

CHAPTER 12

Encouraging the Other: A Successor Interacts with a Predecessor
(For a Smoother Transition in the Congregation You, as a Predecessor, Might Want to Share This Chapter with Your Successor)

Where there is no vision, the people perish.

(Proverbs 29:18)

Each of you should look not only to your own interests, but also to the interests of others.

(Philippians 2:3 NIV)

RETIRED EARLY BECAUSE OF ILLNESS

I'm still in my 50s and have only been with this congregation for 4½ years, but I feel I must retire. My body is giving out before my spirit! This makes me both very sad and scared. I was really having a positive impact in a number of critical areas of this congregation—more so than at my last two pulpits. It's not fair; I'm not ready to quit and leave. And what kind of a life do I have to look forward to—gradually decreasing stamina and independence? Shrinking financial resources? Boredom and loneliness? Who will I be? What will I do? It's just not fair! How many congregants have I counseled over the years about accepting the inevitability of life circumstances? Now it's me!

ف   ف   ف

HOW ARE YOU PLANNING TO . . .

Susan dies and goes to Heaven. St. Peter meets her at the gate and tells her that because they are very crowded in Heaven right now, he must administer a little spelling test to determine whether or not she can get in. "That is fine," she responds, "what do I have to spell?" St. Peter hesitates for a moment and says, "Please spell 'love.'" "That's easy, L-O-V-E." "That's correct," he replies, "You can go in! But I need you to do me a favor. I have to go to the bathroom for a second. Could you just sit here in case somebody comes along? You saw what I did; you can be in charge until I return."

No sooner does St. Peter disappear and Susan settles into his enormous chair then another person appears. She looks up at him only to discover it is her husband. "What happened to you?" she queries. He responds that when he was driving home from the funeral, he was crying so hard that he crashed into a tree and died. "My goodness," Susan replies, "I did not know that you loved me that much. Saint Peter put me in charge for the moment and they are a little overcrowded up here. You have to undergo a little spelling test to get in." "That's fine, what do you want me to spell?" he asks. Susan thinks for a second and responds, "Czechoslovakia."

You never know what questions you will be asked when you come to your new "heavenly" congregation. Let alone you might not know what are the motives behind those questions. This chapter will prepare you for the *trees* that could cause your demise in the new congregation. One nonverbalized question you must be prepared to answer is, "How are you planning to deal with your predecessor?" Even if your predecessor were not universally loved, many congregants liked and admired him. Everyone will watch you with curiosity. We believe that how you deal with your predecessor will tremendously impact how others view your ministry and what they think about your character and moral fiber. Just as importantly, how you treat your predecessor will have enormous effect upon his transition to retirement.

Succeeding as a Successor

In our personal experiences, we have noticed that when a new rabbi succeeds a senior rabbi who was at the helm of a congregation for many years, too often he or she fails. These rabbis arrive with a new suit, a different size prayer shawl, and a metaphorical suitcase packed with different programs and approaches that they mastered at their former congregation. They are met at the door of the synagogue with enthusiasm, encouraging words, and warmth. Many congregants may claim to be glad the old rabbi is gone, and they are sure the new rabbi is everything the former rabbi wasn't. Within a couple of years, this rabbi may be seen driving away dejected and brokenhearted, for he has just been dismissed. Interestingly enough, *his* successor usually becomes the darling that everyone loves. Although we have no statistics to prove this theory, officials in other denominations agree that this seems to be a general trend. Perhaps this is why the concept of *interim* clergy was devised. Of course, some do succeed taking over from a long-serving, beloved rabbi or pastor, but this seems to be more the exception than the rule (unless you were the assistant at the congregation). Why is this so? What does a successor need to know to navigate the minefields in an environment that seems so bright and hopeful at the beginning?

Although you bring new energy and enthusiasm, and you are led to believe that the congregation has been awaiting your arrival with open arms, we suggest that you tread lightly for a period of time. Get a true sense of the lay of the land. The interviewing committee may have told you that your predecessor was lacking in areas where they believe you have strengths. Rather than letting this praise and the warm welcome encourage you to make changes too quickly, discretion is the better part of valor. Remember that many members are still mourning the loss of "their" clergy. There is good reason why most widowers/widows or divorcees do not turn around and get married again immediately. There is a need for a period of adjustment. Even when a widow or widower does remarry, it will never be the same as the marriage of their romantic, innocent youth. Yes, love can be better the *second time around*, as the old Frank Sinatra song goes, but it is a process until it reaches that moment.

As the new clergy, you must comprehend that although you have developed your own style in your former congregation(s), this new congregation does not necessarily want everything foisted upon them immediately. Essentially, congregants would like you to get to know them, learn about their traditions and their worship culture, about things they are used to doing in *their* house before you start redecorating and making it yours. Using the imagery of a new marriage, you are moving into your partner's home. Even though they tell you it is perfectly fine to make changes, they may still be frustrated when you take down their favorite picture without asking first. So it is analogous to life in a new congregation. Live in their house and try your best to appreciate it as if you helped build it. Hear their ideas for change while understanding that change can be hard. Listen to their complaints about the *living room* and *dining room* and try to understand the *cracks in the foundation* and how they got there before you try to draw up a master plan to remodel. Use your first year to familiarize yourself with the congregants, how things have been done, what has worked and what didn't, what changes are needed, why, and how soon. Engage congregants in making initial changes slowly, which will help them feel invested in the congregation's evolution and thereby more likely to embrace you and the transition.

It is essential to understand the worship culture of the congregation and allow that culture to continue until you more fully understand what changes may be desirable. It will take time for your new congregants to trust you as their new leader and understand where you are leading them and why. Do you remember the swimming teacher who told you, "Let go of the side, I'll save you." How long did it take for you to do that? Leave your ego aside as you build trust, and realize that it is not your needs that have to be met, but the congregation's. We suggest that you leave the worship service as is until you understand what they are used to, what is spiritually satisfying and what is not moving. One of my most enlightening moments was when our congregation put together a prayer team to evaluate each service over a month's time. The team met immediately after each service to assess it and discuss what did and did not work, then gathered at the end of the month to appraise the entire process. They then became a transition team to explain to the board what changes should be made and gave a timeline to do so. Many successors will begin moving the pulpit around, inserting new prayers, music, and new traditions within a short time. To be sure, you have your own personality, and it is hard to be the same as your predecessor, but many of the traditions can be kept until the congregants are ready to trust you and leave the side of the proverbial swimming pool. Meanwhile, ask yourself what you can learn from the worship culture that could benefit your knowledge of overall congregational life. Concentrate on your *message* and not on the *style* or form of worship at the beginning.

It is wise to be careful of advice others are sharing with you. As you are having conversations, whether with a board member, a congregant or a colleague, be a little suspicious—curious, not paranoid—about why they are making particular suggestions. Often those who were on the outs with the former clergy suddenly feel a resurgence of power, while those who supported him may suddenly feel disenfranchised. This could be a setting for disaster, for often those who want change have not made significant investments over the years, but they want power. Use your listening skills particularly at the beginning and thoughtfully filter your opinions until you better understand the dynamics of the congregation. Your staff, especially those who have been with the congregation for a period of time, can be very helpful and insightful in educating you about the personalities of various congregants (unless they are just reflecting a negative encounter they had with that person). Again, be cautious and listen before you make a judgment. Deal prudently with those who try to befriend you too quickly. Remember that some congregants truly are kind and caring toward you, and then there are those who find it "significant" to be friends with the clergy and his family.

We know that you want to bring your personality to the congregation, and you should; but it is best to *curb your enthusiasm* and move the congregation ahead at their comfort level and not yours. Remind yourself that this is not your congregation but *theirs*. The work is not only yours, but God's. Appreciate the opportunity that they have given you to help them maintain and even enhance their beloved sacred community.

The following story, related by Linda Hileman in her article, "The Unique Needs of Protestant Clergy Families: Implications for Marriage and Family Counseling," brings home the need to go slowly:

> Joe McKeever relates his experience in a large church in Charlotte, North Carolina a decade ago. Joe had been considered an outstanding preacher in his previous charge, with televised services every Sunday and frequent praise from members of the congregation and the community. His predecessor at the Charlotte church was much loved and, as a consequence, Joe was seen as a usurper. People said hurtful things such as, "We like you, but you've got to do something about your sermons. Some of them are just failures."

His wife was told, "Joe just can't preach." There were other things for which Joe was sharply criticized in a humiliating and public manner, and his tenure at the church in Charlotte was short. It has been ten years since Joe left Charlotte for a very successful ministry in another state, and he relates that the memory of the pain inflicted by the members of that congregation is finally fading. (Hileman, 2008, p. 136)

It is important for you to know why the congregation could not see through their proverbial tears and recognize the strengths that McKeever possessed? What were the underlying factors behind their outrageous criticism and what could McKeever have done differently to win people over?

In preparing research for this book, we were drawn to *Managing Transitions: Making the Most of Change* by William Bridges (2009), a book we suggest you read as well. Bridges speaks about the slow process of change and the need for businesses to go through the "Neutral Zone" (see Chart A below). He teaches that many managers fail because they do not allow the employees to progress through the Neutral Zone with sufficient time to lament the passing of one period in their office life to another. If this is true for the business world and its employees, it can easily translate to congregational life as well. As successors, we must allow people time to adjust to the transition before charging ahead. Bridges suggests,

> The three phases of transition are more like curving, slanting, overlapping strata than like sequential stages. Just so you are aware, each of these three processes starts before the preceding one is totally finished. That is why you are likely to be in more than one of these phases at the same time and why the movement through transition is marked by a change in the dominance of one phase over the other two rather than an absolute shift from one to another. (p. 100)

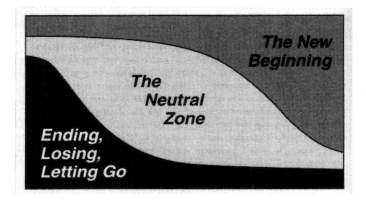

Chart A

Though most of us think of loss only in terms of death, more and more we need to think of nonfinite loss or ambiguous loss (Harris, 2011). Ambiguous loss is most usually precipitated by a disruption of one's assumptive world. This can be intangible loss due to the dashing of one's dreams regarding how the world should be or what we want it to be. Sorrow can occur due to the loss of functionality or diminished self-identity or by the loss of a relationship.

Bridges gives excellent advice, which we as clergy can use to better understand what is happening in the congregation:

> Transitions are the dynamic interludes between one of the seven stages of organizational life and the next. Their function is to close out one phase, reorient and renew people in that time we are calling the neutral zone, and carry people into the new way of doing and being that is the beginning of the next stage. A single transition may not be enough to bring about the complete transformation of the organization and the reorientation of its people. There may instead be a string of transitions, each of which carries the organization a step further along the path of its development. These multi-transition turnings can take years to finish. But however long they take, they make sense to people only in the context of the organization's development. And transitions will need to make sense to people, for otherwise people will resist them and make it far harder for the organization to grow as it must. (2009, p. 82)

A wonderful book you will want to read to understand the task of negotiating change which takes into account that members of the congregation are still grieving for their past equilibrium is *Leading Change in the Congregation* by Gilbert Rendle (1998).

Just as Abraham and Sarah had to leave home before they became great leaders, so we have to convince others to first let go of the present and follow us into an uncertain future. We may not even know where Mt. Moriah is. Abraham and Isaac walked three days toward the unidentified place that God would show them. It all begins with baby steps, the remorse of leaving others behind and facing an uncertain future. If you take the time to build trust with others rather than just assume others will follow you, you will save yourself and the congregation lot of grief.

Advice for Working with Predecessors

Predecessors can be your best ally or your worst enemy, and you can do a lot to make it the former rather than the latter. Even if your denomination requires the former pastor to absent from the congregation for a year or more, his ghost can still haunt you if you fail to comprehend the psychological traumas he and the congregation are going through (see above). A large part of dealing with your predecessor has to do with his emotional acceptance of his *death* in the congregation and his ability to let go of his former role. Some of his reactions will depend upon how you and the congregation support him. We well understand that you have enough on your mind when you first arrive at the congregation— meeting new members, working with staff, planning programs, leading meaningful worship, and promoting the congregation in the community. However, your interaction with your colleague can make or break you.

An important part of your relationship will depend upon how you nurture him while he is in the throes of his transition. For instance, if you need to bury his history to establish your authority and identity, others will sense this. They may be angry with you and come to his defense even if they did not appreciate him during his tenure with the congregation. If, on the other hand, you are able to close the chapter on his contributions to the history of the congregation with an exclamation point, and even carry his honor and vision into the opening pages of this new chapter, people will praise you for your kindness to someone they love and admire. References to your predecessor's prior work and the respectful acknowledgment of his presence, invitations to participate in some worship services and sacred moments, or teach a class, will all be to your credit. Since we fully believe that there is more than enough work in a congregation for one pastor, allowing your predecessor to officiate at weddings and funerals for long-standing members will only heighten their regard for you and help you manage the workload. In some situations, it is more appropriate to co-officiate, but if you do not do so it will always be important to make the appropriate condolence calls or write letters of congratulations for happy occasions. To cement your role does not mean that you have to be at every event in the congregation when you first arrive. The fact that you honor your predecessor and understand the needs of your congregants to connect with someone beloved and familiar at a sacred moment (rather than having a "stranger") will stand you in good stead. With time you will develop your own cadre of followers.

Understand that your predecessor is going through a grieving experience. He is suddenly thrown into a tizzy as he tries to figure out his new roles in life and what he is going to do with his free time. He is confronted with trying to find new meaning in his encore years after having lived a very consequential existence. It is very possible that he never gave a lot of thought to these questions before his retirement date. Maybe he never dove into the existential question of what will give fulfillment to this next stage. You need to know that this is a difficult, slow process. He will experience moments of sadness and grief, as well as the gradual realization of the need to develop a new rhythm of life. You and he are both in a learning curve: he trying to discover a new life, you trying to insert yourself into his former position. Realize that this pastor, who served the congregation with devotion and love for many years, is now experiencing an emotional roller coaster. If you can acknowledge this and allow him to share some things that he cannot share with anyone else then you will have a chance to create an ally for life. If we are instructed to *Do unto others as you would have them do unto you,* then we are obligated to project into the future and ask, "How would I like a successor to treat me someday?" This will give you some insight as to how you can be compassionate and caring toward this colleague. But perhaps the best advice is to arrange time for meaningful conversation(s) with your predecessor; such exchanges will not only reveal critical thoughts and feelings but will be for a healthy relationship.

I share with you what my predecessor wrote about me with the dream that you could create such a relationship with yours:

> The second [blessing] has been having a successor, as I have in Rabbi Daniel Roberts, who treats me with such graciousness, recognition and affection that he couldn't do more if he were my own son. From the beginning of our relationship, when he came as my assistant seventeen years ago, we have been treating each other without rabbinical rank or rancor. He was a rabbi and I was a rabbi, and any member was free to ask him or me or both to officiate in a religious event. He has continued that attitude now that he is the senior. It is most heart-warming to have the human rules of love transcend the suggested Conference guidelines, the cold, who-ranks-first way in which rabbis are to relate to each other in the same temple. It is heartwarming for the congregation, as well. (Green, 1988)

Your predecessor has a wealth of knowledge not only about the history of the congregation and its individual members, but about which programs have worked in the past or failed and why. He knows the staff, how best to interact with them, and who to watch out for because they have an agenda. A retired friend commented that he could have helped his successor in dealing with a staff member who was very difficult. "It was not for me to fix it," he said,

> I didn't want him to think that I was interfering so I waited for him to come to me and perhaps we could have had a heart to heart conversation about anything. All our conversations were always superficial. I wanted to be helpful yet I was feeling my way through the relationship. I would have liked to have been asked to continue contributing to the congregation but I did not want to impose myself. (Personal communication)

You, as the heir, have to make the effort to enlist your predecessor's help if you want it. One meeting or one lunch will not build the relationship. Although we know that you are overwhelmed at the outset with cultivating many other relationships, this is one bond you will want to solidify through regularly scheduled conversations. If possible, assuming your predecessor is still local, share some of your thoughts for the congregation and solicit reactions. You do not necessarily have to accept every piece of advice that is offered. You can choose to do it *your way*, but at least you have brought him into your confidence and you are aware of some potential pitfalls. This would be a good time to fill him in on the NETMA problem (Nobody Ever Tells Me Anything) by bringing him up to date on people in the congregation. Likewise, he could fill you in on what he is hearing that no one else would tell you to your face. Most emeriti simply want to be kept in the loop, for they miss knowing what is happening to people with whom they were once close. For the most part, as retirees, they don't want to do things on a regular basis but they do want to be helpful to the congregation and therefore to you. They don't want to be obligated with being at a certain place at a certain time, but every once in a while they feel compelled to reach out to some members just to show they still care.

You should look at your predecessor's current involvement with members as reinforcement. If your predecessor still lives in the area, his contacts can be helpful, but he needs to make sure that his outreach is perceived as on behalf of both of you. We suggest that you spend some time crafting a clergy contract that would define what responsibilities you would see within his purview and how you would like him to be accountable to you about these activities. Is an email sufficient, a phone call, or a note? Remember that this is the first time in a long while that your predecessor has been held responsible to another clergy and will sometimes be forgetful, especially if he has created a busy life. This may require you to be patient and understanding and to gently remind him of his agreement with you.

Lonely Moments

Bridges (2009) also reminds us that the neutral zone is a lonely place. Your congregants may feel isolated, especially if they don't understand why they are not as comfortable in the church as they once were. For the most part, no one has told them about the grief they might endure. They thought mourning was only for people who died, and they do not comprehend that bereavement is also about relationships that have changed. Often during bereavement, old problems resurface and old resentments spring back to life, so when you think that things are under control, a seemingly minor issue turns into a dilemma. You will likewise feel lonely. In the beginning, you do not know who your true friends are, who to trust, and you are a little suspicious about whether you are liked and accepted. You worry whether this congregation will work out for you.

Wouldn't it be nice if you had someone with whom you could share this emotional roller coaster? Then you might not feel as lonely or as anxious. Such a relationship with an older colleague who could mentor you might afford you the opportunity to get a "scouting report" and learn of the congregation's reactions to change. A predecessor has an ear to the ground that would be a shame to lose; he could be your advocate if you allow it. He can be a friend and a mentor and can offer insights about the leadership style of the congregation. How many people really understand the world of the clergy and with whom you could talk honestly? It is possible that he might not be as caring as you would like, but you will only find that out after a series of interactions and not based on first impressions when both of you are walking on eggshells. The ideal would be to have a regularly scheduled appointment every month or six weeks with your predecessor. Meet in a safe neutral environment where you can be comfortable seeking his opinion and able to confront him should you hear rumors that he is not talking positively about you and the changes you have instituted.

Your predecessor has a great deal invested in the congregation—his hopes and dreams and a lot of blood, sweat, and tears. He steps aside with dread that everything he has built will be for naught. At times he may appear morose or sad as he watches his image of the congregation being dashed by your new vision and enthusiasm. He may also envy your new vigor. It is a reminder of all the things that he had intended to do but didn't have the energy for in his waning years. He may also berate himself as he hears of your new ideas and programs and wonder why he had never thought of them himself. He may even become depressed over his own perceived inadequacies by comparison. There is a lot of grieving going on, so a little compassion and kindness can go a long way toward helping your fellow clergy adjust to a meaningful life off of the pulpit. You might ask him about some of these feelings and how they affect your relationship. He might deny them or he may relish the opportunity to talk with someone who shows understanding. Ask if there are programs or activities that he would like to do that would be helpful and nonthreatening to you. My successor asked me to continue teaching a class for seniors that I had been teaching for years before his arrival. It is a small thing, but it keeps me connected to a group of members and is seen as another offering by the congregation. On occasions when I am not available, he steps in and everyone is comfortable with the arrangement. What most predecessors desire, as you will see in the responses below, is to somehow feel that they have not been put out to pasture entirely.

When a friend retired, he handed the Torah scroll to his successor during his inauguration service and said, "I am giving you a gift and with it goes my heart." He confessed to me that underneath those words was this heartfelt sentiment:

> I am giving you a gift of 28 years of my life in this congregation. I only want you to be a good steward of it and to keep the congregation strong. I hope that you can take these words into your heart as you accept the leadership of this congregation.

Advice to Successors Given by Our Respondents

- Respect the emeritus and refuse to engage in conversations disparaging the emeritus. This should be a hallmark.
- Learn what the person you followed emphasized in their ministry and what their accomplishments were.
- Recognize the inevitable comparisons, both positive and negative, and deal with them openly and honestly.
- Become sensitive to the desires and needs of congregants in maintaining a relationship with their long-time clergy.

- Prepare yourself for some rough roads. I think it is common knowledge that when you are following a long-term pastorate, you may have an uphill climb. It is simply because there always seems to be a time of, "Well, when Pastor Perfect was here, we always had . . . "
- Be as positive as possible about the person you are following. The first pastor I followed had attempted suicide. Some wanted to condemn him, but I refused.
- Invite your emeritus to review the most significant local *minhagim* (traditions) of the congregation with regard to life-cycle ceremonies, the Sabbath, and each of the holidays. Ask questions about origins and such. The purpose would be to help the successor *know* what he's doing when making changes or innovations. In my experience, the successor dropped a number of local *minhagim* without realizing that he was doing so. He didn't ask and no one told him, so it was forgotten. If someone asked about it too late, all he could say was, "Why didn't someone tell me?"
- Do more listening than doing the first year.
- Make the congregation a partner in your activities.
- Be very careful of change that is made too quickly.
- Telephone your predecessor every couple of months for the first year and see how your predecessor is doing.

SUMMARY FOR SUCCESSORS

As a successor, you walk a very thin line between the dreams and energy you have for your new congregation and the mourning that congregants are simultaneously experiencing in the midst of their excitement at your coming to the congregation. It is a thin line between what innovations they can tolerate and which ones would be better postponed until the congregation has left the "neutral zone." You walk the tightrope of showing deference and respect to your predecessor, so you are praised for your humanity and slipping out from under his shadow. This is not an easy time for you, but the more you can communicate and work with your predecessor, the more rewarding your experience will be.

REFERENCES

Bridges, W. (2009). *Managing transitions: Making the most of change*. Philadelphia, PA: Da Capo.

Green, A. S. (1988). *If God were king: The times and words of Rabbi Alan S. Green*. Cleveland, OH: Temple Emanu El.

Harris, D. (Ed.). (2011). *Counting our losses: Reflecting on change, loss, and transition in everyday life*. New York, NY: Routledge/Taylor & Francis.

Hileman, L. (2008). The unique needs of protestant clergy families: Implications for marriage and family counseling. *Journal of Spirituality in Mental Health, 10*(2), 119–144.

Rendle, G. (1992). *Leading change in the congregation: Spiritual and organizational tools for leaders.* Lanham, MA: Rowen and Littlefield.

http://dx.doi.org/10.2190/CLEC13

CHAPTER 13

Encouraging the Other:
A Predecessor Interacts with
a Successor

Transition starts with an ending and finishes with a beginning.
(Bridges, 2009, p. 5)

It's not so much that we're afraid of change or so in love with the old ways, but it's that place in between that we fear . . . it's like being between trapezes. It's Linus when his blanket is in the dryer. There's nothing to hold on to.
Marilyn Ferguson, American Futurist

RETIRED UNDER DURESS

I am angry, hurt, and confused. I have given this congregation some of the best years of my life and thought I was doing an excellent job. Having the congregation's leadership approach me last month about determining an end date for my tenure here shocked me at first. But then my wife reminded me that in anticipation of my 65th birthday a couple of years ago, they raised the issue of my retirement, although in a much more tentative way. Now they want me out! Without much subtlety (or kindness, I might add), they pointed out the reduction in membership as more seniors are dying or moving to warmer climates and the scarcity of younger new members to take their place. They told me I have lost my spark and that my sermons seem like rehashes of things they have heard from me before. They expressed no gratitude for all I have done in the past nor any concern for what my life will be going forward. Is it any wonder that I feel so hurt?

WHO ARE YOU?

Sammy was a very religiously observant person who prayed regularly and observed all the religious laws. When his wife became ill, he diligently took care of her, doing everything to make her life as comfortable as possible. He denied himself any worldly pleasures even though his children encouraged him to continue his activities. Three times a day he went to his congregation to pray and the rest of the time was devoted to her. When his wife died, his family begged

163

him to start living again and enjoy life. So Sammy followed their counsel and bought himself a spiffy Hawaiian shirt and some white pants and matching shoes. He got a haircut and a manicure and shaved off his stubble. Then he purchased a shiny new red Corvette. Shortly after leaving the showroom with his new acquisition, he noticed a very pretty woman standing at the bus stop. He turned his head to gaze at her and wink and . . . boom! Sammy ran squarely into the back of a bus and was killed immediately. When Sammy got to heaven, he asked God, "Why would You take my life after a lifetime of prayers, religious observances, and devotion to my wife all those many years she was ill? Why now? Just as I was beginning to enjoy life again, why did You take me from this world?" God took a closer look at Sammy and hesitantly said, "Sammy? Sammy? I'm so sorry! I didn't recognize you!"

You Have Chosen Another Lover

For you, the predecessor, as much as you may hope for the ongoing success of the congregation that you worked so hard to build and grow, there is always some pain as you see how easily you can be replaced. This is a moment of cognitive dissonance. You are elated to be unburdened of the daily responsibilities but sad that people have stopped relying on your judgment and opinion. In their eyes, you have left them for another lover. You have chosen the world of retirement rather than continuing to minister to them forever. Even as they wish you well, they feel rejected and need to grieve. Even if you had a wonderful relationship, they now sense that a divorce or, at best, a separation is in process. It is possible they will say painful things to you and about you, for they are dealing with their anger at your deserting them. This chapter deals with how emeriti should conduct themselves so that the congregation will continue to blossom during its honeymoon period with a new leader. It is to everyone's benefit that the congregation continues to progress to new, albeit different heights, which deep in your heart is what you really should want to happen. As parents, we should strive to make our children independent so they have the strength and fortitude to continue with life when we pass away. The very worst thought is that our children would be too distraught to carry on without us. This would be dysfunctional parenting. Similarly our dreams as clergy should be that the congregation will continue to grow and flourish after we're gone. We can feel satisfied that we played a significant role in leading the congregation to this point and should wish them continued success.

Though you still wear the title of a clergy, your congregants do not recognize you any more as *their* clergyperson. You are not their "Sammy" who served them for so many years as their minister and caregiver. You may have put away your Sabbath attire, clerical robes, or collar, and now dress casually as a retiree. As authors, we hope that if you are still in the picture when your successor arrives, you will share this chapter on *Encouraging the Other:*

Successor to Predecessor. We suggest that the new clergy allow time for the congregation to go through transition and deal with their loss. Congregants need to know that their former pastor is being treated respectfully and fairly. Also, we suggest that he try to understand some of the psychological issues you are encountering and discuss how to build a respectful working relationship with you. We encourage you to discuss ways you can help your successor succeed.

Moses ordained Joshua and then had to stand outside the Promised Land never to enter it, but to watch Joshua succeed in a way that he never could have. Let us remind you about your conduct as a clergy emeritus so that you can continue to feel meaningfully involved in the congregation yet not allow your ghost to impair the transfer of power to your successor.

Do you want to retire or not?

Some of us really do not want to retire, at least not yet, but we were forced to submit our resignation and months later we still have not recovered from this psychological blow. Others are glad to have this phase of our lives over. Although it was somewhat rewarding, we just never really enjoyed the work, but felt financially trapped in this role until we could afford to leave. Many are physically and mentally exhausted and look forward to our encore years without all the responsibilities. No matter what situation brought about retirement, we all have to learn how to ultimately let go and not *rule from the grave.* If you have a choice about retirement, and family and friends are pushing you even though you really don't want to retire, then *don't!* You will not be fair to anyone, including your successor and the congregation. On the other hand, once you make the decision to retire, you need to set as your goal being the best emeritus you can be. You must not interfere but find other ways to keep your sense of meaning intact.

You need to postulate, "To whom does the congregation really belong: to the pastor or to the membership?" Lawrence Farris answers this question in his book, *Ten Commandments for Pastors Leaving a Congregation:*

> In spite of how we sometimes speak, we know in our heart of hearts that no congregation is "ours." Congregations are not possessions, but partnerships between a pastor and a people. At most, pastors are the stewards of their congregations, those who have been entrusted with their care, well being, and development. Remembering this important truth will allow us, in faith, to release a congregation with our blessing into other hands so that our own hands might be free and open for a new experience of faithfulness in which our spiritual growth will unfold. It is not always easy to trust that the work we began with a congregation will be continued and expanded upon by others, but trust we must.
>
> It is sometimes said that the inability to change the past is the one limitation that God shares with us. The best we can do when it comes to leaving a congregation is to bring the past to as complete and whole a conclusion as possible, so that all may rejoice in what has been good, learn from what has

not, and move freely and faithfully forward into a promising future where
God may be praised and served. (2006, p. 90)

In reality, we only occupy a chapter in the chronicle of a congregation's life,
that is, unless we want the congregation to fold when we leave. We hope we will
not be forgotten and that the deeds we performed will be part of the ongoing
growth of this institution as it lives on after we are gone. Our prayer should be
that the congregation is able to stand tall upon our shoulders as we did upon
those who came before us. As clergy, we were an important part of the growth
and vision of the congregation. To appreciate this growth, it might be helpful
for you and a group of members review old bulletins and record the progress
the congregation made under your tutelage. This process will also benefit your
successor. Then take out two pieces of paper and title one *The Next Chapter
for Me*, and the other one *The Next Chapter for the Congregation*. You might
find it hard to express your feelings and thoughts for your chapter, but you need
to put down at least a few words. Reframe your thoughts as retiring *to* something
rather than *from* something.

The chapter for the congregation is not yours to write, but will be written by
your successor and congregants in the days ahead. Just as you will benefit from
devoting thought to your future, as the current spiritual leader you can encourage
the lay leadership to engage in reflection and visioning as they search for and
work with your successor. Granted, this can be a sensitive conversation, but it
can be valuable for you both. After your years of dedicated service to this community, you have a vested interest in their continued well-being and therefore
should want them to face this transition with a clear vision of their future. Some
congregational leaders may not realize the value of this process of introspec-
tion and imagination. Even if they do, they may find it too emotionally difficult
and therefore procrastinate in doing so. Without pushing your agenda or
perspective, supporting the lay leadership as they engage in such a process can be
one of the finest parting gifts you can give them.

Negotiating the Future

Many clergy report that the hardest thing to do at the beginning of the retirement process is to negotiate their final contract. In our survey, about 50%
already had such a contract in place. This also means that 50% did not. It seems
to us that a written directive is critical for both parties so that everyone will
know what to expect. Consider this as a form of separation agreement.

You and the members of the congregation need to clarify your new title,
roles, and responsibilities, how much your salary will be, what administrative
support you will continue to receive, what activities deserve an honorarium,
and what you would be expected to do gratis. You must also put into print what
expenses the congregation might be willing to pay (see Appendix at the end of
this chapter for issues to discuss during final negotiations). Although you want

to be fair to the congregation, you have the obligation to look out for yourself and your family. Conversely, those elected to negotiate with you must protect the future of the congregation, and they cannot give the "house" away. We share this insight, which you probably already know from past dealings regarding salaries and benefits, that negotiations always produce hard feelings unless both sides can hold a win-win attitude. Reading the book, *Getting to Yes: Negotiating Agreement Without Giving In* by Roger Fisher, William L. Ury and Bruce Patton (2011) is a must for both parties involved. These particular negotiations will not only cover financial commitments and healthcare benefits but also mutual expectations regarding conduct for the next several years.

It would be helpful for each side to write down the dreams each has for this transition and come to some conclusion as to what would or would not work in the days ahead. A year in advance would not be too early to begin this process. Again, both sides need to feel the agreement is fair and satisfied that each won something.

Down the line you will want to share this document of dreams as to your role with your successor and get his reaction and input. Effectively, he will be your new boss and so he too has to be a winner. After the two of you work out your relationship, create a contract that you can jointly present to the congregation's leadership demonstrating your combined effort.

Remember that Moses turned over the leadership of the people to Joshua, who did not have Moses' wisdom nor his strength of character. However, Joshua possessed many skills that Moses lacked. As we confront retirement, it is our obligation to stand aside and let others lead and craft their Promised Land. The congregation's next chapter will be written by the pens of others. So if you are no longer to be Moses, perhaps you can take on the role of Aaron to the new pastor. Every Moses needs a good Aaron, one who understands that he is not the leader but only the ritual subordinate and helper.

We all fear that if our successor does well, congregants might think that we either skated through our final years or that we were not quite as brilliant as they once thought we were. We quickly forget that our successor was chosen because he has different strengths for a different time in the life of the congregation. Often congregants will delude themselves that the new pastor will both embody your strengths and bring many new abilities and ideas to their ministry. That generally is impossible. You will hear of new and inventive things brought to the congregation, even as some of the once-cherished programs of yours have fallen away. You will watch the congregation adapt and become loyal to their new pastor, but you must resist allowing jealousy to engulf you.

Ultimately, the success of the congregation and its new spiritual leader is highly dependent on your commitment as the emeritus to support the new pastor in every way possible. This means that though you would do things differently, you must always be loyal and complimentary of your successor, even when people complain about him. Anything less will not speak well of you. As a predecessor, you have to decide which is more important, the continued success of the institution you helped build or your own ego. If it is the former, put away your sense of self and assist your successor to achieve. If you let your remorse and ego get in the way, others will resent you, and both you and the institution you loved will falter. You will leave on a negative note that people will long remember. Of course, your successor could fail along with your dreams for the congregation. Encourage your successor and the congregation to try new innovations so even if they were to fail, everyone will have learned something from it and will grow closer together.

One of the hardest things you will have to learn is "new tricks" after years of being independent and not having to share with anyone else. In fact, you have been carefully taught about confidentialities, and you may need to learn how to convey such knowledge to your successor. Your duty is to share with him so that he can meet congregants' immediate needs. This is crucial to your relationship, but even more so for the sake of the congregants and the institution as a whole. You are going to have to work very diligently, and you may need to begin by oversharing just to get in the habit. You may feel upset that your successor is not telling you enough and that you have to hear some of the information from your old reliable sources. Understand that he is overwhelmed with the newness of it all. He is meeting new people, trying to remember names, thinking about plans for the congregation, adapting to a new job as well as trying to find meaningful time with his family and getting them acclimated to a new environment. He is in turmoil with his own disenfranchised grief for the world he knew and has left behind. Now he is dealing with the tumult of all that he has yet to learn.

So the question is raised again. Do you want to retire or not? If you were forced out of the congregation, then try to leave in a way so that they will remember your strengths, not your bitter feelings. This will also advance the probability of your receiving a good recommendation if you should ever need one. Later you can deal with your anger and resentment with a counselor, but try to be appreciative for all the years your congregation welcomed you into their lives and paid your salary. If you are ready to retire and welcome it, then you must constantly remind yourself, *I cannot rule from the grave. My successor deserves better.* You have to decide that the future of the congregation is no longer in your control nor is it your responsibility. No matter what decisions the congregation makes with their new leader, they don't want to have to meet your expectations. While you may not get a vote in their decision making, there may be some situations where your input might be helpful. You might want to find a way to respectfully share your opinion, but don't be surprised if they explain to you that you don't know all the details and discount your input.

Be realistic. It is time to move on. Expend your energy in areas that will be more productive and rewarding to you than trying to resurrect what once was. If you are no longer in the community, it might be easier for you, but leaving the community carries its own dilemmas (see Chapter 8). Former congregants will still seek you out, asking you to participate in life-cycle events or just wanting to be friends. If you remain in the community, then you have the advantage of only having to make minor adjustments to your surroundings, but you will have to work much harder with your colleague to secure a warm and caring relationship.

Let's listen to some of our respondents:

- The first interim pastor was threatened by me, but didn't stay long. The last two were fine. One was actually very affirming and did much to help the relationship between my former congregation and myself, making me minister emeritus of church. I never expected this.
- The interim who followed me had been a friend and colleague. But he now seemed rigid in terms of making sure I kept my distance (I still live in the same town as the church I served). I think he felt both appreciative of my ministry and a bit threatened by my presence. The church has just called a full-time pastor and the interim pastor is now gone. I'm trying to be careful about not trespassing beyond the necessary boundaries. He is respectful and friendly to me.
- He has been a complete mensch and a respectful colleague. He is fine with my officiating life-cycle ceremonies as long as I notify him.
- Very cordial and amicable. I followed my predecessor's example of being visible, but not audible. I would do some things differently, but I had my turn and now it's his turn.
- The new pastor asked me to be active in the church and to resume teaching the adult class I had taught for years. After about 8 months, the new pastor asked me to serve on the staff part time, and I have for the last 4 years. I did so with the understanding that I did not want pay, that I didn't have to go to a lot of meetings, and that I was free to be gone when I wanted to. It seems to be working out fine. We are not buddies, but have a good relationship.
- His first comment to me was that he expected me to abide by my agreement not to have anything to do with the congregation. My comment to him was I would abide by my agreement, but that I could not break friendships that had been established during my 18 years as their friend. I would not become involved in the ongoing work of the church or make comments as to what the church was doing or how it was doing.
- We are just very different people. My sense of religious is very different from his, as well as from many of my colleagues whose ministrations I find too "God-oriented." I don't go to services that much anymore.
- I feel no need to be involved in the congregation I served for 39 years. That was then, now is now.
- This is about my present successor. It helps a lot that we like each other. We've had some long talks and I believe we understand each other. I'm extra-careful not to compete, and say only positive things. Fortunately, there

are lots of positive things to say. He is publicly and privately respectful to me and understands that I want him to succeed. He uses me as a resource, but certainly doesn't need me to do his job. My experience was more useful to him at the start. Now he's putting his own stamp on things, as he should. He seems happy when I can help in some way. I love being a mentor, too.

- The interim that succeeded for one year treated me wonderfully and his successor has also treated me wonderfully. I have tried to be helpful when called upon, but to stay out of their way. I think we are all in a good place now.
- I had expected he would call occasionally for information or for advice or support. Instead, he acted as if I did not exist except superficially when I was around.
- The new rabbi does email occasionally for information or an opinion. I try to be helpful, but once or twice, I suggested that a discussion with the Board would be better than a response from the previous rabbi.
- She consulted on unfinished business and situations during her first year, is always delighted to see me when I (rarely) show up, and invited and appreciated my participation in her installation. On the other hand, she never inquired as to whether I would like to be an occasional teaching or preaching resource to the congregation.
- The people are still in positions to look at us as if looking at a history book.
- Would have appreciated more proactive reaching out to me, advice seeking, sharing what is happening, etc. Most contact (occasional lunch, which is always cordial) is initiated by me. Calls come the other way only when the rabbi needs a favor. Over the years there were several incidents involving me which were particularly insensitive and hurtful.
- I kind of expected it would not be totally wonderful, since the new pastor has his hands full with a large congregation and only got larger as some other nearby Catholic churches closed, and members of those churches came to his congregation. I deal only with the realities in this matter, and dreams are not much in the picture. Ideally there would have been a mentoring period with overlap, but we have not gotten that far yet as a church. I surely do not lose any sleep over this. I am happy in what I am now involved with.
- I would have liked a friendly, cooperative relationship. It would have been nice to have a colleague with whom I could engage in conversation and even study. I've come to feel somewhat responsible for the congregation's poor choice of my successor. I tried to scrupulously abide by the guidelines of the CCAR [Central Conference of American Rabbis] and URJ [Union for Reform Judaism] by not being involved at all in the selection process. In retrospect I think I could have helped the lay leadership understand what questions they should be asking and how they ought to conduct the search process though staying out of the actual choice. I think they operated with a regrettable ignorance.

Advice to others:

- For years I took note of how older colleagues were managing the role of emeritus. I tried to learn from both the positive, admirable examples and from the negative examples. I made a list for myself of "do's" and "don'ts." Best advice I repeatedly gave myself —or my wife reminded me: *"It's not 'your' congregation, and it never really was."*
- I would say (as I did), I don't want to skew your perceptions and judgments about the situation or the people, so I don't want to give advice or alerts that may bias your view, but I'm available for consultation about situations and people on the scene, and if you would *want* an advance briefing now, so "you'll know what you're walking into," I'm glad to do it. But first you tell me how you see the situation and how you perceive the people, and we can have a conversation around that, if you like.
- I wouldn't give him that kind of advice unless he asks. I'd sit down and explain what I personally need out of this relationship and clarify what he needs or wants from me. Since we're in the community, my presence is a given for many events. He knows I'm not going to disappear, and I know I'm not centerstage any more. (And by now, I've realized that I don't need to be there anywhere near as much as I used to.)
- If possible, a respectful relationship with your predecessor will in the long run strengthen your position and your security. Both successor and predecessor stand to benefit from mutual respect—and, most of all, the congregation will benefit.
- Ego—if your successor is at least as good as you were, your work will continue—that should stroke your ego more than the "nice" things that people say to you. Enhance the work of your successor and never allow a conversation where they are criticized.
- When people spoke to me and criticized my successor, I did my best to be very noncommittal.
- It is important for the emeritus to know that he is no longer the person in charge. I believe some emeriti find difficulty in accepting this. My successor has done a few things that I did not do in my tenure, but it is his place not mine. I can accept it, because I recognize that times have changed.
- I believe I handled leaving the church very well and prepared them for the future. What I didn't do so well was prepare myself for the stark break it meant for me. I did have "work" in terms of a denominational position and teaching at the divinity school. But I had no idea how much I would miss the daily encounter with so many wonderful people. I think I was so concerned that I left the church well, that I didn't consider how I would feel. It took me awhile to get back on my feet.
- I don't know that I would have done anything differently. I did find that people are sneakier than I expected about wanting to "hang on to me,"

and about finding ways to do that—asking me to conduct a funeral or a wedding, etc., *and* implying they had received permission of my successor to invite me, when that was not the case. I would tell anyone in transition to be especially wary—downright cynical—about that. Be on the lookout for that sort of thing.

- I think you need to plan carefully for retirement. Not only is the financial important but even more the emotional and spiritual side. I made a list of things I would like to try in retirement, a bucket list if you will. I do not know where it is but I remember there were more than 100 things on the list. Some of them I have tried and decided they were not for me, others I never tried, and some of them involve me now. I try to be supportive of my successors but do keep in touch on a more or less regular basis. I think that I have been and continue to be a good emeritus and mentor.

Summary for Predecessors

"Every ending has a new beginning," has to be one's philosophy as a predecessor. Endings are tough, but we have to learn to live with them even though we wish that we could hang on to the world that was. We are best served by investing our time and energy in new beginnings. While mourning the past releases the image of who we once were, now we can dream about the person we would like to become. For those who remain in the same city as their former congregation, the task is rewarding if you can communicate well with your successor. You must learn to keep your opinions to yourself when well-intended congregants flatter you, telling you how much they miss you and wishing that you were still their clergy. You must be the encourager of the next generation and the one to be the mentor. It is a new beginning as you now watch from the sidelines with great hope that this congregation to which you have given so much of your life will continue to grow and remain a strong and vibrant reflection of yours and your predecessor's years of devotion to its well-being.

APPENDIX

Things to think about for Final Contract

- Relevant dates
  - End of commitments to congregation
  - Notification to board/leadership
  - Notification to congregation
- Compensation
  - Severance "bonus" payment?
  - Ongoing retirement payments?
  - Compensation for health care, conference attendance, professional dues, travel, etc.?

- – Conditions for continuation/termination of any of above for surviving spouse
- • Title
- • Responsibilities/authorities (and limitations/exclusions)
- • Office/study in congregation and administrative support if any
- • Farewell celebration(s) and gift

REFERENCES

Farris, L. W. (2006). *Ten commandments for pastors leaving a congregation.* Grand Rapids, MI: William B. Eerdmans.

Bridges, W. (2009). *Meaning transitions: Making the most of change.* Philadelphia, PA: Da Capo.

Farris, L. W. *Ten commandments for pastors leaving a congregation.* Grand Rapids, MI: William B. Eerdmans.

Fisher, R., Ury, W. L., & Patton, B. (2011). *Getting to yes: Negotiating agreement without giving in.* London, UK: Penguin Books.

Furgenson, M. http://www.goodreads.com/quotes/24386-it-s-not-so-much-that-we-re-afraid-of-change-or

PART IV

CONCLUSION

http://dx.doi.org/10.2190/CLEC14

CHAPTER 14

Every Ending a New Beginning

The secret to a rich life is to have more beginnings than endings.

Dave Weinbaum (2013)

Devote yourself to loving others, devote yourself to your community around you and devote yourself to creating something that gives you purpose and meaning.

Tuesdays With Morrie, Mitch Albom (1997)

You might observe that we did not begin this chapter with a humorous quip, for retirement and aging are not funny. Ecclesiastes 3:4 reminds us that there is *a time to mourn, and a time to dance*. Well, retirement is a time when both occur simultaneously, for when we leave the world that has defined us and has been part of our identity for most of our adult lives, we must pass through the process of grief. There will be ups and downs in the months ahead just as there is when we lose a significant person or even a beloved pet. It will be filled with the work of grieving that must be done in order to take us fully into the next stage of our lives. Without taking time out to grieve we risk getting stuck in our former world, longing for it to return.

At the same time, it will be filled with many, many opportunities. Now that we are unencumbered by daily responsibilities, we can *dance with new "partners,"* for we are now liberated to pursue the varied interests and talents we buried over the years or had never even considered for lack of time or energy. There are now myriad opportunities to find new and meaningful activities that will allow you to continue to impact the world and fulfill your needs. You have the blessing of choice: you can get out there and taste the world or just sit around playing computer games and napping in front of the television. They say that old age is not for sissies. Well, neither is retirement. As indicated time after time in this book, a door in your life has closed; but there is a new one waiting to be opened. On the other side of that new door awaits another life filled with a vast array of possibilities—ones that could even take a retired clergyperson like you far away from the world of congregational or organizational life. Perhaps it could bring you even closer to God through self-awareness and service to humanity.

Rather than thinking of yourself as a *stone that was cast away*, retirement is an opportunity for you to become one of those bricks that are part of a magnificent and meaningful edifice. You still have much to contribute and to discover. Even in the latter years of your life, you have the potential to build a legacy for your family and your community. This next period is a time to get in touch with yourself, discover who you really are at this stage in your life, find your talents and develop new interests—all of which might even lead you closer to God. Stephen Covey writes in his book *The 8th Habit*, "If you want to die early, retire to golf and fishing, and sit around swallowing prescriptions and occasionally seeing your grandkids" (2004). Rabbi Rami M. Shapiro, PhD, wrote a beautiful poem entitled *Gates* (1978–1988, p. 79), which succinctly reminds us that moving on is a human experience:

> At each moment of our lives
> we encounter gates behind which beckon the unknown.
> We have little choice but to enter,
> and, as we do,
> the gates swing shut behind us.
> We can never go back.
> The known, the comfortable, the safe
> all these are in the past.
> Only the unknown, the dangerous,
> the mysterious and the terrifying lay ahead.
> Moving on makes us human,
> do so lightly and at peace makes us divine.

How does one move on *lightly and at peace*? Just as with the death of a loved one, at the time of retirement one must take time out to lament and reconcile the loss of mission and purpose, as well as the various people you worked with along the way and adjust to life without these "others." Just as with the loss of a loved one, one must bend with the breeze to the winds of loneliness and start over again without them. Perhaps one way to assist you in moving on "lightly and at peace" in retirement is to get in touch with yourself both spiritually and emotionally, as suggested in Chapters 6 and 7.

One of the great rabbis asked the question, *Who is rich?* His answer was, *He who is happy with his lot!* To be happy with your lot in life, you need to be able to recognize the many blessings you encounter day after day and minute by minute. One way to do this would be to engage in daily prayer or meditation that calls your attention to the blessings God has showered upon you. Then record them in a journal each day and periodically review them so as to remind yourself how truly blessed you are just to be alive. Listing them day in and day out gives you a whole new attitude about life. Rather than feeling unappreciated and unproductive, use your skills and experience to contribute to your community and count your blessings. "Civic engagement is the health club of the new millennium," says Tom Sander (2007), executive director of the Saguaro Seminar at Harvard University, which promotes social involvement. Studies show that acquiring fresh skills later in life helps ward off depression and may even reduce the likelihood of dementia. These will help make you feel needed and necessary.

As indicated so many times before in this book, there is a wealth of possibilities and opportunities awaiting you in the world of retirement. The new reality of life is that the world is no longer the same old environment you once knew. Like the Hebrews in the desert, scrounging for food after fleeing from slavery, they forgot the horrors of their treatment and instead reminisced about the *fish, which we were wont to eat in Egypt for naught; the cucumbers and the melons, and the leeks* (Numbers 11:5). And they clamored to return. At this moment of transition, one needs to recall that Moses did not spend his whole life in the palace of Pharaoh. It was only after he was forced to flee and endure the new world of being a shepherd that he encountered the burning bush and set off on his new and true mission of life. Let us not forget that the Israelites had to spend many days wandering in the desert purposeless until suddenly from afar they viewed the great mountain of the Lord. Even then it was only a mountain until Moses ascended and there encountered God. Upon his descent, he informed the people that they were about to witness God's presence in their midst. The reality of what is ahead of us is that each of us will have to march in our own personal desert until we arrive at our own Mt. Sinai. And even after that, like unto the Children of Israel, there will be more adventures in the desert until we reach our *Promised Land*, a new land and a new life of purpose, meaning, and joy.

Walter L. Hays said, "Opportunity doesn't knock at the door; she answers when you knock" (Anthony & Boersma, 2007, p. 90). We know that some of us may not be ready to do much knocking, for the new life is just beginning. Initially, you may just want to kick off your shoes, put your feet up and relax, enjoying just getting away from the pressure of a lifetime of work or licking your wounds after being forced into retirement. But ultimately, you need to start thinking about what the future holds for you. Yes, take your sabbatical. Like the ancient Hebrews, revel in your freedom until the drudgery of putting one foot in front of the other in the desert sand begins to wear you down, especially if you have no idea where you are going and no spirituality to nourish you. Imagine how different the world must have seemed to the Children of Israel after their Mt. Sinai experience. Yes, there were many, as indicated above, who looked back longingly to what they thought they had for free, but the majority had a dream of freedom and of reaching a land flowing with milk and honey and an entirely new role to play in the world.

We, the authors, know that your new mission is a personal one. We can only suggest what doors you might want to open (see Appendix I), but there are innumerable possibilities out there, geared to your particular talents, interests, and likings. Our intent is simply to encourage you not to think of retirement as a hiatus from life but instead as a wonderful opportunity for discovery, for new adventures, for the reward that comes from hard work by contributing in unique ways that you never would have been able to do before or even thought of doing while you were tethered to the world of work.

We close this book by suggesting that you go online and read the poem *Life is a Journey* (n.d.), written by Rabbi Alvin Fine, which begins "Birth is a beginning and death a destination" and reminds us that life is really a journey with a victory in just making the journey. Yes, life is a sacred pilgrimage, and our adventure is still ongoing in this next stage of life. Enjoy it to its fullest.

REFERENCES

Albom, M. (1997). *Tuesdays with Morrie.* New York, NY: Doubleday.

Anthony, M. J., & Boersma, M. (2007). *Moving on moving forward: A guide for pastors in transition.* Grand Rapids, MI : Zondervan.

Covey, S. (2004). *The 8th habit: From effectiveness to greatness.* New York, NY: Simon & Schuster.

Fine, A. (n.d.). *Life is a journey.* Retrieved from http://home.earthlink.net/~chavele/lifeis.html

Sander, T. (2007). *Forum Magazine* JANUARY/FEBRUARY 2007 URL http://www.hks.harvard.edu/saguaro/pdfs/sanderForumJan07.pdf

Shapiro, R. R. (1978-1988). *Tangents: Selected poems.* Miami, FL: ENR Wordsmith.

Weinbaum, D. (2013, April 19). The secret to a rich life is to have more beginnings than endings. *Jewish World Review.* Retrieved from http://www.jewishworldreview.com/dave/weinbaum041913.php3

Other Resources

Opportunity doesn't knock at the door; she answers when you knock.
                                        Walter L. Hays (Anthony, 2007, p. 90)

Suggested Websites to Visit

Daring Strategy to Protect Your Nest Egg (for those retiring) Michael Kitces, Bottom Line Personal, Vol. 35, #4, February 15, 2014, pp. 7–8. Excellent article on how to approach the financial concept of retirement www. bottomlinepublications.com

Age Wave—Age Wave is the nation's foremost thought leader on population aging and its profound business, social, healthcare, financial, workforce and cultural implications. www. Agewave.com

Kinds of Activities for the Elderly found on: www.eHow.com

Looking for a job go to. www.retirementjobs.com/

Got 10 good years left . . . why not use them to help other people?—Look at the Advanced Leadership Program at Harvard University and then help design such a program at your local university

Living in the Blue Zone—live longer when you have meaning and also social connections. Check out www.bluezone.com

See how work—even volunteer work can extend your life. See: www. DrEddyClinic.com

Be a Tutor to help improve literacy for students in kindergarten through third grade. Check: AARP and Experience Corps, a national leader in engaging older adult tutors to. Call 1-888-687-2277 or go to www.aarp.org/ experiencecorps

Learn a new skill and even get paid for it. Look at Civic Ventures: www.encore.org

Be a Counselor, and offer advice to business owners and potential owners. Go to: www.score.com

Be a Forest Grandparent go www.capbook.org/

Want other suggestions go to: www.encore.org/work/get_started_guide
   – Studies show that acquiring fresh skills later in life helps ward off depression and may reduce the likelihood of dementia

Ethical Wills

Maybe now is the time to start an ethical will. See the book, *So Your Values May Live,* by Jack Reimer and also, Dr. Barry Baines, *Ethical Wills: Putting Your Values on Paper*. Resources for creating an ethical will:

www.ethicalwill.com

www.tinyurl.com/ethicalwills

www.thelegacycenter.net

www.tinyurl/moreethicalwills

Clergy Retirement References

Anthony, M. J., & Boersma, M. (2007). *Moving on, moving forward: A guide for pastors in transition*. Grand Rapid, MI: Zondervan.

Clayton, P. (2008). *Called for life: Finding meaning in retirement*. Herndon, VA: Alban Institute.

Farris, L. W. (2006). *Ten Commandments for pastors leaving a congregation*. Grand Rapid, MI: William B. Eerdmans.

Halaas, G. W. (2005). *Clergy, retirement and wholeness: Looking forward to the third age*. Herndon, VA: Alban Institute.

Lindberg, M. C. (2012). *The graceful exit: A pastor's journey from good-bye to hello*. Herndon, VA: Alban Institute.

Marcuson, M. J. (2009). *Leaders who last: Sustaining yourself and your ministry*. New York, NY: Seabury Books of Church.

Mead, L. B. (2005). *A change of pastors . . . and how it affects change in the congregation*. Herndon, VA: Alban Institute.

Schoenberg, E. S. (2004). *Eit Ratzon: The theory and practice of transition*. Rabbinical Assembly Joint Commission on Rabbinic Placement.

Weese, C., & Crabtree, J. R. (2004). *The elephant in the boardroom: Speaking the unspoken about pastoral transitions*. San Francisco, CA: Jossey-Bass Leadership Network.

White, E. A. (1990). *Saying goodbye: A time of growth for congregations and pastors*. Herndon, VA: Alban Institute.

Generic Retirement References

Astor, B. (2013). *Roadmap to the rest of your life: Smart choices about money, health, work, lifestyle and pursuing your dreams*. New York, NY: John Wiley & Sons.

Bolles, R. N. (1982). *What color is your parachute?* Berkeley, CA: Ten Speed.

Brown, E. (2013). *Happier endings: A meditation on life and death*. New York, NY: Simon & Schuster.

Davis, S., & Handschin, B. (1998). *Reinventing yourself: Life planning after 50 using the strong and the MBTI*. Palo Alto, CA: Consulting Psychologists.

Freedman, M. (2007). *Encore: Finding work that matters in the second half of life.* New York, NY: Public Affairs.

Freedman, M. (2011). *The big shift: Navigating the new stage beyond midlife.* New York, NY: Public Affairs.

Hansen, R. J., & Haas, J. P. (2010). *Shaping a life of significance for retirement.* Nashville, TN: Upper Room.

Hinden, S. (2006). *How to retire happy: The 12 most important decisions you must make before you retire.* New York, NY: McGraw-Hill.

Koenig, H. G. (2002). *Purpose and power in retirement: New opportunities for meaning and significance.* Philadelphia, PA: Templeton Press.

Kotre, J. (1999). *Make it count: How to generate a legacy that gives meaning to your life.* New York, NY: Free Press.

Lloyd, M. (2009). *Super-charged retirement: Ditch the rocking chair, trash the remote, and do what you love.* University Place, WA: Hankfritz.

Merrill Lynch. (2013, May). *Americans' perspectives on new retirement realities and the longevity bonus.* Merrill Lynch retirement study conducted in partnership with Age Wave. Bank of America.

Nelson, J. E., & Bolles, R. N. (2010). *What color is your parachute for retirement?: Planning a prosperous, healthy, & happy future* (2nd ed.). Berkeley, CA: Ten Speed.

Newman, R. (2012). *Rebounders: How winners pivot from setback to success.* New York, NY: Ballantine.

Pauley, J. (2014). *Your life calling: Reimagining the rest of your life.* New York, NY: Simon & Shuster.

Roiter, B. (2008). *Beyond work: How accomplished people retire successfully.* New York, NY: John Wiley & Sons.

Rosenwald, P., & Wendell, L. M. (2013). *When leaders leave: A new perspective on leadership change.* Makeshift.

Schlossberg, N. K. (2004). *Retire smart, retire happy: Finding your true path in life.* Washington, DC: American Psychological Association.

Schlossberg, N. K. (2009). *Revitalizing retirement: Reshaping your identity, relationships, and purpose.* Washington, DC: American Psychological Association.

Sedlar, J., & Miners, R. (2007). *Don't retire, REWIRE.* Indianapolis, IN: Alpha.

Stone, M., & Stone, H. (2002). *Too young to retire: 101 ways to start the rest of your life.* New York, NY: Plume.

Taylor, R. K., & Mintzer, D. (2011). *The couple's retirement puzzle.* Waltham, MA: Lincoln Street Press.

Transition Network & Gail Rentsch. (2008). *Smart women don't retire—They break free.* New York, NY: Springboard.

Wang, M., Henkens, K., & van Solinge, H. (2011). Retirement adjustment: A review of theoretical & empirical advancements. *American Psychologist, 66*(3), 204–213.

Wang, M., & Shultz, K. S. (2010). Employee retirement: A review and recommendations for future investigations. *Journal of Management, 36,* 172–206.

Warren, R. (2002). *The purpose driven life.* Grand Rapid, MI: Zondervan.

Zelinski, E. J. (2009). *The joy of not working: A book for the retired, unemployed and overworked.* Edmonton, Alberta, Canada: VIP.

Zelinski, E. J. (2011). *How to retire happy, wild, and free: Retirement advice you won't get from your financial advisor.* Edmonton, Alberta, Canada: VIP.

Organizational References

Bookman, T., & Kahn, W. (2007). *This house we build: Lessons for healthy synagogues and the people who dwell there.* Herndon, VA: Alban Institute.

Bridges, W. (2003). *Managing transitions: Making the most of change* (2nd ed.). Cambridge, MA: Da Capo.

Bridges, W. (2004). *Transitions: Making sense of life's changes* (2nd ed.). Cambridge, MA: Da Capo.

Cooper rider, D. L., Whitney, D., & Stavros, J. M. (2008). *Appreciative inquiry handbook for leaders of change.* Brunswick, OH: Crown Custom/ Berrett-Koehler.

Lewis, S., Passmore, J., & Cantore, S. (2008). *Appreciative inquiry for change management: Using AI to facilitate organizational development.* Philadelphia, PA: Kogan Page.

The Questionnaire: Survey

We are very appreciative to you for taking the time to share your story about your retirement experience. This information will be very helpful to others as they travel the journey from being fully employed to the new rhythm of being in the retirement adventure.

Although the survey is lengthy please try to complete as much as possible, especially the last page. Since this is not a scientific survey you can stop when necessary. In addition there are several pages that are possible to skip.

We remind you that all answers remain strictly confidential and that we would appreciate as much clarification of your experience as you are willing to share.

Daniel Roberts, Rabbi, Thanatologist
Michael Freidman, Psychologist, Coach

1. How long ago did you retire from your full time position?
   o 1-2 years
   o 3-4 years
   o 5-10 years
   o over 10 years
   o Planning on retiring within the next 2 years
   Other (please specify) _____

2. Age when retired/planning to retire?
   o 55-61
   o 62-64
   o 65-66
   o 67-69
   o 70+

3. What was the process leading to your retirement and/or planning to retire? (choose all that are appropriate)
   o I chose to retire and I set my own date for retirement
   o I was asked to retire, the congregation chose the date
   o I planned on retiring in the future but the congregation determined the date
   o I initiated the retirement process and it went the way I expected
   o I initiated the retirement process but I did not expect the Board of Trustees to react the way it did (please explain below)
   o I am still planning to retire but have not announced it yet
   o I have not thought about retiring but I am hearing grumblings that I should
   Other (please specify) _____

4. What were the factors that led you to choose to retire or be asked to retire? (check all that apply)
   o Age
   o Health issues
   o Budget of the congregation
   o Conditions in the congregation suggested that it was time for me to move on
   o I could financially afford to
   o I was 'burned out' and tired of daily and weekly preparations
   o I was 'compassionately fatigued' and congregational life was getting difficult
   o The congregation desired to have another Clergy person (i.e., younger, different, etc.)
   o The congregation/organization has a required age for clergy to retire
   o The congregation/organization suggested I move to another congregation and I decided that this was my last move
   o I was looking for a new challenge
   o I wanted to travel and do other things while I still could
   o I wanted to spend more time with my family
   o I wanted to investigate new possibilities in my life
   o I wanted to pursue new educational opportunities
   o I wanted to move to a new community
   Other please specify _____
   We would like to know about your final moments in the congregation. (if you are still planning on retiring please skip to page 8)

5. Do you have a have a formal retirement agreement
   o Yes
   o No
   o Not yet retired
   If yes, can you share some of the details in it (i.e., process, how accomplished, terms, etc.)
   _____
   _____

6. How would you have liked your retirement process to have been handled differently? (e.g. with the board of trustees, the congregation as a whole, the announcement of your retirement, etc.)
   o It was fine the way it was
   o I was unhappy with the process
   Please elaborate on your experience: _____

   _____

7. Share with us some of the things that brought you real joy or real sadness at your final event (i.e., the final service, letters received, saying good bye, presents received or not received, the tributes, etc.).

   _____
   _____

8. Tell us about the experiences of closing your office. (check all that apply)
   o It was emotionally upsetting and draining for me
   o It hardly phased me
   o I was delighted to be closing this chapter of my life
   o I was swamped with memories
   o I had great difficulty deciding what to keep and what to throw away
   o I became angry
   o I had difficulty saying my last goodbyes to my co-workers
   o It hurt emotionally when I closed the doors for the the last time
   o I felt relief that the moment was finally over and I will be able to start a new chapter in my life
   Other reactions and/or please clarify your checked reaction (please specify)

   _____

   Tell us about your adventures in life after your retirement.

9. What are some of the biggest adjustments you had to make after retiring? (Check all that apply)
   o What to do with my free time
   o Finding new meaning
   o Not having to go to the office every day
   o Boredom—not know what to do
   o Dealing with a health issue that occurred since retirement
   o Meeting and making new friends
   o Finding a new hobby
   o Finding the right educational venue in which to learn and/or to teach
   o Finding a good volunteer position for me
   o Finding another job/occupation
   o Not feeling needed

o Feeling that it was so easy to replace me
o Not hearing from former parishioner(s) or friend(s)
Other adjustments and/or please clarify your checked answer (please specify)

_____

_____

10. Besides financial concerns, what are some of the most pressing issues that you had to deal with in the first six months after your retirement? (Check all that apply)
   o My boredom
   o Overall feelings of depression
   o Readjusting my schedule
   o Getting used to a new rhythm of time
   o Sleeping too much
   o Readjusting home duties with partner
   o Making new friends
   o "Wasting" time and feeling OK about it
   o Too busy to think
   o Couldn't get motivated
   o Thought my hobbies would be enough but they weren't
   Other concerns and/or clarify your checked response (please specify)

_____

_____

11. Have you continued to worship at your previous congregation(s)? (Click all that apply)
   o Yes
   o No
   o If no and it was your choice, check here & elaborate below
   o If no and you were requested to stay away, check here & elaborate below
   o If you remained at the congregation, what kind of emotions and feelings did you experience sitting in the pew? (Check here & explain below)
   o If you no longer worship at your former congregation, please relate the process of finding a new spiritual home. (Check here & explain below)
   Please elaborate on your answer

_____

_____

12. After your retirement did you move from your former community?
   o Yes (go to question 13)
   o No (go to question 14)

13. If yes to question 12 please:
    Share with us some of the reasons for moving

    _____

    Share with us how it affected you emotionally

    _____

    Share with us your pleasures and/or regrets in your decision

    _____

14. Did you take another clergy position following retirement?
    o Yes; nearby (less than 20 miles)
    o Yes; far away (more than 20 miles)
    o No

15. After retirement as clergy, did you seek another form of employment?
    o Yes, a job in the secular world
    o Yes, a job in education
    o No, I tried but could not find one
    o No, I did not want another job
    o I am happy to not be working
    o Could not work due to health or other reasons
    Other (please specify)

    _____

    Tell us about your partner's reaction (if you do not have a partner, please skip to the next section)

    _____

16. To what degree was your partner involved in the following decisions and planning for your retirement?

    When to retire

Highly	Appropriately	Indifferent	Not Involved at all	Not Applicable
o	o	o	o	o

    Financial planning for life in retirement

Highly	Appropriately	Indifferent	Not Involved at all	Not Applicable
o	o	o	o	o

    Where to live

Highly	Appropriately	Indifferent	Not Involved at all	Not Applicable
o	o	o	o	o

What congregation to join

Highly   Appropriately   Indifferent   Not Involved at all   Not Applicable

o   o   o   o   o

Whether or not to leave the community

Highly   Appropriately   Indifferent   Not Involved at all   Not Applicable

o   o   o   o   o

The final retirement ceremonies

Highly   Appropriately   Indifferent   Not Involved at all   Not Applicable

o   o   o   o   o

Other choices partner highly involved in (please specify)

_____

_____

17. What are some of the issues that your partner had to deal with after your retirement? (Mark all that are appropriate)
    o Felt upset at no longer playing a significant/unique role in the congregation
    o Relieved at no longer having the focus on him/her
    o Angry at how she/he was treated at the end
    o Angry at how you were treated at the end
    o Felt some depression now that she/he is no longer active in the congregation
    o Glad that you no longer have major responsibilities that take you away from the family
    o Sad because people who you thought were friends no longer are friendly to you
    o Adjustment to retirement has caused some friction in your family
    o Sad or upset because lost spiritual home
    o Your being home more hours has caused him/her to make significant adjustments
    o Has a sense her/his style is being cramped
    o Seems to have inordinate worries over your adjustment to retirement
    o Upset because you had to move
    o Wasn't asked for input in final decisions for the retirement ceremonies
    Others and/or expand on checked items (please feel free to add to the list)

_____

_____

18. What are some adjustments that you and your partner had to make in the first six months after retirement? (Check all that apply)
    o New domestic rules about sharing chores (e.g., cleaning house, putting dishes away, care of the yard)
    o "Lunch Hour" (who makes)
    o Sharing space in the house

o Sharing office space
o Sharing a computer
o Adjusting to a new rhythm of time
o Each feeling guilty that leaving and doing own 'things'
Please explain or expand

_____

_____

19. What advice would you give to fellow clergy about post retirement adjustment for one's partner?

_____

_____

We would appreciate knowing the story of the adjustments you had to make to this new world of retirement

20. What were/are some of your emotional reactions?
o Initially
o After 6 months
o More long term (if appropriate)

21. What new joys in life have you discovered since retirement? (i.e., family life, volunteer opportunities, new hobbies, etc.)

_____

_____

22. There is something called "disenfranchised grief" (grief that you experience but others do not recognize or acknowledge). Did you experience such grief over your retirement that others did not understand?
o Yes
o No
If yes, would you share some of those emotions or experiences below?

_____

_____

23. Since your retirement have you found a new "raison d'etre" (meaning/purpose) in life?
o Definitely
o I think I have
o I am still searching
o I have yet to find that meaning
o I am anxious that I have yet to find one
o I still wonder what it might be
Please explain why you chose what you chose

_____

_____

24. If you answered positively to the previous question, what was the process through which you discovered this new meaning? (Check all that apply)
    o Analytical approach
    o Happenstance
    o Was suggested to me by a friend, relative or fellow clergy
    o Was approached by someone else in the organization
    o Felt I was directed by God to do this
    o Read something about the organization and was inspired to participate
    o Prayer
    Other (please explain)

    _____

    _____

25. What volunteer activities or projects have you become involved in since your retirement?

    _____

    We are interested in your relationship with your successor and your suggestions to future successors as to how that relationship might be improved.

26. How would you rate the treatment you received by the clergy who succeeded you?
    o Wonderful
    o Appropriate
    o Respectful
    o As expected
    o Just OK
    o No relationship
    o Lacked respect for my feelings and what I was going through
    Please expand your answer and share your dreams of what you would have liked the relation to be?

    _____

    _____

27. If you could give advice to a successor, what suggestions would you offer about the future of the congregation, about your retiring, about how to handle the transition or any other area important to you?

    _____

    _____

28. If you were to offer suggestions to others who are transitioning about things you did or did not do or that you wish you had done differently, what would they be? (e.g., you were not kind enough, you did not leave a final report, you spoke negatively about your successor, you tried to turn him/her into a reincarnation of you, you did too much for congregants after you left thereby

not giving your successor room to develop his/her own relationships, etc.
Please remember this survey is anonymous.)

_____

_____

29. How should or could you have treated your successor differently than you
did or are doing now?

Left detailed instructions about the history of the congregation, who was
sick, who had died, new members in last year, etc.

I could have	I should have	I wish I had	I did
o	o	o	o

Taken him/her out for a meal

I could have	I should have	I wish I had	I did
o	o	o	o

Been more informative when I received news about a member

I could have	I should have	I wish I had	I did
o	o	o	o

Consulted with him/her before accepting a life cycle event

I could have	I should have	I wish I had	I did
o	o	o	o

Identified longstanding traditions and persistent struggles that have shaped
the congregation

I could have	I should have	I wish I had	I did
o	o	o	o

Left an evaluation of the congregation's strengths and weaknesses

I could have	I should have	I wish I had	I did
o	o	o	o

Left a schedule of annual events that were absolutely central to the
congregation

I could have	I should have	I wish I had	I did
o	o	o	o

Left a list of issues in the community

I could have	I should have	I wish I had	I did
o	o	o	o

Left a list of other organizations with whom the congregation has a
relationship

I could have	I should have	I wish I had	I did
o	o	o	o

Left a list of resources you found helpful

I could have	I should have	I wish I had	I did
o	o	o	o

Other things wish did or did that please you. (please specify)

_____

_____

We would like to know about the primary issues you are facing, if any, as you look forward to retirement. (If retired please skip to page 9)

30. Besides financial, what concerns, if any, do you have about retirement? (e.g., what to do with spare time, not being in the limelight, the transition of using time differently, making new friends, moving, etc.)

_____

_____

31. What concerns, if any, do you believe your partner has? (If you do not have a partner please skip this question.) Please check all that apply.
   o Financial—-not enough to sustain current lifestyle.
   o Having to leave friends
   o A change in relationship with current congregants
   o Finding a new spiritual home
   o Moving
   o Making new friends
   o Aging
   o Health matters
   o What to do with free time
   Other (please specify)

_____

_____

32. Please describe some of the dreams you have for the future.

_____

_____

33. In anticipation of your retirement, tell us about your involvement with the planning for this transition? Please include any outstanding ideas, programs, or methods of negotiation that others might find useful.

_____

_____

We cannot express how appreciative we are for your taking time to share with us and others your life story and emotional reactions. Please rest assured that your information will remain confidential.

34. Please share with us an interesting story about your retirement (either positive or negative)

_____

_____

35. Please indicate your denomination: (please clarify in the box below)
    o Catholic (which denomination)
    o Protestant (which denomination)
    o Muslim (which sect?)
    o Jewish (which denomination)
    o Unitarian
    o Fundamentalist (which denomination)
    o Mormon
    Please clarify _____

36. The following information is optional and will be used only in event that we would like to contact you to better understand your answer(s) or to request your permission to quote one of your responses. If we do use an anonymous quote from your survey, we will be pleased to send you a complimentary copy of the book.
    Name: _____
    Address 2: _____
    City/Town: _____
    State: _____
    ZIP: _____
    Country: _____
    Email Address: _____

37. If you would like to receive a summary of the results of this survey, please check the box below.
    o Yes, I would like a summary of the results of this survey

Author Biographies

Rabbi Daniel Roberts, DD, DMin, FT, is rabbi emeritus of Temple Emanu El in Cleveland, Ohio, where he served for 35 years. Rabbi Roberts received his ordination from Hebrew Union College in Cincinnati (1969) and his DMin from Pittsburgh Theological Seminary where his thesis was on comforting the mourner. He earned a Fellow in Thanatology Certification awarded by the Association for Death Education and Counseling and is its immediate past treasurer. In retirement, he was elected rabbi of a monthly congregation in Sharon, them Pennsylvania, serving 10 years until he was able to help successfully merge with a nearby congregation. In 2014 he served as the interim rabbi of Temple Adath Israel in Lexington, Kentucky. Throughout his career Rabbi Roberts has been intrigued with the field of Thanatology. He has lectured frequently at the King's College International Conference on Death and Bereavement in London, Ontario, and has been a keynote presenter there, as well as at the Association for Death Education and Counseling's National Convention. Rabbi Roberts has contributed to numerous books, (all published by Baywood) *Personal Care in an Impersonal World: A Multidimensional Look at Bereavement* (ed. John D. Morgan, 1993); *What Shall We Do? Preparing the School Community to Cope with Crises* (ed. Robert Stevenson, 2000); *Ethical Issues in the Care of the Dying and Bereaved* (ed. John D. Morgan, 1996); and *Living, Loving, and Loss: The Interplay of Intimacy, Sexuality and Grief* (eds. Brad DeFord and Richard Gilbert, 2013). He has also produced a video on teenage suicide prevention, "Inside, I Ache," which has been used in schools throughout the country.

Michael Freidman, Ed.D, is an applied psychologist who served over 15 years in the public sector as an educator, psychologist and administrator and has over 30 years of clinical experience. He created and manages an independent practice that provides a unique blend of organizational consulting and clinical intervention for individuals and families as well as business and organizational leaders. He is both a certified school psychologist and licensed psychologist. Dr. Freidman has an extensive background in organized congregational and community life. Active involvement in his own synagogue included serving as community life. Active involvement in his own synagogue included serving as congregational president. He is past president of the Philadelphia Federation of the Union of reform Judaism (URJ) and currently is a member of URJ's North America Board of trustees after serving on the Oversight and Long-Range Planning committees. Michael has consulted with the Central Conference of american Rabbis (CCAR), American Conference of Cantors (ACC) and numerous congregations and organizations. He is particularly interested in applying his professional skills and experience to work with clergy, congregations and organizations and has recently created Congregational Consulting Network as an independent service provider to the community. Dr. Freidman seeks to draw continued vision and purpose in these endeavors through greater understanding of the Bible and ancient texts. His current coaching with clergy includes those preparing for their retirement.

Bishop Patrick G. White served as a Parish Priest in the Anglican Dioceses of Toronto, Canada and Bermuda for 40 years and as Bishop of Bermuda for 4 years before retiring in 2012. He has a Doctor of Ministry from The Toronto School of Theology (1994). In retirement he has been serving part-time in interim ministries as well as Chaplain to the Retired Clergy in his Episcopal Area in the Diocese of Toronto. The other "part" of his time he and his wife Elizabeth enjoy travelling and looking after their grandchildren.

Linda Rabinowitch Thal is the author, with Rabbi Rachel Cowan, of *Wise Aging: Living with Joy, Resilience and Spirit*, which was recently named a finalist for the Myra H. Kraft Memorial Award by the Jewish Book Council. She is primary author of Vetaher Libeynu: The Institute for Jewish Spirituality Curriculum for Nurturing Adult Spiritual Development. She teaches and conducts workshops throughout the United States and abroad.

Index

Page references followed by n indicates a note and f indicates a figure.

Aaron, 167
abandonment, feeling of, 147–148
Abraham, 100, 156
Abraham, Israel, *Hebrew Ethical Wills*, 73
Abram, 67
Achenbaum, W. A., 30
activities plan, 32, 122, 177
addictions, 97
Addison, Howard Avruhm, 86
adjustment
  period for clergy and spouse, 114
  period for congregation, 13, 153
  period needed for retirement, 2, 5
  to retirement, 21, 75, 122
After the Ecstasy, the Laundry (Kornfield), 91
"Age-Proof Your Brain" (Howard), 66
aging. *See also* health, mental; health, physical
  acknowledging, 42, 57–58, 68–69
  adult children and, 129–130
  advantages of, 32
  anxiety about, 148
  daily activities and, 72
  fear of, 14, 66
  grief of, 2, 15
  pain of, 34, 150
Alabama, 99
Albom, Mitch, *Tuesdays With Morrie*, 177
aloneness (*hitbodedut*), 87–88
Alzheimer's disease, 66, 72
ambivalence, 61

anger
  about retiring, 11, 168
  about working, 61
  after retirement, 14, 15, 43, 56, 59–61, 119, 148
  with congregation, 46, 61–62, 107
  from congregation, 116
  counseling for, 168
  at denominational leaders, 61
  depression turned inward, 60
  at sacred moments, 59
  writing letters to release, 60
anguish, 2, 82, 109
Anonymous, *Cloud of Unknowing*, 91
Anthony, Michael J., 44, 46–47, 179
anticipation
  feelings of, 2, 11, 31
  of grief, 15, 44
anxiety
  about aging, 148
  about finances and estate planning, 111
  about new daily routine, 10
  of congregation, 47
  due to retirement changes, 5, 56, 120
  before retirement begins, 19
Appreciative Inquiry, 21–22, 141
Ariel, David, 81
Artist, The (movie), 77
attending services at old congregation, 13, 34
Au, Noreen C., 85
Au, Wilkie, 85
awareness, self, 20, 24

Bach, Richard, 65
baggage and luggage, for experiences, 96–98

199